GENDER EQUALITY AND WELFARE POLITICS IN SCANDINAVIA

The limits of political ambition?

Edited by Kari Melby, Anna-Birte Ravn and
Christina Carlsson Wetterberg

First published in Great Britain in 2008 by

The Policy Press
University of Bristol
Fourth Floor
Beacon House
Queen's Road
Bristol BS8 1QU
UK

Tel +44 (0)117 331 4054
Fax +44 (0)117 331 4093
e-mail tpp-info@bristol.ac.uk
www.policypress.org.uk

© Kari Melby, Anna-Birte Ravn and Christina Carlsson Wetterberg 2008

British Library Cataloguing in Publication Data
A catalogue record for this book is available from the British Library.

Library of Congress Cataloging-in-Publication Data
A catalog record for this book has been requested.

ISBN 978 1 84742 066 4 hardcover

Cover design by Robin Hawes.
Front cover: image kindly supplied by Paul Green.
Printed and bound in Great Britain by MPG Books, Bodmin.

Contents

List of tables

Preface

This book has been developed within the framework of the research project 'Gender Equality and Welfare Politics in Scandinavia', which was part of the Welfare Research Programme (*Velferdsforskningsprogrammet*) run by the Nordic Council of Ministers for the period 2000–05. Initially, we would like to express our gratitude towards the Council for its generous funding of the project, funds primarily used as research grants, and sponsoring of recurrent working seminars, which made Scandinavian cooperation and comparison possible. We want to underline that the book to a great extent is a collective product, and to direct our sincere appreciation to all participants for interesting discussions and very good cooperation. We are also very pleased and grateful that two well-known welfare researchers kindly agreed to comment on the book: Keith Pringle, who also attended our final working seminar, and Ruth Lister, who read and commented afterwards. You have both been of great help! Annette Andersen has been of invaluable assistance in the last phase of the project, proofreading and adapting the entire manuscript to the house style of The Policy Press. Thank you very much indeed, Annette! Last but not least, it has been a pleasure working with The Policy Press. We really appreciate the fact that we always met with professional treatment, and in a most personal and friendly manner.

Kari Melby, Anna-Birte Ravn and Christina Carlsson Wetterberg
August 2007

Notes on contributors

Charlotte Andersen, MA in Social Sciences and Psychology 1998, Aalborg University, Denmark. She worked on the project 'Gender Eqaulity and Welfare Politics in Scandinavia' as a research assistant for nine months in 2003-04.

Trine Annfelt, MA in Pedagogics, PhD in Gender Studies, is Associate Professor at the Department of Interdisciplinary Studies of Culture, Norwegian University of Science and Technology (NTNU), Trondheim, Norway. Selected publications: *Kjønn i utdanning. Hegemoniske posisjoner og forhandlinger om yrkesidentitet i medisin og faglærerutdanning* [*Gender in education. Hegemonic positions and negotiations about Identity among students in medicine and home economics*] (DrPolit thesis, 1999); 'More gender equality – bigger breasts? Battles over gender and the body', *NORA: Nordic Journal of Women's Studies*, vol 12, no 3 (2002); 'From soft fathers to the rights of the sperm? Biologism as a heteronorming resource', in E. Magnusson, M. Rönnblom and H. Silius (eds) *Critical studies of gender equalities: Nordic dislocations, contradictions and dilemmas* (Gondolin, 2007). She has also co-edited the anthology *Når heteroseksualiteten må forklare seg* [*When heterosexuality has to explain itself*], (Tapir forlag, 2007). Her research interests include ethnicity, heteronormativity and gender equality in education and family politics. From 2007 she is affiliated with the Nordic Centre of Excellence 'The Nordic Welfate State – Historical Foundations and Future Challenges'.

Anette Borchorst, PhD, is Associate Professor at FREIA, Centre for Feminist Research, Aalborg University, Denmark. Her primary research interest relates to welfare state models and welfare policies in Western Europe, particularly in relation to parenting. She was part of the Danish Power and Democracy Study and edited a book on gendered power in 2002. Among her publications are *Equal democracies? Gender and politics in the Nordic countries* (Scandinavian University Press, 1999) (co-editor and co-author); 'The public–private split rearticulated: abolishment of the Danish Daddy Leave', in A.L. Ellingsæter and A. Leira (eds) *Politicising parenthood in Scandinavia: Gender relations in welfare states* (The Policy Press, 2006) and 'The women-friendly welfare states revisited', *NORA: Challenges to Gender Equality in the Nordic Welfare States*, vol 10, no 2 (2000) (with B. Siim). From 2007 she is affiliated with the Nordic Centre of Excellence 'The Nordic Welfate State – Historical Foundations and Future Challenges'.

Ann-Dorte Christensen, PhD, is Associate Professor in Political Sociology at FREIA, Centre for Feminist Research, Aalborg University, Denmark. She wrote her PhD thesis on women's political identities in social movements (1990). Among her publications are: *Equal democracies? Gender and politics in the Nordic countries* (Scandinavian University Press, 1999) (co-editor and co-author); 'The

Danish gender model: between movement politics and representative politics', in J. Andersen and B. Siim (eds) *Gender, democracy and citizenship – Politics of empowerment and inclusion* (Palgrave Macmillan, 2004) and 'Gender, class, and family: men and gender equality in a Danish context', *Social politics: International studies in gender, state, and society* (in press). Together with Anette Borchorst she edited the book *Kønsreflektioner [Reflections on gender]* (Aalborg University Press, 2006). She is presently working on The INTERLOC Project: Gender, Class and Ethnicity. Inter-sectionality and Local Citizenship. From 2007 she is affiliated with the Nordic Centre of Excellence 'The Nordic Welfate State – Historical Foundations and Future Challenges'.

Christina Fiig holds a PhD in Political Science and Gender Studies. She is Assistant Professor at FREIA, Centre for Feminist Research, Aalborg University, Denmark. The topic of her PhD thesis was a theoretical and empirical analysis of the recent Habermasian theory of the public sphere based on the critiques of feminist political theory and a Danish media debate on contemporary feminism and gender. Her research interests include theories of democracy and the public sphere in a gender perspective, leadership and gender, media and gender, and politics and gender. She is currently working on gender and leadership in relation to the financial sector. She participates in the Danish part of the European Commission's 6th Framework Programme EUROSPHERE – Diversity and the European Public Sphere. Towards a Citizens' Europe. Her recent publications include: 'Det vigtigste er debatten' ['The central debate: feminist voices in the Danish public sphere'] in A. Borschorst and A.-D. Christensen (eds) *Kønsrefleksioner [Reflections on gender]* (Aalborg University Press, 2006) and 'Women in Danish politics: challenges to the notion of gender equality', in J. Gelb and M.L. Palley (eds) *Women and politics around the world: A comparative encyclopedia* (ABC-CLIO, 2008). From 2007 she is affiliated with the Nordic Centre of Excellence 'The Nordic Welfate State – Historical Foundations and Future Challenges'.

Ruth Lister is Professor of Social Policy at Loughborough University, UK. She was formerly the Director of the Child Poverty Action Group and a member of the Commission on Social Justice. Her book *Citizenship – feminist perspectives* (Palgrave Macmillan, 1997) appeared in a second, extended edition in 2003. Her recent publications include *Poverty* (Polity, 2004) and, as co-author, *Gendering citizenship in Western Europe* (The Policy Press, 2007).

Åsa Lundqvist, PhD in Sociology at Lund University (2001), Associate Professor in Sociology (2007), teaches at the Centre for Gender Studies at Lund University, Sweden. Among her publications are: 'Conceptualising gender in a Swedish context', in L. Davidoff, K. McClelland and E. Varikas (eds) *Gender and history: Retrospect and prospect* (Blackwell, 2000); *Bygden, bruket och samhället: Om människor och organisationer i brukssamhället Böksholm 1900–1979 [Community,* mill and Society: People and organisations in the rural industrial community Böksholm 1900–1979] (Arkiv förlag, 2001); 'Önska, vilja, våga. Om beslutet att skaffa barn' ['Wanting, willing, daring: on the decision to have a child'], *Sociologisk Forskning*, no 1 (2003) (with C. Roman) and *Familjen i den svenska modellen* [*The family in the Swedish model*] (Boréa förlag, 2007). Her research interests include analysis of the history of the welfare state and welfare policies, especially social and family policies within the 'Swedish Model'. From 2007 she is affiliated with the Nordic Centre of Excellence 'The Nordic Welfate State – Historical Foundations and Future Challenges'.

Kari Melby is Professor of History, Department of Interdisciplinary Studies of Culture/Centre for Feminist and Gender Studies, and Vice-Dean for Research, Faculty of Arts, Norwegian University of Science and Technology (NTNU), Trondheim, Norway. A main area of research is gender and political participation/gendered policies in a broad sense. Her books include analyses of women's professional and voluntary organisations published in *Kall og kamp. Norsk Sykepleierforbunds historie* [*The history of the Norwegian Nurses' Association*] (Cappelen, PhD dissertation, 1990), *Kvinnelighetens strategier. Norges Husmorforbund 1915–1940 og Norges Lærerinneforbund 1912–1940* [*Strategies of femininity. The Norwegian Housewives' Association and the Norwegian Association of Women Teachers*] (University of Trondheim, 1995), and *Inte ett ord om kärlek. Äktenskap och politikk i Norden ca. 1850–1930* [*Not a word about love: Marriage and politics in the Nordic countries, 1850–1930*] (Makadam, 2006) (with A. Pylkkänen, B. Rosenbeck and C.C. Wetterberg). The main conclusions of the last-mentioned are published in 'The Nordic model of marriage', *Women's History Review*, vol 15, no 4 (2006). From 2007 she is affiliated with the Nordic Centre of Excellence 'The Nordic Welfate State – Historical Foundations and Future Challenges'.

Diana Mulinari is Associate Professor in Sociology working at the Centre for Gender Studies, Lund University, Sweden. Her research interests are located in the fields of feminist/postcolonial/global studies. Her doctoral dissertation explored the politicisation of motherhood during the Sandinista revolution in Nicaragua: *Motherhood and politics in revolutionary Nicaragua* (Bokbox, 1996). She has conducted several studies on the relationship between gender, class and 'race'/ ethnicity, exploring the specificity of both the 'Nordic welfare model' and Nordic feminism(s). Among her publications are: 'Uno hace cualquier cosa por los hijos. Motherwork and politics in Sandinista Nicaragua', in H. Ragone and W. Twine (eds) *Ideologies and technologies of motherhood: Race, class, sexuality and nationalism* (Routledge, 2000); 'The new Swedish working class. Swedish unions and migrant workers', *Race and Class*, no 3 (2003) (with A. Neergaard) and *Intersektionalitet* [*Intersectionality*] (Liber, 2004) (with P. de los Reyes).

Keith Pringle is Professor in Sociology at Mälardalen University College, Sweden, Research Professor at the Department of Applied Social Sciences, London Metropolitan University, UK; Honorary Professor at Aalborg University, Denmark, and Honorary Professor at Warwick University, UK. He has researched and written widely in the fields of men's practices, children, ethnicity and intersectionality. He has authored or co-authored five books and co-edited four with two more currently in press. He has co-ordinated or co-managed several transnational research networks for organisations such as the European Commission and the Nordic Council of Ministers.

Anna-Birte Ravn is Associate Professor in Gender Division of Work and Social Change at FREIA, Centre for Feminist Research, Aalborg University, Denmark. Her area of research is gender history, with a focus on women's movements and the development of the welfare state. She took part in a comparative project on women's waged work and protective labour legislation, published in U. Wikander, A. Kessler-Harris, and J. Lewis (eds) *Protecting women: Labor legislation in Europe, the United States, and Australia, 1880–1920* (University of Illinois Press, 1995). Her work includes 'Gender, taxation and welfare state in Denmark 1903–63(83)', in K. Melby et al (eds) *The Nordic model of marriage and the welfare state* (Nordic Council of Ministers, 2000), and 'Køn og klasse – om nytten af begrebet intersektionalitet' ['Gender and class: on the uses of the concept of intersectionality'], in A. Borchorst and A.-D. Christensen (eds) *Kønsreflektioner* [*Reflections on gender*] (Aalborg University Press, 2006). From 2007 she is affiliated with the Nordic Centre of Excellence 'The Nordic Welfate State – Historical Foundations and Future Challenges'.

Christine Roman is Professor in Sociology at Örebro University, Sweden. A main area of research is continuity and change in gender relations in work and family. Her doctoral dissertation, *Lika på olika villkor* [*Equal treatment: Different opportunities*] (Symposion, 1994), addresses questions concerning relations between working life and family life, as well as intersections between class and gender. She has conducted several studies within this research field, including in-depth studies of negotiations between heterosexual couples, studies of the interplay between the social sciences and family policy, and studies on feminist theory on intimate relations. Among her publications are *Hemmet, barnen och makten* [*The home, the children and the power*] (Fritzes, 1997) (with G. Ahrne), and *Familjen i det moderna. Sociologiska sanningar och feministisk kritik* [*Families in modern society: Sociological truths and feminist critique*] (Liber, 2004). From 2007 she is affiliated with the Nordic Centre of Excellence 'The Nordic Welfate State – Historical Foundations and Future Challenges'.

Birte Siim is Professor in Gender Research in the Social Sciences at FREIA, Centre for Feminist Research, Aalborg University, Denmark. She has published extensively on gender, welfare and democracy. Her recent publications include: *Gendering citizenship in Western Europe: New challenges for citizenship research in a cross-national context* (The Policy Press, 2007) (co-author); 'Contesting citizenship: comparative analyses', Special Issue of *CRISPP, Critical Revue of International Social and Political Philosophy*, vol 10, no 4 (2007) (with J. Squires); *The Politics of inclusion and empowerment: Gender, class and citizenship* (Palgrave, 2004) (co-editor); *Contested concepts in gender and social policy* (Edward Elgar, 2002) (co-editor) and *Gender and citizenship. Politics and agency in France, Britain and Denmark* (Cambridge, 2000). Her research includes an investigation of the political mobilisation of ethnic minority women for the Danish Power Study, and she is currently the Danish partner of two EC-funded research projects: 'VEIL – Values, Equality and Diversity in Liberal Democracies. Debates on Muslim Women's Headscarves in Europe' and 'EUROSPHERE – Diversity and the European Public Sphere: Towards a Citizens' Europe'. From 2007 she is affiliated with the Nordic Centre of Excellence, 'The Nordic Welfate State – Historical Foundations and Future Challenges'.

Christina Carlsson Wetterberg is Professor of History at Örebro University, Sweden. Her research deals with social, cultural and political aspects of modern history, with a special focus on the women's movement, social welfare and family law. She is also working within the area of biographical research. Among her later publications are: 'Att biografera en kvinnlig intellektuell' ['Writing a biography on an intellectual woman'], in *Med livet som insats* (Sekel, 2007); *Inte ett ord om kärlek. Äktenskap och politik i Norden ca. 1850–1930* [*Not a word about love: Marriage and politics in the Nordic countries*] (Makadam, 2006) (co-author); the main conclusions of this book are published in 'The Nordic model of marriage', *Women's History Review*, vol 15, no 4 (2006); *Rummet vidgas. Kvinnors väg ut i offentligheten ca. 1880–1940* [*The widening room: Women entering the public sphere 1880–1940*] (Atlantis, 2002) (co-editor). She is presently working on a biography of the author and feminist Frida Stéenhoff (1865–1945). From 2007 she is affiliated with the Nordic Centre of Excellence, 'The Nordic Welfate State – Historical Foundations and Future Challenges'.

A Nordic model of gender equality?
Introduction

Kari Melby, Anna-Birte Ravn and Christina Carlsson Wetterberg

The challenges of today

The overall objective of this book is to analyse the meanings of gender that underpin policies for the achievement of gender equality in the Scandinavian welfare states, ie Denmark, Norway and Sweden. The book focuses on similarities as well as differences between the countries and discusses the relevance of talking about *a Nordic model*. Different meanings of gender equality and the relationship between discourse and practice are analysed. The book is interdisciplinary and includes historical perspectives and comparative analyses. Its primary focus is on reforms and legislation related to the family, so crucial to the understanding of the welfare state. The book is policy oriented, but is also directed towards a broader discourse, and it focuses on the relationship between equality policy and family policy in the Scandinavian countries. The ambition of gender equality has been more explicitly expressed and applied in the Scandinavian countries than in other countries of Europe. But gender equality in the early 20th century to a great extent meant equality based on gender difference. The book raises the question whether the hallmark of the Scandinavian welfare model is a special combination of gender equality and gender differentiation. It stresses the importance of viewing the concept of equality in its historical context and investigates the changing meanings of equality based on sameness and/or gender difference.

The analysis takes its point of departure in a period when gender-equality policies were formulated for the first time. Gender equality – in the sense of formal equal rights – had already achieved increasing political support in the Nordic countries during the last decades of the 19th century, and around 1920 women had obtained formal equal rights with men in terms of education and government posts, voting and political positions. Between 1909 and 1929 the marriage legislation in all Nordic countries was also thoroughly reformed, modernising the institution of marriage, enhancing women's individual rights and ending the husband's legal power over his wife. The reformed legislation also gave married women the obligation to provide for the family, which was unique, as seen in a European perspective, and questions the application of a male-breadwinner model to this formative period of the Scandinavian welfare states.

Until the 1930s the employment rate among women was relatively similar in all Scandinavian countries, but from then on and until the 1960s the rates were higher in Sweden than in Denmark and, especially, Norway, where also the childcare system was far less developed (Haavet, 2006; Åmark, 2006). On the other hand, Norwegian women gained more rights as mothers at an early stage. Today the overall similarities between the Scandinavian states are conspicuous; gender equality prevails when it comes to education, employment and political participation rates, and welfare systems are well developed. However, two contradictions serve as a challenging starting point for the book. First, despite a long tradition of gender-equality policy, the labour market is highly gender segregated in the Scandinavian countries. Second, there are substantial differences between Sweden and Norway on the one hand and Denmark on the other when it comes to the development of contemporary official gender-equality policies. While this field is regulated in detail in the former countries, it is not the case in Denmark. This poses the question in what way discourse, policies and practice are related. The book will include analysis on all these levels and thereby hopefully throw some light on the links between them and make a comparison easier and more fruitful. In some of the chapters the main focus is on discourse or politics, while others concentrate on practice.

It has been argued that the early modernisation of gender relations through gender-equality reforms was an important historical precondition for the Scandinavian welfare state model (Bradley, 1996; Melby et al, 2001). This book will continue the discussion of the special characteristics of the official equality policy in the Scandinavian countries and its relationship to the development of the welfare state. In Scandinavia, it has been argued, there is a strong belief that one can rely on the state to attend to gender equality (Bradley, 1996; Bergqvist et al, 1999). Is this really the case in all three countries? Can we follow a tradition of 'state feminism' as far back as the marriage law reforms of the 1920s? The book critically investigates and discusses the Scandinavian 'success story' portrayed in normative political theory and in historical analysis of the development of gendered citizenship rights. The notion of the Scandinavian welfare states as 'woman-friendly' (Hernes, 1987) will be discussed through historical and contemporary comparative analyses presented in Part One.

The importance of integrating other aspects than gender, for example class or ethnicity, when analysing gender-equality politics is a common point of departure for the authors of this book. The first part primarily highlights the interrelationship between gender and class. Other aspects come to the fore in Part Two, which deals with contemporary challenges to gender-equality policies raised by recent developments in Scandinavia. Gender-equality policies are today criticised for ignoring other aspects of discrimination related to, for example, fathers, ethnicity, class, sexuality and generation. The chapters in this part critically discuss the Nordic equality model by confronting it with three crucial challenges in terms of equal rights for fathers, multiculturalism and a critical young generation. Expanding the rights of the father is today a central aim in Scandinavian family policy, and one of the questions is what this means for equality between men and women. Another central debate is related to growing immigration to the Scandinavian count over the past decades, and concerns the relationship between gender equality ethnic differences. In this debate it has been argued that gender-equality pol actually functions as an ethnic borderline between 'them' and 'us'. The relationship between gender, class and ethnicity is an important issue in feminist and gender research in the humanities and social sciences and will also be discussed here. The question of generation is a third theme. The younger generations are socialised to believe that the Scandinavian welfare states have reached equality, but the way some young women experience personal gender inequality in everyday life points to a paradoxical gender relationship even in present-day Scandinavia.

A Nordic model?

Although analyses from 'inside' the Nordic area tend to underline differences between the countries, the ambition in this book is to highlight similarities as well as differences through a comparative perspective. In research on the welfare state, the claim of a Nordic model is associated with the name of Gøsta Esping-Andersen (1990). His identification of a social democratic Nordic welfare regime is well established, though not without debate. Lately he has also included the gender dimension in his analysis. The Nordic model 'may be famous for its generosity and universalism, but what really stands out is its emphasis on employment and the "defamilialization" of responsibility for providing welfare', Esping-Andersen writes (2000, p 4). He claims that this emphasis on employment in the Nordic model, together with the defamilialisation, maximises women's economic independence (see also Rosenbeck, 2005).

Esping-Andersen's contention of a Nordic model has been a central point of departure for research on social policy and the welfare state. However, social scientist Mikko Kautto and his colleagues hold a more pragmatic view, giving attention to differences among the countries. They prefer to talk about 'groupings of nations that to varying degrees share common historical and cultural experiences' (Kautto et al, 1999, p 12). Greater diversity has developed through the 1990s, due to different tracks in economy and politics in Sweden and Finland on the one hand, and Denmark and Norway on the other. Nevertheless, they conclude that there are more similarities than differences; the Nordic welfare state model continues to exist with its traditional hallmarks still alive (Kautto et al, 1999, p 271; Kautto et al, 2001, pp 264f). The historians behind the research project 'The Nordic Model of Welfare – a Historical Reappraisal' conclude similarly; their working hypothesis on a model with five exceptions proved to be a fruitful approach (Christiansen and Åmark, 2006, p 351). Through historical and comparative studies they find it timely, however, to question Esping-Andersen's thesis that the Nordic model is social democratic. The Nordic countries took different roads to modernity in the 20th century, they argue; there were variations between them and it is a political fact that 'all major welfare reforms have been passed by broad parliamentary majorities' (Christiansen and Åmark, 2006, p 352). The research group underlines the importance of cooperation and internal comparison within Nordic politics in the framing of a Nordic model; Nordic cooperation is seen as essential in shaping the idea of a Nordic welfare model (Petersen, 2006; see also Rosenbeck, 2000). The investigation of the use of inter-Nordic comparison in political debates and decision making is defined as methodically new in comparative studies. On this point Nordic research represents unique possibilities, due to the fact that Nordic regional cooperation probably is unique in the world (Christiansen and Åmark, 2006, p 335). Most researchers seem to balance similarities and diversities and conclude on a Nordic model of welfare. One exception is probably Christina Bergqvist et al (1999), who in their study on gender-equality policy underline the variations within and between the Nordic countries.

The research project on 'The Nordic Marriage Model' also claims that it is justified to talk about a Nordic model (Melby et al, 2006). Although the laws enacted in each Nordic country were not completely identical, the similarities are striking. In a comparative European perspective, the contours of a specific Nordic marriage model are clear.[1] The Nordic model of marriage was in fact a demonstration of inter-Nordic comparison as a political strategy. The marriage model was a product of intense work of an all-Scandinavian law committee. The importance of comparison is underlined when we know that Finland later chose to follow the Scandinavian model, not the German one, in reforming its marriage law, as did Iceland. Concerning the Nordic marriage model, there were indeed a common project and a master plan, which obviously was not the case in welfare state politics in general (Christiansen and Markkola, 2006, p 29). Furthermore, this process illustrates that Nordic cooperation between independent states took place even before the First World War, just a few years after the dissolution of the union between Norway and Sweden.[2] Family law and gender relations stand out as issues of the highest priority concerning Nordic harmonisation and cooperation. That, in turn, clearly demonstrates the political importance of gender issues, which is often not acknowledged. Gender relations was an area where efforts to harmonise the legal framework were distinctive, indicating that gender equality is one of the most prominent hallmarks of the Nordic model.

When explaining the Nordic model, the homogeneity in terms of ethnicity and religion is often underlined. So is a long tradition of political democracy and Lutheranism, and increased attention is today being paid to the impact of Lutheran traditions on the emerging welfare model and the position of women in the public, welfare and religious spheres throughout the centuries (see, for example, Markkola, 2001). It is claimed that Protestantism, more than social democracy, shaped universalism and the Nordic model of welfare (Knudsen, 2000). The Nordic marriage Acts, for example, were enacted in political consensus; neither social democracy nor social liberal traditions could provide an overall political explanation. This corresponds with the view held by, especially, Norwegian scholars of the welfare state and by the Nordic research group behind the recent historical reappraisal of the Nordic welfare state (see, for example, Seip, 1984, 1994; Bjørnson and Haavet, 1994; Christiansen et al, 2006). Others suggest that it is rather a question of political culture. For example, the concept 'Agrarian Enlightenment' has been deployed to point out the existence of a political culture based on popular mobilisation and social inclusion, and not on differentiation along the boundaries of public and private (Sørensen and Stråth, 1997). The modernisation process in the Nordic countries was characterised by a unification of equality and individual liberty. Although marked by a legal tradition in which the protection of individual liberties as protective rights against state intervention was relatively weak (Kulawik, 2002), individualism stands out as a distinct but often-overlooked element in the Nordic political culture (Sørensen and Stråth, 1997; Christiansen, 2000, p 201). In fact, a responsible and self-disciplined subject was a precondition for the gradual establishment of universal social rights (Kulawik, 2002). The Nordic model is distinguished by individualism combined with state responsibility for the common welfare through social reform and state intervention. The Nordic model is also characterised by a close interaction between the state and civil society, finding its expression in the strength of voluntary organisations (Sørensen and Stråth, 1997; Berven and Selle, 2001). In sum, we are talking about a political culture in which it was a state responsibility to reform society, relying on the active participation of the citizens.

The closeness and subtle boundaries between public and private, local and national, the state and civil society gave space for women's agency in the Scandinavian countries. This should be seen in the light of the late modernisation of the Nordic countries. The process of modernisation – including industrialisation, the development of an urban middle class and legislative reforms – went in parallel with the process of democratisation and the growth of popular movements. Nordic women seem to have been integrated in the democratic process through voluntary organisations with access to the political sphere rather early (Jordansson and Vammen, 1998). During the 19th century, all Nordic societies underwent changes that dissolved patriarchal structures. Towards the end of the century, women's citizenship was discussed in relation to legal changes concerning family and heredity. The claim for equality between men and women was introduced when the women's organisations were established in the 1870s and 1880s. Different views on details certainly existed, but there was less principal resistance to the need for the emancipation and independence of women than in many other European countries. Already the marriage reforms early in the 20th century could be interpreted as a sort of 'state feminism', as a political response to important challenges for society. When family and marriage were perceived as being in crisis, the political answer in the Nordic countries was equality. The democratic integration of women in civil society was a hallmark of the Nordic political culture, as much as women's agency is one among several factors that explain this culture.

A dual breadwinner model?

In the Nordic countries today women's labour market participation is almost the same as men's, women constitute from one-third to one-half of Nordic parliamentary assemblies and governments, and their strong position in all areas of society is facilitated by public care services (Christiansen and Markkola, 2006). When explaining the relatively high fertility rates and economic productivity of the Nordic countries, Gøsta Esping-Andersen points to public childcare etc, or in general terms the 'defamilialization' of women, as the most important reason (Esping-Andersen, 1999). Feminist scholars have accentuated especially the Swedish welfare state's capacity for promoting a 'gender-encompassing' right to provide and to care (Kessler-Harris, 2003). The combination of high fertility rates, working mothers, and parent insurances allows not only mothers, but also fathers to take care of small children at home. Together with low poverty rates for lone mothers, these factors constitute a specific characteristic of the Nordic countries of today (Christiansen and Åmark, 2006).[3]

Between 1920 and 1980, women's labour market participation in all the Nordic countries rose slowly towards an internationally high level (Åmark, 2006), but the three Scandinavian countries followed different roads towards a clear-cut dual breadwinner model and modern gender relations. Focusing on the formation of Norwegian family policies in a comparative Nordic perspective, Inger Elisabeth Haavet concludes that in Norway a 'maternalist' policy endured for quite a long period (Haavet, 2006). In Denmark the number of married women in the labour market fell during the 1950s, not only relatively, but also in absolute figures (Borchorst, 1980), indicating a pronounced housewife ideology also in this country.

The paradox is that, while in international comparison women's labour market participation today is extremely high, the horizontal and vertical gender segregation of the Nordic labour markets is pronounced and among the highest in the world (Christiansen and Markkola, 2006, p 24). Even if Nordic men take more responsibility for household chores, including care for children, than their European counterparts, women are still responsible for the main part of work and care in the home (Bonke, 1995, 1997). The paradox has given rise to two radically different interpretations of the capacity of the Nordic welfare states to support gender equality: on the one hand, the Norwegian Helga Maria Hernes has characterised these states as potentially 'woman-friendly' (Hernes, 1987), that is, women are not subjugated to harsher choices between children and work than men; on the other, Swedish historian Yvonne Hirdman has argued for a continuous reproduction of a segregating and hierarchical 'gender-system' (Hirdman, 1988, 2001).[4] In this volume, we take a closer look at the historical construction of the dual breadwinner model in Scandinavia, a main point being that this model was already established in the early 20th century, and that the paradox was built into it from the start.

In the recent historical reappraisal of the Nordic model of welfare, Niels Finn Christiansen and Klas Åmark cautiously conclude that a fundamental transformation from 'a male breadwinner *ideal* to a dual breadwinner *model*' occurred during the 20th century (2006, p 341, italics added). The male breadwinner ideal was not part of 'tradition', but emerged with the industrialisation process in the final decades of the 19th century (Wikander, 1988; Sommestad, 1992, 1997). A Swedish commission report of 1938, mentioned by Åsa Lundqvist (Chapter Four, this volume), probably echoes the traditional understanding of obligations to provide for families, when stating that by the late 1930s the former 'multiple breadwinner model' had been replaced by a new ideal of the father as sole provider. The ideal was institutionalised in tax and civil servants' legislation in the early 20th century, as shown by Anna-Birte Ravn (Chapter Three, this volume). It was strongly supported by the Scandinavian social democratic parties, but it was also strongly contested, for instance by women within the social democratic labour movement, and for large numbers of families it never materialised.

Around 1900 the question of protective labour legislation came up in the Nordic countries and, inspired by international developments, Scandinavian governments proposed laws to protect women from work in factories. These proposals caused a heated debate in the parliaments as well as protests from women's organisations across class and national boundaries. Unlike in all other European countries, the USA and Australia, a special prohibition on women's night work was never included in Norwegian and Danish factory laws (Wikander et al, 1995). This may be seen as a protection of women's right to work, reflecting a multiple breadwinner model – or as reflecting the fact that the Scandinavian countries around 1900 were still primarily agrarian and relatively poor, and that all hands were needed to secure family provision (Sommestad, 1997). In these early years, class was clearly more important in family policies than gender. A night-work prohibition was enacted by the Swedish parliament in 1909, but against the strong protests of social democratic women. To this early contour of a Nordic gender model should be added the inclusion of maternity leave in early factory legislation (Hageman, 1995; Karlsson, 1995; Ravn, 1995).

In Chapter Two of this book Christina Carlsson Wetterberg and Kari Melby argue – in contrast to the common understanding that a male breadwinner model prevailed during the first half of the 20th century – that the marriage reforms of the 1910s and 1920s represented a 'modified dual breadwinner model'. The reforms established an economic equality between husband and wife, resting on two fundamental principles: first, the principle of deferred community property, which made husband and wife independent, formally equal owners of their respective property during marriage and stipulated a division of assets into two equal parts in case of divorce; second, the principle of joint responsibility for family provision, legally recognising women's unpaid work in the home as a contribution to family maintenance on a par with maintenance by money. The economic equality of these early marriage reforms rested on gender difference, but unlike marriage legislation in the rest of Europe, which gave the husband alone the responsibility to provide for his family and stated his guardianship over his wife (and children), they recognised married women as individuals in their own right. In the first half of the 20th century, women's work in the home did contribute substantially to family maintenance, especially in the many small family businesses (farming etc), and to talk about a 'modified dual breadwinner model' thus better conceptualises social practice as well as legal frameworks in this period of time.

The marriage laws gave married women in Scandinavia the freedom to choose waged work irrespective of their husbands' will, and in practice many wives, especially in poor working-class families, were engaged in part-time work (Åmark, 2006). Also, single women, including lone mothers, were expected to work to provide for themselves and their children. However, the seemingly inconsistent policy towards married and unmarried mothers respectively makes sense within an overall concern that families – and not the state – should be responsible for provision to the extent possible. This may account for the contradictory policies – trying to balance women's claims for individuality with considerations for family needs – of the Scandinavian welfare states in relation to regulations on family provision. The overall concern of the legislature seems to have been to secure families' self-provision, in the first half of the 20th century, complemented by the national interest in the size and quality of the population, in the final part of the century, directed by a focus on productivity and economic growth as a precondition for welfare.

Another apparent inconsistency in the family policies of the emerging Scandinavian welfare states appears when comparing the marriage reforms of the early 20th century with tax legislation in the same period (see Ravn, Chapter Three). According to the former, married women gained equality and were treated as family providers on a par with their husbands and as individual economic citizens vis-à-vis the state; the second type of legislation bestowed on the married man alone the role of family provider and, especially in the Danish case, relegated married women to mere accessories to their husbands, to non-persons without citizens' rights or obligations. Moreover, in the progressive tax systems, joint taxation of spouses made married women's gainful employment outside the home less attractive, and from the 1930s this 'penalty on marriage' had consequences also for working-class families with average incomes. Scandinavian tax legislation can be read as the MPs' vision of a male breadwinner society, which never fully matured, however.

Another reading of the Scandinavian tax laws of the early 20th century makes the inconsistency or outright contradiction between marriage reforms and tax law systems less obvious. When conceptualising the model of family provision as a 'modified dual breadwinner system', the work performed in the family by housewives was productive work, and husband and wife constituted a complementary unit of production that could not be separated. This reading would also account for the strange fact that in Norway, where married women's roles as housewives were more pronounced in discourse and practice, they were acknowledged as individual providers/producers in the tax-law system in 1959 more than 10 years before separate taxation of spouses was enacted in Denmark and Sweden (1967, 1970).

Inspiration for an alternative family policy in the Nordic countries came from Sweden, where during the 1930s Alva Myrdal and others turned the theoretical discussions, which were taking place in the entire industrialised world, of married women's right to paid work upside down, arguing for working women's right to motherhood (Haavet, 2006, pp 205–6). In this volume Åsa Lundqvist (Chapter Four) shows how in Swedish governmental commission reports of the 1930s and 1940s ideas of a 'brand new family' emerged – a family where society had taken over responsibilities for childcare, leaving both spouses free to be gainfully employed. All over Scandinavia, governments and legislators were concerned about declining birth rates, and the 'brand new family' was the Swedish experts' solution to facilitate family formation and increase birth rates by furthering gender equality.[5] The Swedish debates of the 1930s on the crisis of family formation, or the population question, were echoed in Denmark and Norway. Lundqvist shows how, between 1940 and 1960, the idea of a 'brand new family' was substituted in Sweden by a focus on women as the 'caring heads' of the family and men as family providers. If a male breadwinner model ever existed as a dominant part of the political ambitions of Scandinavian welfare state builders, it would have been in the immediate post-war period, when Swedish and Danish government commissions on tax-law reform for the first time questioned the concept of married women's household work as productive work (Ravn, Chapter Three).

However, in the wake of the economic boom and the need for more women in the labour market, these ambitions were soon replaced by the construction of a clear-cut dual breadwinner model. From the late 1950s the problem of 'women's two roles' as mothers and workers became part of family policy discourses, and the 1960s witnessed a shift in both discourse and political praxis towards a new ideal of gender neutrality (Lundqvist, Chapter Four). A main conclusion in Christine Roman's chapter in this volume (Chapter Five) is that the discursive shift in Swedish family policies from the late 1960s made individual family members, rather than the nuclear family as such, the target of reform, and that in this process questions of gender equality increasingly replaced questions of equality between social classes. Eventually, the family policies of the three Scandinavian welfare states became more and more directed towards facilitating a clear-cut dual breadwinner model, giving freedom of choice to both men and women – or, in other words, a 'gender-encompassing right to provide and to care'.

A thoroughly gender-segregated labour market, along with women's continued main responsibility for family care and household chores, show that this formal right – institutionalised in gender-neutral family policies – is far from the social practices of women and men in the Scandinavian countries today, however. The problem is that while labour market policies turned women's right to provide into an obligation, no family policies turned men's rights to care into obligations. In this respect, the countries differ, however, as shown by Anette Borchorst (Chapter One). She discusses similarities and differences between the Scandinavian welfare states of today with regard to care policies and gender-equality visions. Drawing on Nancy Fraser (1997), she concludes that, while Danish care policies have for many years been solidly based in a universal- (that is, dual) breadwinner model, Swedish policies have more consistently embraced gender equality and therefore not only furthered a universal-breadwinner model, but also took steps towards a universal- (that is, dual) caregiver vision. Norwegian care policies have been marked by ambivalence concerning the gainful employment of mothers, and Norwegian mothers were integrated in the labour force despite the lack of public care services. Nevertheless, Norway was the first country in the world to take steps towards a universal-caregiver model, adopting a 'daddy quota' as early as 1993.

New perspectives on parenthood

The question of parenthood is another key area where gender politics meets with family policies. In a comparative perspective, the traditional right of the father to guardianship of children in marriage and after divorce was substituted by increased rights for mothers in the Scandinavian countries; in Norway and Denmark, even before the marriage reforms of the first decades of the 20th century. As shown by Christina Carlsson Wetterberg and Kari Melby (Chapter Two), these reforms introduced (or confirmed) a distinction in custody within marriage, giving parents equal rights to decide on daily care, while the father retained the right to decide in matters of economic custody. As regards custody after divorce, the marriage reforms opened up the possibility for women to be full guardians – a right that unmarried women had already obtained. Today joint custody of children within marriage as well as after divorce is the principal rule.

All the Scandinavian/Nordic countries differ from the rest of Europe in the early change of view of the unmarried mother from sinner to victim, the offender now being the father of the 'illegitimate' child (Kofoed, 2002; Poulsen, 2002), and all three countries implemented reforms aimed at disciplining fathers to take responsibility for the maintenance of 'illegitimate' children. In Norway and Denmark, moreover, the state supplied economic support in case the father did not pay (demanding the father to reimburse the expenses), but only in Norway did children born out of wedlock gain the right to inherit from the father and to carry his name in this early period (1915). In Denmark, reforms to this end were carried out in 1937. At this time an income maintenance law for children of unwed mothers was also introduced in Sweden, but not until 1969 did they obtain the same rights as children born in wedlock.

Behind the mother's responsibility – formal or substantial – for young children during most of the 20th century lay prevailing understandings of what was in 'the best interest of the child'. In the last decades of the century, however, the argument of the child's best interest was used to bolster fathers' rights to custody or access to children after dissolution of marriage or partnership. In all three Scandinavian countries, the father's right to children after divorce or dissolution of partnership was strengthened in the late 20th century. So mothers had a preferential right to their children in a strictly limited period. Trine Annfelt (Chapter Six) and Charlotte Andersen and Anna-Birte Ravn (Chapter Seven) analyse changes in family laws regulating custody and access, and the discursive strategies brought into use in the political debates on family policies leading to these reforms (see also Roman, Chapter Five). Focusing on Norway from 1981 till 2000, Annfelt shows how this institutional change was legitimated also by a fundamental change in the way gender equality was used in discussions of fathers' and mothers' rights, her main point being that gender equality increasingly lost importance as a discursive resource for women, while it gained importance for men. This shift was possible because the concept of 'equality' was released from its original connection to women as the underprivileged gender in socio-economic terms. When equality became a benefit in itself, it could be, and was, de facto, used by politicians of all political affiliations to argue for men as the underprivileged gender in need of equality. Andersen and Ravn's analysis of the Danish case, focusing on institutional and discursive changes from 1968 to 1995, confirms this shift in the meaning of equality. The political debates of the late 1960s, the 1970s and early 1980s took for granted that the mother was the prime childcarer, and that this work contributed to her underprivileged position in the labour market, making her custody of the child the most 'fair' solution. In the 1990s, these arguments not only lost discursive power, but also mothers were portrayed as a problem because of their alleged obstruction of fathers' access to their children. Christine Roman addresses ambiguities in Swedish gender-equality policies by bringing to the fore that the new rights gained by biological fathers might serve to reproduce power relations between women and men. In her words, the discourse on the importance of the biological father has become hegemonic. The male gender seems to overrule class.

Women's economic citizenship – a key issue

The question of economic citizenship or economic independence serves as another entry to the conceptualisation of equality. The concept 'economic citizenship' is suggested by Alice Kessler-Harris (2003) as a response to the fact that traditional concepts of citizenship fail to address the gendered application of economic rights. According to T.H. Marshall's classical definition, economic rights include the civil right to work, that is, 'the right to follow the occupation of one's choice' and the social right to economic security (Marshall, 1992, pp 10f). Kessler-Harris argues that although these two sets of economic rights – the civil and the social – are seen as complementary, their gendered application is obvious: 'Who gets what kinds of economic rights (whether civil or social) has rested on sometimes hidden, normative assumptions about who "cares" and who "works"' (Kessler-Harris, 2003, p 159). In the concept of 'economic citizenship' she combines the right to work in the occupation of one's choice – including childrearing and household maintenance – with the right to an income adequate for the support of self and family. Economic citizenship in this sense is probably the most important issue in regard to women's empowerment and human dignity in the 20th century; it has been pivotal for women's full integration into the community of citizens.

In this volume we analyse the realisation of economic citizenship for women in the Scandinavian countries in the 20th century and identify different strategies: on the one hand, the claim for civil rights to occupational work; on the other, claims for attaching economic rights to care work, either indirectly to women as family members or directly as individual economic rights for women. We know from previous research, and this is confirmed in the present volume, that, in practice, full civil citizenship for married women – that is, the right to independent economic maintenance through an occupation – was carried through in the second half of the 20th century (Hagemann, 2002). Until the 1960s the important demarcation line of civil citizenship seems to have been drawn between married and unmarried women. As shown by Christina Carlsson Wetterberg and Kari Melby in Chapter Two, a claim for civil rights in the sense of rights to occupational work did not gain great support in the early decades, but was more important in Sweden than in Norway. Even in Sweden, however, married women's entry into the labour market was not a political issue until the 1950s, as Åsa Lundqvist shows in Chapter Four. In the 1960s, Swedish government commissions introduced the idea of 'freedom of choice', and Christine Roman (Chapter Five) identifies the important shift from class to gender equality as a primary goal of family policies in the late 1960s. Only from this time did the individual, and not the nuclear family, come into focus in family reforms, and married women's gainful employment become normative in Sweden and Denmark (see also Ravn, Chapter Three). In Norway this shift took place around a decade later.

A more important strategy in the first half of the 20th century to strengthen married women's economic position was to attach economic rights to care. From the very beginning of the century, women became a target of social policy, related to the fact that they were key to reproduction. With inspiration from Foucault, Bente Rosenbeck has indicated that motherhood became an important strategy, and women's fertility a policy field, when declining fertility became a political challenge in the Nordic countries at the turn of the 19th century (Rosenbeck, 1992). The mother and housewife played the lead in efforts to improve the quality and quantity of the population. The Nordic marriage Acts, adopted between 1909 and 1929, exemplify a strategy where economic rights were attached to care. New rights should strengthen the economic position of the wife, but were given to women as family members, indirectly and through the management of men. In

Sweden there were hardly any reforms in favour of individual mothers' rights in this period, but the Norwegian laws took steps to further strengthen women's economic position as housewives and enhance individual mothers' rights. These laws indeed increased married women's economic independence, but in a strictly limited way. When it came to economic security, married women were far from equal to men, as Christina Carlsson Wetterberg and Kari Melby write in Chapter Two. The marriage reform established gender equality, but married women did not become economically independent.

In Chapter Three, Anna-Birte Ravn delves deeper into married women's economic dependence on the basis of the right, or rather lack of right, to pay taxes. She reveals that this lack of economic citizenship resulted in the loss of other forms of citizenship: in Denmark married women's ability to exercise new political rights on a local level remained dependent on their husbands' paying of local taxes until the 1960s. It is an important observation that this obvious political discrimination, following from married women's legal status as subordinate persons in the tax-law system, makes sense only within a special form of gendered thinking on the relationship between individual, family and state. The gendered tax system – as well as other economic regulations of the family – affected not only discourse or 'imagination'. By disadvantaging married women's paid work, the tax-law system contributed to the material preservation of a heterosexual male provider/female housewife family model and to keeping married women in 'their place'.

On the other hand, material changes came to affect the regulation of the gender arrangement. In Chapter Five, Christine Roman states that in the late 1960s the gap between state regulations and family life was obvious in Sweden. Family laws were still based on gendered division of work, while rising female labour market participation, increasing divorce rates, and the expansion of social rights and benefits had changed the family. A proposal for a gender-neutral marriage Act expressed the processes of individualisation and defamilialisation. Gender equality was no longer compatible with the ideal of mothers as housewives, with consequences for women's economic rights. Due to the gender neutrality principle, women lost some specific rights attached to their caring work, with the right to maintenance after dissolution of marriage as one example. Another is the proposal of gender-equal parental leave. In other words, the 'fight to abolish housewifery' not only resulted in a transformation of former private concerns – such as childcare – to the political; it also abolished economic rights attached to care, distributed to women indirectly through marriage.

Today the concepts of gender equality and women's citizenship, as well as gender-equality policies are strongly challenged. One challenge is represented by the debate on parenthood (as previously). Another is formulated by the younger generation: women and men brought up with apparently achieved gender equality. Not least are gender-equality politics and concepts of citizenship challenged by increasing cultural, religious and ethnic diversity in Scandinavia.

A generational uproar?

Two chapters in this volume deal with generational differences and conflicts of today, resulting in debates challenging the contemporary equality and family policy. In Chapters Ten and Eleven, Ann-Dorte Christensen and Christina Fiig indicate that some young women of today want to restore the division between private and public, and do not want the state to interfere in how people organise their private lives and family relations. This policy is quite contrary to the actual one, with its roots in the 'state feminism' of the 1930s and in the women's movement of the 1970s.

The young women in Christensen's study expect equal rights for women and men, and they value equality. Their expectations as to their future work and family life are driven by autonomy and individualisation, and they stress the importance of being independent of a male provider. Nevertheless, they reject the pronounced focus on career and want to combine family and work in a way that differs from the dominant equality policy. While previous generations of women experienced family responsibilities and care as a barrier to public life and equal rights, these young women emphasise the right to put greater focus on the family, where they expect individuality and autonomy to have room to flourish. Also Birte Siim (Chapter Eight) identifies a tendency among young ethnic-minority women in Denmark to define gender equality as belonging to the public sphere and to see the strong equality norm as a barrier against respecting different family cultures. Can we expect, then, that claims for attaching economic rights to care – as, for example, the relatively popular Norwegian cash benefit for care of small children (see Borchorst, Chapter One) – will gain increasing support in the future? If so, we can see clear connections to the solutions of the 1910s and 1920s.

While young women not self-defined as feminists are the focus in Christensen's study, Fiig analyses the defined feminists who initiated a media debate on feminism in the Scandinavian countries around the end of the 20th century. They addressed the concept of equality from another direction, challenging the strong public consensus on the achieved gender equality not by rejecting the focus on career, but by highlighting inequalities in the Scandinavian welfare states – in schools and other educational institutions, in workplaces, and in the public sphere. This new feminism reveals that private problems in fact are not private and that the slogan of the 1970s is still relevant, even though the questions and solutions are not totally in line with official equality policy, focusing much more on intimate questions relating to body, sexuality and violence. Contrary to the feminist movements of the 1970s, however, they insist on feminism as an individual and not a collective project. The focus on individuality and diversity seems to be a common feature characterising the claims for citizenship of the young generation of women.

Is it a common tendency today to define gender equality as belonging to the public sphere, while the private/family is reserved for individuality and diversity

– a kind of 'refamilialisation'? If the answer is 'yes', this may in turn have politi consequences.

Ethnicity – diversity and Nordic gender-equality models

Welfare politics, including equality politics, contains liberating elements as well as elements of control and even discrimination. At the same time as the marriage laws declared husband and wife as equals, some people were forbidden to marry on eugenic grounds. In Chapter Four Åsa Lundqvist shows that the egalitarianism of the Swedish family policy of the 1930s and 1940s was conditional: poor and old women, and women with many children as well as mentally ill men and women were all constructed as different from 'normality'. The controlling and discriminating aspects of the Scandinavian welfare states have come to the fore in welfare state research lately. A vast amount of coercive sterilisation during the 1930s and 1940s, especially in Sweden, has been revealed, questioning the picture of the all-good and benevolent welfare state (Broberg and Roll-Hansen, 1996; Tydén, 2002). The theoretical consequences of this new knowledge are not obvious. While some researchers stress the aspects of control, others still hold that freedom and security are central aspects of the welfare state (Åmark, 2001; Koch, 2001; Kulawik, 2002;).

Historically then, equality politics has meant empowerment and inclusion of some women, and marginalisation and exclusion of others. A central question in relation to this today, addressed by Birte Siim (Chapter Eight) and Diana Mulinari (Chapter Nine), is the marginalisation of migrant women in present-day Denmark and Sweden. The two authors discuss the challenges from migration and multiculturalism to the Nordic welfare and gender models, characterised by universal social citizenship, participatory democracy and so-called woman-friendly policies. They both point to discriminatory practices that affect minority women living in Denmark and Sweden respectively, and their analyses show that the Scandinavian welfare states tend to support gender hierarchy among ethnic 'others' and to construct difference, quite contrary to the aims of the official equality policy.

Birte Siim looks at the specific tensions between gender equality and diversity in the Danish approach to migration, and the barriers and potentials with regard to including minority women in democracy and society. Between 1983 and 2002, Danish migration policies changed radically from being among the most liberal to being among the most restrictive. The overriding principle became that of economic self-sufficiency, resulting for example in an 'introductory grant', breaking with a major Danish welfare-state principle of universal social rights, as well as with the equal treatment principle in the Human Rights Convention. According to Siim, the increased emphasis in migration legislation on assimilating minorities to presumed Danish values and ways of life creates tensions between the gender-equality model and respect for cultural diversity. During the 1990s, migrant families became the target of highly gendered political reforms and a discourse framed by the dichotomy of liberated Danish majority women versus oppressed minority women lacking self-determination. Siim concludes that, while the dual breadwinner model and strong gender-equality norm can hold a potential for equal treatment of young migrant women, they can at the same time be a barrier to respecting the diversity in family cultures, norms and values. But maybe the problem with the Scandinavian gender-equality model is not that it does not acknowledge family ties, but that it does not secure gender equality in the family?

Within the last two decades, Denmark and Sweden have moved in opposite directions in relation to migration policies. Even so, Diana Mulinari shows how notions of gender equality in Sweden are used as a central feature of defining boundaries between who belongs to the nation and who does not. The Swedish welfare state is racialised, argues Mulinari, and calls for more empirical research and theoretical work on this theme. Focusing on refugee women from Latin America, who were active in resistance movements and fighting for gender equality before they arrived in Sweden, Mulinari shows how a culturalist discourse constructs these women as part of an undifferentiated category of 'migrants' with assumed 'cultural' traits, distinguishing the 'west' from the 'rest' and 'them' from 'us'. More specifically, 'other' cultures are constructed as patriarchal, and thereby 'gender equality' has developed as a central ethnic signifier of national belonging and maybe the most important boundary between 'them' and 'us'.

The results of Siim's and Mulinari's investigations raise new questions about the relationship between Nordic welfare institutions and gender equality from the perspective of migrant women. They indicate that, in spite of different multicultural policies and discourses in Sweden and Denmark, there are common problems connected to gender equality and respect for diversity. These problems also occur in Norway, in spite of yet another political scenario in relation to migration, though more similar to the Swedish one than to the Danish. This actualises once again the complex relation between discourse, politics and practice.

Politics, science and everyday life

The marriage laws adopted during the early decades of the 20th century were secular, relying on liberalism and modern science rather than religion. First and foremost, the medical profession played an important role in giving the prerequisites for the formation of marriages. This can be seen as a first sign of a tendency, more explicit from the 1930s, towards a scientifically legitimated political decision making. From this time, the social sciences became increasingly important as a basis for welfare politics. This is what Anne-Lise Seip has called the 'scientification of politics' (Seip, 1989).[6] Of course, it is not a one-way relationship. Politicians favour some discourses over others, and policy influences academic discourse.

Traditionally, we think that there are marked differences between the countries on this topic. Extensive use of experts is usually seen as something typically Swedish. But actually how unique is the system with science-based official reports as a basis for policies? The study of the parallel law processes in the Nordic countries towards the marriage-law reform shows that experts were consulted in all countries. Could we say that a distinctive role of experts is an element of the Nordic model?

Two chapters in the present volume focus on the relationship between science and politics, not unexpectedly dealing with Swedish cases. Åsa Lundqvist (Chapter Four) provides an analysis of the development of Swedish family politics between the 1930s and the early 1970s. More concretely, the amalgamation of political ambitions, social reforms, and ideas and suggestions brought forward by experts in governmental commissions, are analysed. Christine Roman (Chapter Five) examines the impact of academic discourse on political discourse since the 1970s. First, her analyses demonstrate that the social sciences played an important mediating role between the Swedish welfare state and social movements that challenged established boundaries between private and public. Second, she points out the significance of sociology and gender research in the discursive shifts that took place in family and gender-equality politics during the investigated period, as well as the new truths about gender relations and the parent–child relationship that were established in the process.

A positive attitude towards state intervention in combination with reform-oriented and active social movements has been seen as another hallmark of Nordic political culture, with the marriage legislation as an early example. In sharp contrast to other European countries, in the Nordic countries the state crossed the border into the private sphere in order to regulate the relationships within the family. This was a regulation with the complex ambition to defend the interests of married women, of the family and of the nation. As many of the chapters in this book show, the marriage reform was the rather modest beginning of a process leading towards a more profound state intervention in private life. This intervention can be analysed in terms of equality, freedom and social security as well as in terms of control: for example, on the one hand, the maternity insurances, and on the other, sterilisation laws emerging in the 1930s; children's allowances paid to the mother after the Second World War; the parental leave introduced later on; and today a discussion about distributing this leave between the mother and the father.

We shall not forget, though, that as new regulations are emerging others disappear. Compulsory sterilisation is not accepted today, almost all eugenic hindrances to entering marriage have disappeared, and marriage as such has lost importance via laws on cohabitation and same-sex partnership. Even if the heterosexual family is still the norm, there are today other accepted ways of living together.

As stated many times in this book, discourse, political ambitions, laws and so on are not identical to how things work in practice and how ordinary people think and act in everyday life. Often certainly there has been, rather, a gap; a gap that 'social engineers' strove to bridge by fostering ambitions and social reforms (Hirdman, 1989). That the marriage laws were adopted can be explained by the fact that different kinds of interests could be satisfied by the reform. It was seen both as a way to stabilise marriage and secure reproduction and/or as a way to strengthen married women's individual rights. On these grounds one could establish consensus among politicians from different camps, legal and medical experts, and women's organisations. Whether the reform had support among people in general is difficult to say. One leading lady within the Danish women's movement, Astrid Stampe Feddersen, questioned in an interesting way young women's rationality when it came to marriage:

> What the young women are thinking of is to meet the man who will be their sweetheart, and with whom they can share their life, and they are totally convinced that whatever disaster befell other women, the two of them will stand up to it. They do not want to hear about a marriage settlement. (Beretning, 1914, p 40)

From the assembly room, with its rhetoric of rational choices, equality and economic independence, we tumble straight into a daily life governed by quite different rules. Love enters as something irrational that the law has to fight against. According to Stampe Feddersen, the law should guarantee that people, even if they were blindfolded, should have their rights and, in the case of women, should also be protected (Beretning, 1914).

The concept of gender equality in a historical context

This book stresses the importance of looking at 'gender equality' as a historical concept. How equality is conceptualised varies according to time and place, and within a specific historical context as well. When equality was claimed in the context of early 20th-century marriage reform it was, openly or not, based on the assumption of gendered division of work. The gendered imagination taking for granted the heterosexual male-provider/female-housewife family as the norm of civil society favoured a specific form of masculinity and femininity: the married man as the head of his household and providing for his family, and the married woman as wife, housewife and mother. Equality in this context usually meant that married women's work and care within the family was valued as different but equally important as men's work outside.

The heterosexual male-provider/female-housewife family was set up as a norm, but poor families and families without a male provider could seldom live up to the norm. In these 'abnormal' families women were supposed to work outside the home. Accordingly, different discourses on equality coexisted within the political debate; the dominant discourse related to gender difference, another was based on sameness in relation to work, and a third took its point of departure from caring responsibilities. Åsa Lundqvist's analysis of Swedish family politics in the 1930s and 1940s (Chapter Four) confirms that the dominant discourse stressed the functions of the gender-divided nuclear family, but that the egalitarianism was conditional: poor and old women, women with many children as well as mentally ill men and women were all constructed as different from 'normality'.

In Scandinavia the rhetoric of equality was successful from the 1910s. The Nordic marriage-law reform expressed the dilemma of modernity: a dilemma between gender division and equality, between a housewife norm and an equality norm, between family orientation and individualism. The result was, not surprisingly, rhetorical inconsistencies, as when the rhetoric of women's independence and gender equality prevailed, together with a naturalisation of women's housework and a strong housewife norm. Until the 1960s the gendered division of work was rarely thoroughly questioned. According to Lundqvist, equality was emphasised in an ideological way in Sweden in the 1940s and 1950s, that is, in theory it was assumed that in a sophisticated, modern society all citizens should be equal. However, in practical politics and discussions, gender difference was emphasised in order to improve social conditions. The dilemma of modernity, trying to unite a rhetoric of equality with a fundamental gender division, was still evident. During this phase, the concepts of equality and difference were altered. On the one hand, experts trained in social psychology interpreted differences between women and men in novel ways. In discussions regarding women's role as mothers and carers for the children, women were seen as the 'natural' carers. These experts legitimised women as the 'caring head' of the family, while other experts stressed the dual roles of women, in a time where women's participation in the labour market became increasingly more important. Ideological and material changes in the 1960s brought family policy into a phase dominated by gender neutrality, with a focus on both women and men. At the beginning of the 1970s, men were brought into the debate on gender equality and family policy in Sweden in connection with a debate on parental leave (see Roman, Chapter Five). From that time on, the conflict between family and work was officially defined as concerning men as much as women. During the 1980s the focus of equality policy shifted from the family to work life. And as is shown in the chapters dealing with parenthood, generational conflicts and ethnicity, this new understanding of gender equality is today to some extent contextualised.

All over Scandinavia, from the very beginning of the 20th century, women became a target for social policy, related to the fact that they were a key to reproduction. This brings the interrelation between family politics and gender-equality politics and the discursive frameworks that shaped these politics to the fore. While the concept of family policy is used and presented as gender-equality policy in Norway and Sweden, the concept is not well established in Denmark, and the two policy areas seem to be largely separated. While gender-equality policies are regulated in detail in the former, this is not the case in the latter. This brings about a discussion of how discourse, policies and practice are related. The countries have in many respects adopted policies that are quite similar, but they also differ in terms of visions of gender equality, policy logics and the role gender equality has played as an explicit policy goal. Path-dependent processes, the timing of specific policies and the role of specific discourses may explain these differences. Cultural factors such as the degree of secularisation have been of importance, and the influence of specific actors such as women's organisations and political parties also contributes to explaining the differences (Borchorst, Chapter One).

While state intervention in the family traditionally has been one hallmark of the Scandinavian welfare state, studies among the younger generation give reason to question whether a new privatisation of families is going on. As Christensen's study (Chapter Ten) shows, young women's approach to gender equality is characterised by a strong endeavour for autonomy and individualisation, which means that neither men, the state, nor predefined equality discourses are allowed to make decisions on their behalf. Christensen discusses whether young women of today question some of the key issues in the development of the 'woman-friendly' Scandinavian welfare states. She finds that it appears as if they find it important to reinstall the border between private and public.

Notes

[1] This view is held also by other observers, among them British scholar David Bradley, who declares that there was no counterpart in other democratic societies to the proactive and wide-ranging approach to family reform in the Nordic countries. According to Bradley, there were comparable features in other European jurisdictions, but these were more isolated phenomena (Bradley, 2000, p 45. See also Bradley, 1996, 2001).

[2] See Christiansen and Åmark (2006, p 336) on this point. Concerning the union between Norway and Sweden and its dissolution, see Sejersted (2005) and Stråth (2005).

[3] According to Esping-Andersen (1999), parental leave for fathers does not explain the high degree of gender equality in the Nordic countries.

[4] For a critical discussion of Helga Hernes' thesis, see Borchorst and Siim (2002). See also discussions on Yvonne Hirdman's theory by Wetterberg (1992); Blom (2002); Borchorst et al (2003) and Hagemann (2003).

[5] See also Hirdman (1989).

[6] In a recent publication on Nordic welfare state history, the role of scientists does not seem to be a main perspective. Rather, political explanations are underlined; when dealing with health, and especially the hospital sector, the 'logic of modern medicine' explanation is abandoned (see Christiansen and Åmark, 2006, pp 339–40).

Bibliography

Åmark, K. (2001) 'Trygghet och tvång', *Nyhedsbrev. Netværk for Nordisk Velfærdsstatshistorie*, vol 16, pp 2–10.

Åmark, K. (2006) 'Women's Labour Force Participation in the Nordic Countries during the Twentieth Century', in N.F. Christiansen, K. Petersen, N. Edling and P. Haave (eds) *The Nordic Model of Welfare. A historical reappraisal*, Copenhagen: Museum Tusculanum Press, pp 299–333.

Beretning fra det 2. Nordiske Kvindesagsmøde i København den 10. og 11. Juni 1914 (1914) Copenhagen.

Bergqvist, C., Borchorst, A., Christensen, A.-D., Ramstedt-Silén, V., Raaum, N.C. and Styrkárdóttir, A. (eds) (1999) *Equal Democracies? Gender and politics in the Nordic countries*, Oslo: Scandinavian University Press.

Berven, N. and Selle, P. (eds) (2001) *Svekket kvinnemakt? De frivillige organisasjonene og velferdsstaten*, Oslo: Gyldendal akademisk.

Bjørnson, Ø. and Haavet, I.E. (1994) *Langsomt ble landet et velferdssamfunn: trygdens historie 1894–1994*, Oslo: Ad notam Gyldendal.

Blom, I. (2002) 'Stereotypienes tyranni', review of Y. Hirdman (2001), *Nyhedsbrev. Netværk for Nordisk Velfærdsstatshistorie*, vol 20, pp 12–15.

Bonke, J. (1995) *Arbejde, tid og køn – i udvalgte lande*, Copenhagen: The Danish National Institute of Social Research.

Bonke, J. (1997) *Dilemmaet arbejdsliv – familieliv i Norden*, Copenhagen: The Danish National Institute of Social Research.

Borchorst, A. (1980) *Kvinder som arbejdskraftreserve – politisk floskel eller social realitet?*, Aarhus: Aarhus University Press.

Borchorst, A. and Siim, B. (2002) 'The women-friendly welfare states revisited', *NORA. Nordic Journal of Women's Studies*, vol 2, pp 90–8.

Borchorst, A., Christensen, A.-D. and Siim, B. (2003) 'Diskurser om køn, magt og politik i Skandinavien', in A. Borchorst (ed) *Kønsmagt under forandring*, Copenhagen: Hans Reitzel Publishers, pp 247–66.

Bradley, D. (1996) *Family Law and Political Culture. Scandinavian laws in comparative perspective*, London: Sweet & Maxwell.

Bradley, D. (2000) 'Family Laws and Welfare States', in K. Melby, A. Pylkkänen, B. Rosenbeck and C. Wetterberg (eds) *The Nordic Model of Marriage and the Welfare State*, Nord 2000: 27, Copenhagen: Nordic Council of Ministers, pp 37–67.

Bradley, D. (2001) 'Evaluations of the projects "The Nordic Marriage Model in a Comparative Perspective" and "Women's Right to Work, Social and Private Security in the Nordic Countries and the European Union"', in K. Ståhlberg (ed) *The Nordic Countries and Europe III. Evaluations*, Nord 2001: 24, Copenhagen: Nordic Council of Ministers.

Broberg, G. and Roll-Hansen, N. (eds) (1996) *Eugenics and the Welfare State. Sterilisation policy in Denmark, Sweden, Norway and Finland*, East Lansing, MI: Michigan State University Press.

Christiansen, N.F. (2000) 'What is Nordic about the Nordic Welfare States?' in K. Melby, A. Pylkkänen, B. Rosenbeck and C. Wetterberg (eds) *The Nordic Model of Marriage and the Welfare State*, Nord 2000: 27, Copenhagen: Nordic Council of Ministers, pp 197–205.

Christiansen, N.F. and Åmark, K. (2006) 'Conclusions', in N.F. Christiansen, K. Petersen, N. Edling and P. Haave (eds) *The Nordic Model of Welfare. A historical reappraisal*, Copenhagen: Museum Tusculanum Press, pp 335–54.

Christiansen, N.F. and Markkola, P. (2006) 'Introduction', in N.F. Christiansen, K. Petersen, N. Edling and P. Haave (eds) *The Nordic Model of Welfare. A historical reappraisal*, Copenhagen: Museum Tusculanum Press, pp 9–29.

Christiansen, N.F., Petersen, K., Edling, N. and Haave, P. (eds) (2006) *The Nordic Model of Welfare. A historical reappraisal*, Copenhagen: Museum Tusculanum Press.

Esping-Andersen, G. (1990) *The Three Worlds of Welfare Capitalism*, Cambridge: Polity Press.

Esping-Andersen, G. (1999) *Social Foundations of Postindustrial Economies*, Oxford: Oxford University Press.

Esping-Andersen, G. (2000) 'A Welfare State for the 21st Century. Ageing societies, knowledge-based economies, and the sustainability of European welfare states', Paper.

Fraser, N. (1997) *Justice Interruptus. Critical reflections on 'postsocialist' conditions*, New York and London: Routledge.

Haavet, I.E. (2006) 'Milk, Mothers and Marriage. Family policy formation in Norway and its neighbouring countries in the twentieth century', in N.F. Christiansen, K. Petersen, N. Edling and P. Haave (eds) *The Nordic Model of Welfare. A historical reappraisal*, Copenhagen: Museum Tusculanum Press, pp 189–214.

Hagemann, G. (1995) 'Protection or Equality? Debates on Protective Legislation in Norway', in U. Wikander, A. Kessler-Harris and J. Lewis (eds) *Protecting Women: Labor legislation in Europe, the USA, and Australia, 1880–1920*, Urbana and Chicago, IL: University of Illinois Press, pp 267–89.

Hagemann, G. (2002) 'Citizenship and Social Order: gender politics in twentieth-century Norway and Sweden', *Women's History Review*, vol 11, no 3, pp 417–29.

Hagemann, G. (2003) 'Moderne og postmoderne', in G. Hagemann, *Feminisme og historieskrivning*, Oslo: Universitetsforlaget, pp 75–90.

Hernes, H. (1987) *Welfare State and Woman Power: Essays in state feminism*, Oslo: Norwegian University Press.

Hirdman, Y. (1988) 'Genussystemet – reflexioner kring kvinnors sociala underordning', *Kvinnovetenskaplig tidskrift*, vol 3, pp 49–63.

Hirdman, Y. (1989) *Att lägga livet till rätta – studier i svensk folkhemspolitikk*, Stockholm: Carlssons.

Hirdman, Y. (2001) *Genus – om det stabilas föränderliga former*, Stockholm: Liber AB.

Jordansson, B. and Vammen, T. (eds) (1998) *Charitable Women – Philanthropic Welfare 1780–1930*, Odense: University Press of Southern Denmark.

Karlsson, L. (1995) 'The Beginning of a "Masculine Renaissance": The debate on the 1909 prohibition against women's night work in Sweden', in U. Wikander, A. Kessler-Harris and J. Lewis (eds) *Protecting Women: Labor legislation in Europe, the USA, and Australia, 1880–1920*, Urbana and Chicago, IL: University of Illinois Press, pp 235–66.

Kautto, M., M. Heikkilä, B. Huinden, S. Marklünd and N. Ploug (eds) (1999) *Nordic Social Policy. Changing welfare states*, London and New York: Routledge.

Kautto, M., Fritzell, J., Huinden, B., Kvist, J and Uūsitalo, H (eds) (2001) *Nordic Welfare States in the European Context*, London and New York: Routledge.

Kessler-Harris, A. (2003) 'In Pursuit of Economic Citizenship', *Social Politics*, vol 10, no 2, pp 157–75.

Knudsen, T. (ed) (2000) *Den nordiske protestantisme og velfærdsstaten*, Aarhus: Aarhus University Press.

Koch, L. (2001) 'Tvangssterilisation i Danmark 1929–67', in H.R. Christensen, U. Lundberg and K. Petersen (eds) *Frihed, lighed og tryghed. Velfærdspolitik i Norden*, Aarhus: Skrifter udgivet af Jysk Selskab for historie nr. 48.

Kofoed, N. (2002) 'Synd og forsørgelse. Seksualitet uden for ægteskab i Danmark 1700–1850', *Den jyske Historiker*, nos 98–99, pp 45–65.

Kulawik, T. (2002) 'The Nordic Model of the Welfare State and the Trouble with a Critical Perspective', *Nyhedsbrev. Netværk for Nordisk Velfærdsstatshistorie*, no 21, pp 2–8.

Markkola, P. (2001) 'Lutheranism and the Nordic Welfare States in a Gender Perspective', *Kvinder, Køn & Forskning*, vol 2, pp 10–19.

Marshall, T.H. (1992/orig. 1950) 'Citizenship and Social Class', in T.H. Marshall and T. Bottomore, *Citizenship and Social Class*, London: Pluto Press, pp 3–54.

Melby, K., Pylkkänen, A., Rosenbeck, B. and Carlsson Wetterberg, C. (eds) (2000) *The Nordic Model of Marriage and the Welfare State*, Nord 2000: 27, Copenhagen: Nordic Council of Ministers.

Melby, K., Rosenbeck, B. and Carlsson Wetterberg, C. (2001) 'Ekteskapslovreform: En forutsetning for velferdsstaten?', in H.R. Christensen, U. Lundberg and K. Petersen (eds) *Frihed, lighed og tryghed. Velfærdspolitik i Norden*, Aarhus: Skrifter udgivet af Jysk Selskab for historie nr. 48.

Melby, K., Pylkkänen, A., Rosenbeck, B. and Carlsson Wetterberg, C. (2006) *Inte ett ord om kärlek. Äktenskap och politik i Norden ca. 1850–1930*, Göteborg and Stockholm: Makadam.

Petersen, K. (2006) 'Constructing Nordic Welfare? Nordic Social Political Cooperation 1919–1955', in N.F. Christiansen, K. Petersen, N. Edling and P. Haave (eds) *The Nordic Model of Welfare. A historical reappraisal*, Copenhagen: Museum Tusculanum Press, pp 67–98.

Poulsen, P.P. (2002) 'Bagerjomfruen og hornblæseren. Uden for ægteskabet i Gødvad i 1800-årenes anden halvdel', *Den jyske Historiker*, nos 98–99, pp 131–43.

Ravn, A.-B. (1995) '"Lagging Far Behind All Civilized Nations": The debate over protective labor legislation for women in Denmark, 1899–1913', in U. Wikander, A. Kessler-Harris and J. Lewis (eds) *Protecting Women: Labor legislation in Europe, the USA, and Australia, 1880–1920*, Urbana and Chicago, IL: University of Illinois Press, pp 210–34.

Rosenbeck, B. (1992) *Kroppens politik. Om kön, kultur og videnskab*, Copenhagen: Museum Tusculanum Press.

Rosenbeck, B. (2000) 'Modernization of Marriage in Scandinavia', in S. Sogner and G. Hagemann (eds) *Women's Politics and Women in Politics. In honour of Ida Blom*, Oslo: Cappelen Akademisk Forlag, pp 69–85.

Rosenbeck, B. (2005) 'Velfærdsstatsforskning og køn', in N. Bredsdorff and N.F. Christiansen (eds) *Det kritiske blik*, Copenhagen: Tiderne Skifter, pp 184–204.

Seip, A.-L. (1984) *Sosialhjelpstaten blir til. Norsk sosialpolitikk 1740–1920*, Oslo: Gyldendal Norsk Forlag.

Seip, A.-L. (1989) 'Politikkens vitenskapeliggjøring. Debatten om sosialpolitikk i 1930-årene', *Nytt Norsk Tidsskrift*, vol 3, 210–25.

Seip, A.-L. (1994) *Veiene til velferdsstaten. Norsk sosialpolitikk 1920–1975*, Oslo: Gyldendal Norsk Forlag.

Sejersted, F. (2005) *Norge og Sverige gjennom 200 år*, bind 2: *Socialdemokratiets tidsalder. Sverige och Norge under 1900-talet*, Oslo: Pax.

Sommestad, L. (1992) *Från mejerska till mejerist. En studie av mejeriyrkets maskuliniseringsprocess*, Lund: Arkiv.

Sommestad, L. (1997) 'Welfare State Attitudes to the Male Breadwinning System: The United States and Sweden in comparative perspective', *International Review of Social History*, vol 42, no 5, pp 153–74.

Sørensen, Ø. and Stråth, B. (eds) (1997) *The Cultural Construction of Norden*, Oslo-Stockholm-Copenhagen-Oxford-Boston: Scandinavian University Press.

Stråth, B. (2005) *Norge och Sverige genom 200 år*, band 1: *Union och demokrati. De förenade rikena Sverige-Norge 1814–1905*, Oslo and Stockholm: Pax/Nya Doxa.

Tydén, M. (2002) *Från politik till praktik. De svenska steriliseringslagarna 1935–1975*, Stockholm: Acta Universitatis Stockholmiensis, Stockholm Studies in History 63.

Wetterberg, C.C. (1992) 'Från patriarkat till genussystem – och vad kommer sedan?', *Kvinnovetenskaplig tidskrift*, vol 3, pp 34–48.

Wikander, U. (1988) *Kvinnors och mäns arbeten: Gustavsberg 1880–1980*, Lund: Arkiv förlag.

Wikander, U., Kessler-Harris, A. and Lewis, J. (eds) (1995) *Protecting Women: Labor legislation in Europe, the USA, and Australia, 1880–1920*, Urbana and Chicago, IL: University of Illinois Press.

Part One
Meanings of gender equality in Scandinavian welfare policy

Woman-friendly policy paradoxes? Childcare policies and gender equality visions in Scandinavia

Anette Borchorst

Introduction

Since the late 1980s, feminist scholarship has reconceptualised the equality–difference dilemma, which has plagued feminist activists and policy makers for many decades. They have been confronted with the claim that they should choose either difference or equality as the route to achieving gender equality, because the two should be regarded as logically incompatible. The dilemma has been closely interconnected with the gendered division of breadwinning and unpaid care work and the public–private split, which has been attached to it.

The rethinking of the dilemma has generated a broad consensus that it is neither universal nor static, and that it varies in significance and appearance according to time and place. Furthermore, most scholars agree that the dilemma rests on a socially constructed dichotomy. This calls for contextualised studies of how the dilemma is constructed in time and space.

In this chapter I focus on the political construction of the equality–difference dilemma in so-called woman-friendly Scandinavian welfare policies. I address different policy logics of childcare policies in Sweden, Norway and Denmark and the visions of gender equality underpinning them. I commence with the rethinking of the dilemma in feminist scholarship during the past decades. Subsequently, I discuss whether the notion of one coherent Scandinavian welfare model should be challenged, and I critically address the term 'woman friendliness' and discuss its conceptual strength. The following sections explore the underlying visions of gender equality of day-care policies, parental leave and homecare cash benefits, and I focus on the varying timing and context of these policies in the three countries. Finally, I offer some perspectives on the political construction of the equality–difference dilemma in the Scandinavian countries, and how woman-friendly policies are presented in a European context.

Equality versus difference – a contextual and socially constructed dilemma

For centuries, feminists have grappled with the equality–difference dilemma both as activists and as scholars. Political scientist Carole Pateman named this dilemma after Mary Wollstonecraft, a feminist pioneer who struggled with the problem both personally and in her activism for female suffrage in Britain. Pateman's point of departure was women's problems with achieving full citizenship, and she described Wollstonecraft's dilemma as follows:

> The dilemma arises because, within the existing patriarchal conception of citizenship, the choice always has to be made between equality and difference, or between equality and womanhood. On the one hand, to demand 'equality' is to strive for equality with men (to call for 'rights of men and citizens' to be extended to women), which means that women must become (like) men. On the other hand, to insist, like some contemporary feminists, that women's distinctive attributes, capacities and activities be revalued and treated as contribution to citizenship is to demand the impossible; such 'difference' is precisely what patriarchal citizenship excludes. (Pateman, 1992, p 20)

Pateman concluded that the two routes are incompatible within the confines of the patriarchal welfare state, and it makes it impossible for feminists to choose. She asserted that female subordination and a public–private separation were cemented by the patriarchal welfare state. Her conclusion related to liberal countries, such as Britain, Australia and the US, where liberalism had permeated society and shaped public policies around a public–private dichotomy. Scandinavian countries had experienced a somewhat different development, since women had moved nearer to, but not yet achieved, full citizenship in these countries. As a more general statement, Pateman claimed that only public or collective provisions can secure full citizenship (Pateman, 1989, pp 180, 203).

Wollstonecraft's dilemma has been challenged and reinterpreted theoretically and empirically by many feminist scholars, and it has been argued that difference is opposite not to inequality, but to sameness. The allegation that equality and difference are mutually incompatible is accordingly false, and has been constructed to curtail women's options (Scott, 1988). In a similar vein, political scientist Carol Bacchi argued that the choice between the two notions is a trap that obscures the fact that there are other options for achieving gender equality (Bacchi, 1990). The equality–difference issue diverts the attention from the inadequacy of the market and the state to cope with social reproduction. In a comparison of American, Australian and British feminist arguments for gender equality, she concluded that the Americans in particular have been divided into two contending camps. This has, above all, been exposed in debates about pregnancy and parental leave.

The reason why American feminists more often than Australian and British have been trapped in heated debates about equality and difference is the limited regulation of pregnancy and parental leave in the US. In line with Pateman's argument, Bacchi argued that the character and significance of the dilemma in different contexts is interconnected with variations in the character of the public–private split and with the strength and power of feminist agency and women's movements.

The rethinking of the equality–difference dilemma since the late 1980s has fostered valuable insights into how the dilemma operates, and a widespread consensus has emerged among feminist scholars that it is a dynamic and socially constructed phenomenon. All of the above-mentioned scholars point to the political construction of the gendered division of care and breadwinning as salient for the character of the problem.

The solution to Wollstonecraft's dilemma: visions for shared caregiving and breadwinning

The philosopher Nancy Fraser has offered a very thought-provoking reconceptualisation of the dilemma, drawing on normative theory of justice, post-structuralism and a critical socialist standpoint (Fraser, 1997). She explores the role of sameness and difference in different gender-equality visions and assesses their strengths and weaknesses in fostering gender equality. Her position is that both recognition of cultural difference and redistribution directed at reducing economic inequality should be pursued simultaneously in the struggle for gender equality:

She argues that gender differences have both cultural–valuational and political–economic dimensions that generate two analytically different kinds of injustice. She insists that both economic redistribution that removes some of the material differences between the genders and recognition of gender specificities should be pursued simultaneously (Fraser, 1997, p 21).

Fraser, too, addresses the equality–difference dilemma as a social construction, and she rejects the idea that equality or difference or any other single value may foster gender equality. She proposes instead a plurality of different normative principles related to poverty, exploitation, income distribution, leisure time, respect, marginalisation and androcentrism, which foster recognition of difference as well as economic redistribution as markers to assess the strengths and weaknesses of different feminist visions for gender equality. They differ particularly in the organisation of care work. One vision, *the universal-breadwinner model,* aims at universalising the breadwinner role. It is based on moving care work from the family to the market and the state. Another vision, *the caregiver parity model,* keeps care work in the family context and seeks to revaluate informal care work through public funding, such as caregiver allowances. Whereas the first emphasises sameness and intends to make women into citizen workers like men, the second preserves the gendered division of caregiving and breadwinning, but seeks to make difference costless. The purpose is to upgrade women as citizen carers. Neither vision adequately manages post-industrial dilemmas or fulfils the different dimensions.

Fraser claims that a third vision has the potential to foster gender equality in the post-industrialist phase of capitalism, where women have been or are being integrated in breadwinning. *The universal-caregiver model* aims at removing the gendered separation by making women's life patterns the norm of both women and men. It is based on shared parental roles of care and breadwinning. Her allegation is that this vision combines the best part of the two other visions and that it dismantles the gendered opposition between care and breadwinning. This could be labelled as a solution to a post-industrial version of Wollstonecraft's dilemma, with the goal of promoting full participation by women in politics and civil society on a par with men. Like the aforementioned scholars, she regards collective solutions as necessary to reduce gender inequalities.

The visions are analytical categories, that may coexist, but their policy logics are to some extent contradictory, especially as far as the universal-breadwinner and the caregiver-parity vision are concerned. This has to do with the fact that the two visions are constructed around very different perceptions of whether care of dependent persons should be located solely within the realm of the family, or whether public responsibility for care is crucial for achieving gender equality.

Gender equality and Scandinavian welfare states

Gender equality has been regarded as a hallmark of the Scandinavian welfare states, and it has often been considered part and parcel of the welfare state model that has characterised these countries. Comparative welfare state research, and, above all, sociologist Gøsta Esping-Andersen, has concluded that these welfare states represent a specific social democratic cluster that distinguishes itself from the liberal and the conservative–corporatist welfare state models (Esping-Andersen, 1990). The configuration of state, market and civil society in welfare provision is distinctive for the three welfare models, since each model tends to ascribe more importance to one of these arenas compared to the other models. The key concept for differentiating between them is the degree of decommodification. This concept takes stock of the state–market connection by measuring the capacity of welfare states to render the living standards of individuals independent of pure market forces (Esping-Andersen, 1990, p 3). Esping-Andersen concludes that the Scandinavian social democratic model has the highest degree of decommodification. The model is characterised by an activist and interventionist state that provides many universal transfer payments and care services to its citizens.

The conclusions about distinct welfare models have been remarkably resilient, but a vast number of scholars have criticised the typology and its core assumptions and concepts. Feminist scholars have criticised the theory for neglecting the gendered suppositions of welfare states, for ignoring the role of the family and for missing central differences by discarding public care services.

Esping-Andersen has added defamilialisation as a criterion for ranking the welfare states. The concept measures the degree to which regimes unburden households and diminish the dependence of kinship (Esping-Andersen, 1999, p 51). On the basis of family allowances, tax deductions and care services for children and the elderly, he concluded that the Scandinavian countries were also uniquely defamilialised. It is, however, also questionable whether defamilialisation captures all nuances in the development in Scandinavian countries, since they have also fostered refamilialisation through relatively generous parental leave schemes, which have prolonged the period working mothers may care for the newly born. Similarly, granting statutory rights to fathers has also increased the role of the family in caring for small children.

Woman-friendly welfare states or modernised patriarchies?

In 1987, political scientist Helga Hernes concluded that the Scandinavian welfare states had a woman-friendly potential and that reproduction 'had gone public in these countries'. Hernes stated that a woman-friendly welfare state would not force harder choices on women than on men and would open other roads to self-realisation than motherhood (Hernes, 1987, p 15). The term 'woman friendliness' was catchy, but its conceptual strength, normative foundation and empirical validity have been questioned. In the years after it was published, Hernes' book served as an eye-opener for feminist-state theorists to become more aware of comparative variations in the gendered impact of welfare policies. However, her conclusions have been criticised for being biased towards the political culture, institutions and gender model of the Nordic countries and for being premised on a vision of a universal-breadwinner model. Furthermore, the relation between gender equality and woman friendliness is not made clear (Borchorst and Siim, 2002).

Hernes emphasised the role of women's agency and the drastic changes in women's lives, and she downplayed gender structures and patterns of continuity. This is contrary to historian Yvonne Hirdman's analysis. In her contribution to the Study of Power and Democracy in Sweden, she concluded that basically no major changes had occurred in the gender system in the post-war period (Hirdman, 1990). According to her, the gender system theory was reproduced through two different logics – segregation and hierarchy – based on a male norm. This theory aroused considerable theoretical controversy too, because, among other things, it neglected human agency. Furthermore, the lack of a comparative perspective on the Swedish welfare state contributed to an extremely pessimistic picture of Sweden.

Seen together, Hernes and Hirdman raised interesting questions about the implications of emphasising the role of either structure or agency. Furthermore, the span between the two trajectories that Hernes and Hirdman pictured may be attributed to the fact that the former focused on the role of politics and of political actors, whereas the latter concentrated her analysis on the market. A realistic diagnosis of the Scandinavian countries probably lies in between the two scenarios.

The bottom line is, however, that the Scandinavian (and Nordic) case seems to constitute a specific model, when regarded in a larger perspective. Whether they (ie the Scandinavian countries) are measured against the strength of breadwinning, eligibility criteria or specific dimensions such as the ability to maintain autonomous households as single mothers, or the level of public care services, they have often been singled out as a distinct model.

Understanding difference

In much of the recent debate about Wollstonecraft's dilemma, differences – not only between the genders but among women and among men – have become a leading theme. Since women (and men) do not constitute a single, undifferentiated group, it is problematic to argue that they have common and collective interests as both Hernes and Hirdman did. It is, however, noteworthy that Hernes also stated that in a woman-friendly welfare state injustices based on gender should be eliminated 'without an increase in other forms of inequality such as among groups of women' (Hernes, 1987, p 15). The question is how patterns of inequality related to class, gender and race intersect. Different types of inequality are intertwined, but they do not operate by the same mechanisms, and the achievements of different welfare policies in eradicating different types of inequalities may vary.

An interesting question is whether Scandinavian welfare policies are better equipped to reduce class-based and gender-based inequalities than ethnic inequalities. These welfare states were established on compromises between different classes, and the 'passion for equality' that has characterised these countries has, above all, related to reducing class inequalities. Gender inequality was gradually put on the political agenda, but it was not till the 1960s and 1970s that gender equality became a central political objective in the wake of the comprehensive political mobilisation of women. The role of ethnicity has, until recently, been neglected in the welfare discussions, possibly because these countries have been relatively homogeneous in terms of race and ethnicity and have been reluctant to acknowledge the development towards multicultural societies. In recent years, ethnicity has become subject to increased political and scholarly focus. The question is whether the visions of gender equality in Scandinavia are based on political values of the majority population. Another issue is whether multiculturalism in itself challenges redistributive social policies in general and the distinctive features of the Scandinavian welfare states in particular (Kymlicka, 2006). In terms of gender, the question is whether the woman-friendly policies also benefit women from ethnic minority groups, or whether they are based on visions of gender equality for middle-class women from the majority population (see Siim, Chapter Eight, and Mulinari, Chapter Nine in this volume).

Gender visions of Scandinavian care policies

The overall question is, then, whether Scandinavian welfare policies have dismantled the equality–difference dilemma as Pateman, Bacchi and Hernes indicated, and whether they have done so in similar ways. In this chapter, I focus on the policy logics of different childcare policies in the three countries and explore their underlying visions of gender equality.

The three countries have adopted at least three types of care policies: maternity and parental-leave schemes, day-care services and homecarer allowances. All involve some degree of state intervention and tax financing, supplemented by other types of funding, such as parents' payment (day care) or wages (parental-leave compensation). However, day-care services and cash benefits such as parental-leave and homecarer allowances have different impacts on who provides the care and in which arena the care is located (Leira, 2002).

Day-care services are performed by public employees, and may accordingly be regarded as defamilialisation that, above all, stimulates a universal-breadwinner vision. Homecarer allowances and parental leave enhance familialisation, but in different ways. In spite of its gender-neutral underpinning, the modest compensation of homecarer allowances makes it a non-option for fathers. It promotes a caregiver-parity model that is founded on gender-differentiated parental roles. Parental-leave schemes are founded on a universal-breadwinner vision. They provide a relatively high economic substitution tied to previous income. Attachment to the labour market is also supported by regulations against layoff during leave. The level of compensation and the gendered construction are decisive for whether fathers are encouraged to take part in the care of newborns or not. Collective agreements, especially in the female-dominated sectors, also supplement the economic compensation up to the normal wage level, and collective agreements in some job sectors also guarantee old-age pension contributions. Furthermore, schemes that earmark leave periods for the father that are not transferable to the mother are embedded in a universal-caregiver policy logic.

In the following, I will explore which mix of gender visions and care policies has been adopted in the three countries, and whether and how they have solved the equality–difference dilemma.

Maternity and parental leave

All three countries adopted *maternity leave* schemes at the end of the 19th century, involving a few weeks' mandatory leave with restricted access to economic compensation. The interwar period and the immediate post-war period only saw small changes. Working-class mothers had to engage in gainful employment, and they had to tackle the problems with bridging motherhood and waged work individually. When the mass entry of women into the labour force took off, the issue reappeared on the political agenda. This happened in the early and mid-1960s in Sweden and Denmark and some 15 years later in Norway (see Appendix, Table 4).

In the 1960s, *Sweden* took the lead in terms of integrating women in gainful employment, and was the first Scandinavian country to carry out a major policy reform of parental leave. In 1974, the leave was extended to six months, and fathers were granted statutory rights to leave. The arguments in favour of the decision strongly emphasised that bridging family life and working life was, above all, a problem for women, and integrating men in care responsibilities was decisive for achieving gender equality. The legislation was entirely gender neutral. During the 1970s, proposals for earmarking part of the leave for fathers were promoted by several actors, motivated by the argument that the reform had only affected gendered leave practices very modestly. The Social Democratic Party was subject to a heated debate, when the party leadership rejected the pressure from the women's caucus for a daddy quota (Karlsson, 1996).

During the following years, the role of fathers was subject to increased politicisation. A daddy group appointed by the Social Democratic government in 1982, focused on making men into fathers. In 1994, one month's daddy leave was passed by a right-wing government and above all promoted by the Liberal Party, which was very committed to gender equality. The daddy leave was framed as a means to change the so-called 'in principle' attitude of men towards gender equality (Bergman and Hobson, 2002; Klinth, 2002). The small extreme right-wing party, New Democracy, was the only party to frame it as coercion. When Sweden underwent an economic crisis in the early 1990s, cutbacks in social benefits were implemented, including parental leave. In January 2002, Sweden extended the daddy leave to two months. All the right-wing parties opposed the proposal.

Norway was the first Scandinavian country to grant mothers economic compensation during parental leave (Sainsbury, 2001). It happened in 1909, 20 years before both Sweden and Denmark. Still, political discourse over many subsequent decades strongly emphasised the role of women in the family, framing Norway as 'the country of housewives'. Despite an economic upturn during the 1960s, the country did not witness a large-scale entry of women into the labour force, as the two other countries did. This happened some 15 years later, in the wake of the oil boom. In 1978, the leave was extended to 18 weeks, and fathers obtained statutory rights; but until 2001, fathers' entitlements were determined by the mother's employment situation. A major policy shift took place when Norway, in 1993, was the first country in the world to adopt a one-month daddy quota. The idea was launched in 1989 by a government committee focusing on the role of men, and it was also promoted in a long-term government programme on gender equality for the early 1990s. The argument was that the gender-equality project could not be furthered if only the role of women was in focus. The quota was presented as mild and benevolent coercion, and it was framed as a win–win solution for child, father and mother. When it was passed in parliament, it was not very controversial. The Conservative Party, which voted against the proposal, voiced some concern on parental choice, but it was in favour of strengthening the responsibility of fathers, like the rest of the parties (Oftung, 1996; Leira, 2002; Ellingsæter, 2006).

Denmark was the laggard in expanding maternity leave and in granting fathers statutory rights to parental leave. Throughout the 1970s, visions of a universal-caregiver model gained influence in the new feminist movement, and a broad political mobilisation in favour of a reform of parental leave emerged. Proposals to prolong the leave and grant fathers statutory rights were repeatedly put on the political agenda, but they were rejected by the centre and right-wing parties (Borchorst, 2003). The arguments against the reform were mainly economic, since the country in 1973 was hit by a severe economic crisis, with massive unemployment and public cutbacks. In 1980 maternity leave was extended to 18 weeks, and in 1984 Danish fathers obtained statutory rights 10 and 6 years after the Swedish and Norwegian fathers. The law stipulated that fathers had the right to two weeks after the birth and to share 10 weeks of the parental leave with the mother. The politicisation of fatherhood was limited in Denmark, and, unlike the other two countries, no government committee was set up to focus on the role of men and fathers. Denmark was also the last country to adopt a daddy leave. It happened in 1997, when parental leave was prolonged to 26 weeks, of which the last two were earmarked for the father. A right–left split appeared for the first time in political negotiations on parental leave, but the decision went largely unnoticed by the public. In 2001, the daddy leave was abolished at the same time as the leave was extended to 52 weeks. This decision also generated a right–left split, but this time it prompted a heated debate. The right-wing parties that took power shortly after framed the daddy leave as a violation of the family's free choices, and a discourse about entitlement of fathers never gained ground as a competing discourse, among other reasons because the Social Democrats were internally divided on the issue (Borchorst, 2006).

Day-care services

The three welfare states have, over a long span of years, provided public funding for childcare facilities. Throughout the first part of the the 20th century, policies in the three countries were residual and targeted at poor families. Still, for many decades to come, childcare facilities were few in number and of poor quality.

In *Denmark*, an alliance between Social Democratic politicians and progressive childcare pedagogues produced a broad political consensus to subsidise childcare. The economic prosperity of the 1960s provided an impetus for a policy shift, and many different actors argued for the integration of women into the labour force (Borchorst, 2002). For a short time, two competing discourses were at play as to who should care for the children. One position held that mother and child should stay together for at least three years and that childcare facilities were harmful for children. According to the other discourse, children would benefit from good-quality day-care services. Meanwhile, all political parties in parliament supported the adoption of a fundamental break with the previous legislation, which was passed in 1963. The new law was based on universalist principles and framed public childcare provisions as a children's right. It was not formally linked to considerations for women's employment, although the right-wing politicians especially were motivated by the unmet demand for labour. The law triggered a rapid expansion of high-quality childcare provisions, and since the mid-1960s Denmark has had record high provision for children under three (see Appendix, Table 10). The growing number of childcare facilities and the integration of women were simultaneous and mutually reinforcing processes.

Sweden witnessed a similar process when the activity rates of women started to increase in the early 1960s. The women's caucus in the Social Democratic Party strongly advocated expansion of public childcare as a vehicle for achieving gender equality. The Swedish trade unions also pressured strongly for public day care during this period, when some of the right-wing parties opposed state-sponsored childcare during the 1960s. However, the increasing number of working mothers appeared to be an irreversible process, and a considerable number of working mothers engaged in gainful employment before universal childcare was adopted in 1972. The motivation related to women's employment and to the social-pedagogical value for children, but Swedish politics tended to ascribe greater emphasis to the role of the family in caring for the newborn than did the Danish, and the parental-leave reform implied that children would be cared for in the home during the first year (Bergqvist et al, 1999).

Norwegian politics has for many years been marked by ambivalence towards publicly provided childcare, and there has not been a broad political alliance promoting the issue. In the 1970s, there was strong opposition towards expanding public childcare, but in 1975 a universalist law was adopted. However, it did not trigger any significant extension of childcare facilities. The level of public provision has remained substantially lower than in the two other countries, especially for children under three (see Appendix, Table 10). A substantial number of working mothers engaged in gainful employment during the 1970s and 1980s without childcare options (Leira, 2002; Ellingsæter, 2006). In 2003, a price reform was passed, reducing payments made to the parents, and this increased the pressure for expansion of the number of childcare facilities.

Homecarer allowance

In all three countries proposals for homecarer allowances have been on the political agenda for several decades, initially aimed at mothers, but in recent decades the legislation has been couched in gender-neutral rhetoric even though the take-up rate by fathers is extremely modest.

In *Norway*, women in the Christian People's Party, in particular, supported by the traditional extra-parliamentary women's organisations, have advocated a homecarer allowance that would encourage mothers to stay at home and care for small children. For many years, this proposal failed to obtain sufficient support, but in 1997, when the party headed a centre-right government, a cash-for-care allowance was adopted as an alternative to public childcare provisions. The proposal was supported by the parties to the right. The Social Democrats, above all, the women, strongly opposed the reform. The scheme was constructed as a means to strengthen the free choice of families, and it was not aimed solely at the parents.

In *Sweden*, a homecarer allowance was proposed by the Social Democrats in the early 1960s, and the women's caucus was internally divided on the issue. This division disappeared later when they united in a demand for childcare provisions. At this time, some right-wing parties argued for a homecarer allowance, with free choice in relation to care as a strong rhetoric. They did not, however, gain sufficient support (Bergqvist, 1999; Klinth, 2002). The proposal reappeared in the 1990s and it was passed by a right-wing government in 1994, when the Liberal Party, which supported a daddy month, reached a compromise with its coalition partner, the Christian Democratic Party. When the Social Democrats regained power later the same year, the scheme was removed before it was implemented. Since then, the issue has not played a significant role.

In *Denmark*, the Social Democrats proposed a homecarer allowance in the 1960s, but over the next decades liberal and conservative politicians proposed a removal of state subsidies from childcare services in favour of letting the money follow the child. The proposal did, however, disappear from the political agenda. During subsequent decades, municipalities were allowed to pay mothers to mind their own children, but the compensation was very modest, and relatively few parents opted for it. In 1993, a childcare leave scheme was adopted together with an educational and a sabbatical leave arrangement integrated in a plan to reduce unemployment. This scheme, which was abandoned in 2002, was more comparable to parental-leave schemes. It promoted a universal-breadwinner policy logic, with its regulations of job return and its relatively generous economic compensation.

Post-industrial policy paradoxes

The Scandinavian welfare states have generated unmistakable gains in terms of gender equality, and Pateman's and Bacchi's conclusions that Wollstonecraft's dilemma has become less intricate are probably precise, since childcare policies have made it possible to reconcile caring responsibilities with working life. Still, the dilemma has far from disappeared; it appears as paradoxes and inconsistencies between different policy logics. Gender equality is largely taken for granted as a norm in these countries, but it is, however, also clear that gender equality has not and will not progress in a linear movement, and the state feminist project that Hernes described suffers from visible shortcomings.

Gender equality as a political project has been more consistent in *Sweden* than in the two other countries, and Swedish policy paradoxes have mainly appeared in the discrepancy between the strong rhetoric of gender equality and the gendered social practices. The policy logics have, above all, embraced a universal-breadwinner model through the reforms of parental leave and the expansions of childcare provisions. A step towards a universal-caregiver vision was taken with the adoption of the daddy month. Shared parenthood as a prerequisite for shared power between the genders gained a strong foothold in Swedish political discourses during the 1990s (see Lundqvist, Chapter Four, and Roman, Chapter Five in this volume). Objectives for reaching gender equality have been integrated in political negotiations about childcare policies, and Swedish politics have been characterised by a party competition that has kept gender high on the political agenda. The pressure for reforms mainly originated within the political parties and with the women's caucuses as a strong pressure group. The decrease in female representation at the 1991 election prompted a comprehensive debate on the subordinate position of women, and several parties subsequently boosted their gender-political image. New feminist organisations emerged, first in the form of a secret group and later as a political party that ran for election in 2006. However, it did not gain sufficient support to obtain parliamentary representation.

A caregiver-parity vision of gender equality has never gained a strong foothold in *Danish* policies, either in the political system or in the women's organisations. Policies have for many years been solidly based on a universal-breadwinner model with a very high level of public child provision as the key pillar. By this means, Danish politics has gone furthest in terms of defamilialisation and is characterised by a reluctance to acknowledge gender as a relevant political criterion, which has created policy paradoxes in the mismatch between the gender-neutral debates and the gendered construction of, particularly, parental leave. Parental leave earmarks a relatively longer period for the mother than the two other countries, whereas the daddy leave has been abolished. This implies that Denmark is the only Scandinavian (and Nordic) country that has downplayed a universal-caregiver gender vision. The restricted role of gender equality in Danish politics may, among other things, be ascribed to the unfavourable opportunity structures that prevailed during the formative years of Danish policies of gender equality. The so-called landslide election in 1973 coincided with the economic crisis, and it altered the political climate profoundly and undermined the prevailing consensus on gender equality. Today no political parties profile themselves on gender equality.

In *Norway*, gender equality has constituted a hegemonic discourse, but the country has opted for all three visions in childcare policies, and this exposes the longstanding ambivalence towards gainful employment of Norwegian mothers

(Leira, 2002; Ellingsæter, 2006). Policy logics have been founded on a reluctant-breadwinner model, since Norwegian mothers were integrated in the labour force despite the lack of services; but the country was, however, the first to take steps towards a universal-caregiver model by adopting a daddy quota. The cash-for-care allowance, on the other hand, promoted a caregiver-parity model. This ambivalence mirrors a strong maternalist position that can be traced back to discussions in the early 20th century (see Carlsson Wetterberg and Melby, Chapter Two, in this volume; Sainsbury, 2001).

It has been demonstrated that the policy logics of the Scandinavian welfare states share a number of characteristics that explain why they are often clustered together when gender equality is in focus. The similarities are, among other things, a product of their similar political cultures and the fact that women's organisations, political parties and experts have engaged in policy learning (Melby et al, 2006). Since the early 1970s this coordination has been institutionalised among the state machineries of gender equality in the three countries under the auspices of the Nordic Council of Ministers.

The analysis also illuminates that the Scandinavian countries do not constitute a coherent model. The variations may be explained by the different economic, political and discursive opportunity structures. The fact that Denmark was hit earlier and harder by an economic crisis in the 1970s implied that gender equality never obtained the same political significance as in the two other countries. Sweden underwent an economic crisis much later, when gender equality had already gained a strong foothold in Swedish politics. Furthermore, social democracy has been much stronger in Sweden and Norway in comparison with Denmark, and this has strengthened gender equality as a political objective. A distinctive feature of the Swedish situation is that a right-wing party has very actively supported gender equality. The extreme right has, on the other hand, been strongest in Denmark, where the Progress Party, which voiced open resistance to gender equality, gained considerable political representation in the so-called landslide election in 1973. A sister party was later established in Norway, but it never became as influential as the Danish party. In Sweden, New Democracy only obtained parliamentary representation from 1991 to 1994. Furthermore, religion has played a far greater role in Norway, where the Christian People's Party was formed in the 1930s and has been far more significant than its Danish sister party, which was established in the early 1970s. Furthermore, religion has had greater political significance than in the two other countries. Freedom of religion has also been used as legitimisation for including decisive exceptions in the legislation of gender equality (Skjeie and Teigen, 2005).

Perspectives on the Scandinavian policy paradoxes

The Scandinavian welfare model in itself has fostered new types of inequalities that have reproduced Wollstonecraft's dilemma in new forms.

The gendered character of the public–private division has been reproduced in the labour market, and this has exacerbated the gender segregation of the labour market, which is more conspicuous than in other countries. Woman-friendly arrangements are much more widespread in the public sector than in the private sector, such that relatively many women are attracted to public employment. During the past decades, salaries in the public sector have fallen behind those in the private sector, which means that the wage gap between the genders persists, despite women's relatively higher education levels compared to those of men. Many women are hit by a 'child penalty', which implies that childbirth and parental leave, career opportunities, wages and pension earnings are intertwined in a complex way. Women miss out on wage increases, career opportunities and old-age pension contributions the more children they have. Furthermore, the development towards insurance-based old-age pensions has and will increase gender-income inequalities in old age, due to women's lower salaries, shorter working hours per week and shorter working lifetime.

Still, it is widely accepted that the Scandinavian welfare policies have been at the forefront in fostering gender equality, and they are sometimes constructed as a model for other countries. This was suggested after the Lisbon summit in March 2000, when woman-friendly welfare policies were presented as a means to making the EU the most competitive and dynamic knowledge-based economy in the world. The strategy was designed to comply with challenges such as globalisation and the aging of populations. After the summit, some experts were asked to make policy recommendations for making the strategy operational, and they suggested that woman-friendly policies, including affordable day care, paid maternity and parental leave, and provisions for work absence when children are sick, have the potential to achieve several objectives at the same time. The woman-friendly policies were framed as a win–win strategy: they secure economic competitiveness by increasing the labour force, reduce the greying of populations and combat social exclusion and poverty (Esping-Andersen et al, 2002, ch. 3).

Truly, the Lisbon benchmarks for women's employment rates at 60% in 2010 were met several decades earlier in the Scandinavian countries (see Appendix, Table 4), and they have adapted to a dual-breadwinner family model, which has also contributed to a relatively high fertility rate. It is, however, questionable whether the model is exportable. Furthermore, the picture of woman-friendly policies as simultaneously inclusive and competitive has been challenged by neo-liberal discourses about the need for welfare reforms during an era of globalisation. These discourses have gained ground in many countries, and the right-wing government takeovers in Denmark in 2002 and in Sweden in 2006 have led to a rearticulation of a public–private split, and arguments for free choice are voiced more loudly.

Hence, the Scandinavian welfare states have weakened Wollstonecraft's dilemma. But they have not resolved it. It has survived in a post-industrial version.

Bibliography

Bacchi, C.L. (1990) *Same Difference: Feminism and sexual difference*, Sydney: Allen & Unwin.

Bergman, H. and Hobson, B. (2002) 'Compulsory Fatherhood: The coding of fatherhood in the Swedish welfare state', in B. Hobson (ed) *Making Men into Fathers*, Cambridge: Cambridge University Press, pp 92–124.

Bergqvist, C., Kuusipalo, J. and Styrkarsdottir, A. (1999) 'The Debate on Childcare Policies', in C. Bergqvist, A. Borchorst, A.-D. Christensen, V. Ramstedt-Silén, N.C. Raaum and A. Styrkárdóttir (eds) *Equal Democracies? Gender and politics in the Nordic countries*, Oslo: Scandinavian University Press/Nordic Council of Ministers, pp 137–57.

Borchorst, A. (2002) 'Danish Childcare Policy: Continuity rather than Radical Change', in S. Michel and R. Mahon (eds) *Childcare Policy at the Crossroads: Gender and welfare state restructuring*, New York: Routledge, pp 267–85.

Borchorst, A. (2003) *Køn, magt og beslutninger. Politiske forhandlinger om barselsorlov 1901–2002*, Aarhus: Magtudredningen/Aarhus University Press.

Borchorst, A. (2006) 'The Public–Private Split Rearticulated: Abolishment of the Danish daddy leave', in A.L. Ellingsæter and A. Leira (eds) *Politicising Parenthood in Scandinavia*, Bristol: The Policy Press, pp 101–20.

Borchorst, A. and Siim, B. (2002) 'The Women-Friendly Welfare States Revisited', *Nordic Journal of Women's Studies*, vol 10, pp 90–8.

Ellingsæter, A.L. (2006) 'The Norwegian Childcare Regime and its Paradoxes', in A.L. Ellingsæter and A. Leira (eds) *Politicising Parenthood in Scandinavia*, Bristol: The Policy Press, pp 121–44.

Esping-Andersen, G. (1990) *The Three Worlds of Welfare Capitalism*, Cambridge: Polity Press.

Esping-Andersen, G. (1999) *Social Foundations of Postindustrial Economies*, Oxford: Oxford University Press.

Esping-Andersen, G., Gallie, D., Hemerijck, A. and Myles, J. (2002) *Why we need a New Welfare State*, Oxford: Oxford University Press.

Fraser, N. (1997) *Justice Interruptus. Critical reflections on the 'postsocialist' condition*, New York/London: Routledge.

Hernes, H.M. (1987) *Welfare State and Women Power. Essays in state feminism*, Oslo: Norwegian University Press.

Hirdman, Y. (1990) 'Genussystemet', in *Demokrati och Makt i Sverige*. Maktutredningen huvudrapport, SOU 1990:44, Stockholm, pp 73–114.

Karlsson, G. (1996) *Från Broderskap til Systerskap. Det Socialdemokratiska Kvinnoförbundets Kamp för Inflytande och Makt*, Lund: Liber Förlag.

Klinth, R. (2002) *Göra Pappa med Barn. Den Svenske Pappapolitiken 1960–95*, Umeå: Borea.

Kymlicka, W. (2006) 'The Multicultural Welfare State', Paper to Fourth International Conference on Political Theory: Globalisation and the Political Theory of the Welfare State and Citizenship, Aalborg University.

Leira, A. (2002) *Working Parents and the Welfare State*, Cambridge: Cambridge University Press.

Melby K., Rosenbeck, B., Pylkkänen, A. and Carlsson Wetterberg, C. (eds) (2006) *Inte ett ord om kärlek. Äktenskap och politik i Norden ca. 1850–1930*, Stockholm: Makadam förlag.

Oftung, K. (1996) 'Fedrekvote – Et Virkemiddel for Likestilling', *Arbeidsnotat 14/1996*, Høgskolen i Lillehammer.

Pateman, C. (1989) *The Disorder of Women*, London: Polity Press.

Pateman, C. (1992) 'Equality, difference, subordination: the politics of motherhood and women's citizenship', in G. Bock and S. James (eds) *Beyond Equality and Difference*, New York: Routledge, pp 17–31.

Sainsbury, D. (2001) 'Gender and the Making of Welfare States: Norway and Sweden', *Social Politics*, vol 8, pp 113–43.

Scott, J.W. (1988) 'Deconstructing Equality-Versus-Difference: or, the uses of poststructuralist theory for feminism', *Feminist Studies*, vol 14, pp 33–50.

Skjeie, H. and Teigen, M. (2005) 'Political Constructions of Gender Equality: Travelling Towards … a Gender Balanced Society?', *Nordic Journal of Women's Studies*, vol 13, no 3, pp 187–97.

TWO

The claim of economic citizenship: the concept of equality in a historical context

Christina Carlsson Wetterberg and Kari Melby

In the beginning of the 20th century, marriage legislation was reformed in all the Nordic countries. Male privileges were abolished and equality was declared. Some changes in the old marriage laws had been accomplished already at the end of the 19th century, especially in Denmark and Norway, where the wives had attained their majority. Married women in all the countries had also been given the right to dispose of their own private property and income, but husbands maintained complete disposal of the common estate, as well as custody of the children. All this was changed during the reform process that followed, starting in 1909 in Norway and ending during the 1920s[1] (see Appendix, Tables 1 and 2). This early introduction of basic equality between spouses was in contrast to the situation in the rest of Europe, where it was not until the 1960s that similar legislation began to take shape (Bradley, 1996; Melby et al, 2000). This makes it relevant to talk about a Nordic model of marriage. But there were also significant differences between the Nordic countries. This chapter compares how the reform was justified ideologically and how it was designed in Norway and Sweden respectively, highlighting similarities as well as differences. The focus will be on questions regarding economic equality and equality in relation to the custody of children. Our point of departure is the widely held assumption in research that Norwegian policy, much more than its Swedish counterpart, has been and still is framed by a housewife ideology and rhetoric of gender difference (Sainsbury, 2001; Borchorst et al, 1999; Haavet, 1999). Is this seen also in the marriage reform, and if so, what do the differences mean in terms of equality?

Equality now and then

What is striking in the marriage-reform process in the Nordic countries is the very strong emphasis on equality in the motivations and discussions. But it is important to notice that equality meant something else at that time than it does today. From the beginning of the century, a norm saying that married women's primary duty was to take care of the home and the children while husbands supported the family through their work received increased support in society.[2]

When equality was claimed in the context of marriage reform it was, openly or not, usually based on the assumption of this kind of gendered division of labour. From this point of departure, equality meant that work and care within the family or, to be more precise, within what was counted as 'normal' families, was valued as different from but as important as work outside. However, this kind of equality, based on gender difference, was not attainable for those families that at the time were seen as 'deviant', those of unmarried women, lone mothers and poor wives from the working class, where the assumption was the same as today, namely, that they should/could work outside the home.[3] In other words, this concept of equality was conditional, depending on whether the woman had a male provider or not, and, thereby, also, indirectly, on class. The heterosexual male provider/female housewife family (see Ravn, Chapter Three, this volume) was set up as a norm, but with exceptions.

Custody was, besides the economic relationship, a key issue for gender equality related to the family. Even here the contrast between now and then is striking. According to very old marriage laws, the father had custody of children within marriage and, if he was not totally unsuited, also after a divorce. In this area also Danish and Norwegian women obtained expanded rights earlier than their Swedish counterparts, and some of these rights were carried through even before the common reform process started. The legal reforms in the Scandinavian countries changed the concept of *custody within marriage* and divided it in two parts: daily care and economic guardianship. The reforms made mother and father equal in terms of daily care and everyday decisions, but the father remained sole guardian in economic matters. This division persisted until the 1950s. When it came to *custody after divorce* the marriage reforms opened up the right for women to be full guardians.[4] In this case, Norway chose its own path by stating the mother's priority for the custody of small children. In the other Nordic countries the parents were made formally equal in relation to the children after divorce, and if they could not agree the courts would decide. It is interesting to contrast the situation at the beginning of the 20th century, when women's quest for custody of their children was a central claim, with the situation today, where, as Trine Annfelt argues in Chapter Six, the situation is the opposite and the debate focuses on men's rights.

The assumptions – in relation to economy and work, and in relation to fatherhood and motherhood – underlying the marriage laws today are thus quite different compared with the beginning of the 20th century. At that time equality was supposed to be reached through an economic union between the spouses, while today the assumption is that equality ideally is best promoted if the economic bonds between the spouses are as few as possible – and the laws are slowly undergoing changes in this more individualistic direction (Westerhäll-Gisselsson, 1985).[5] With custody of children it is the other way around, however. Joint custody is today the principal rule not only in marriage but also after divorce in both Norway and Sweden (Bergman and Hobson, 2002, pp 101–3).

Male breadwinner model or dual breadwinner model?

The economic equality between husband and wife in the Scandinavian marriage reform of the 1910s and 1920s rested on two fundamental principles. The first was the idea of deferred community property, which stated that husband and wife were independent and *formally equal owners* of their private property during marriage, and in case of dissolution of marriage the assets were *divided into two equal parts unless otherwise agreed in a marriage settlement*. The other principle was that the spouses were *jointly responsible for family maintenance* and that subsistence maintenance was declared equal to maintenance by money. By legally recognising women's unpaid work at home as family support, the marriage reform actually presented what we, in our book *Inte ett ord om kärlek* (Melby et al, 2006a), identify as a modified dual breadwinner model (see also Melby et al, 2006b). This is in contrast to the common understanding that a male breadwinner model prevailed during the first half of the 20th century. Here, we will develop this discussion further.

The marriage law reform declared the equality of husband and wife, but the law was also designed to secure the economic position of the housewife. The reason was, of course, that even if subsistence maintenance and maintenance by money were declared to be equal, there was little doubt that the woman was the economically dependent spouse. It was acknowledged that she supposedly seldom owned or earned significant means. The solution was *to furnish her with 'housewife's rights'* by defining the commitment of the *male breadwinner*. During marriage she had the right to get money from her husband for household expenses and for personal use. If he failed to provide adequately for the family, the court could issue him with an obligation to do so. This was a real change and a reasonable consequence of the joint responsibility for family maintenance (Utkast (N), 1918, p 55). The shared maintenance responsibility obviously necessitated a dual as well as a male breadwinner model.

Another aspect of the model was the strengthening of the housewife's economic position. The standard of living of all family members was supposed to be the same during and after marriage. The law established that the wife should have *the necessary amount of money at her disposal* to cover household expenses and her personal needs and that necessary means should be accessible for the wife 'in appropriate amounts at a time'. An economically responsible and reliable housewife was the norm. Women's extended rights were designed to give them both individual freedom of choice and better conditions to perform their maternal role. One justification was the well-being of the family; another was that it was urgent to give married women a more independent position.

On the other hand, however, *the wife's economic rights were carefully restricted*. Indeed her husband was obliged to give her money during marriage, but what was to be her property was in fact limited to what she received to cover personal needs. She was, after some discussion, not given property rights over the means for household expenses. As we shall see, the female members of the national committees were not content with this solution and tried to enlarge wives' property rights.

Joint responsibility for family maintenance and equal status of the two forms of maintenance constitute the main bases for claiming a dual breadwinner model. Rather than a pure economic or property rule, *an economic and a social community* were established. But there was little doubt that the woman was the economically dependent spouse, despite the formal declaration of the two forms of maintenance as equal. The reform prepared for a gender arrangement based on gendered division of work, where women's reproductive work in the home was an explicit assumption. The equality norm met with a housewife norm.

Different meanings of gender equality

The marriage reform proposals, as well as the resulting laws, contained inconsistencies in relation to what was defined as gender equality. The reforms were driven through during a time of great changes, not least in relation to gender, where women, mostly unmarried, were entering the labour market on a large scale. Even though the employment rates for married women were far below 10% during the 1910s and 1920s, an economically independent wife was not beyond contemporary imagination.[6] A rhetoric of equality as sameness can also be found in the debates on marriage reform. Both the Norwegian and the Swedish proposal draw the picture of the modern, working and independent woman and welcome emancipating reforms. And the rule stated in both is that, in theory, the wife should use her own income to cover her personal expenses (Utkast (N), 1918, p 52; Lagberedningen, 1918, p 22). The marriage reform was presented as an adaptation to a modernised gender relationship. Actually, the reform can be seen as an early example of 'state feminism', where gender equality was presented as a positive and necessary value for modern society. But unmarried women's increased rights were also seen as a threat. One central argument for a marriage reform was that it was necessary to give married women a more independent and equal position in order to prevent women from completely giving up plans to marry (Melby et al, 2006a, chs 6 and 7).

Combined with the picture of profound changes in gender relations, with more and more women entering the labour market and with less gender-differentiated legislation, the proposals construct a marriage where equality is based on difference, not on sameness. In the Norwegian proposal the gender division and housewife position was even presented as natural. It stated that: 'using her labour directly in the common household is for the wife *the more natural* way to fulfil the obligation to support, rather than seeking occupation outside the household' (Utkast (N), 1918, p 49). The naturalisation of women's housework was part of the *housewife norm*, more distinct in the Norwegian proposal than in the Swedish. The Swedish proposal also presented the housewife solution as the happiest one for the family, but at the same time as only one among alternatives.

The delegates wrote: 'If the wife, who has no independent income, in the interest of the family takes up the care of the household and the children, and there is no urgent need for her occupational work, her work in the home should be seen as sufficient contribution to family maintenance' (Lagberedningen, 1918, p 191). The inconsistency in the Norwegian proposal is more obvious, since the rhetoric of women's independence and gender equality prevailed together with the perception of women's housework as natural and a strong housewife norm, which is absent in the Swedish proposal. However, the difference between the two countries on this point is minuscule.

'Economic citizenship' – for the few

Civil rights include the rights to individual freedom, religious freedom, freedom of speech and the right to own property (Marshall, 1950). The early 20th-century Nordic marriage Acts increased married women's civil rights in the economic field when the spouses were declared as independent and formally equal owners of their own property during marriage. However, the basic civil right required for economic independence was the right to work, defined by Marshall as 'the right to follow the occupation of one's choice in the place of one's choice ...' (Marshall, 1950, p10). For married women, though, the right to independent economic maintenance through an occupation was not carried through in practice until the second half of the 20th century (Hagemann, 2002). At the time, a married woman was – in practice – dependent on her husband's willingness to support her economically. Neither in Sweden nor in Norway did she gain property rights over what she received to cover household expenses. The important demarcation line of civil citizenship in the economic field was marriage; the line was drawn between married and unmarried women. Or, more precisely, having a male provider made the difference: unmarried women, lone mothers and poor wives from the working class were expected to maintain their families through work outside the home. The male provider/female housewife family was dominant, favouring the specific form of masculinity where the married man was the provider and the specific form of femininity where the married woman was the housewife and mother. Nevertheless, it appears that class overruled the heterosexual norm of gender division; women without a male provider were expected to practise civil citizenship.

The fact that women's rights in the economic field were acknowledged late, especially in the US, is Alice Kessler-Harris's (2003) argument for suggesting a new category of citizenship. The history of past struggles for economic independence and social justice for women has shown the gendered character of the conceptual framework for citizenship. Although the civil as well as the social aspects of economic rights – in Marshall's terms the civil rights protected economic independence through work and the social rights, the (right to) economic security – are seen as general and complementary rights, their gendered implication is obvious: 'Who gets what kinds of economic rights (whether civil or social) has rested on sometimes hidden, normative assumptions about who "cares" and who "works"', Kessler-Harris writes (p 159). She calls for a 'gender-encompassing' concept and suggests that T.H. Marshall's three traditional categories – civil, political and social – be supplemented by a category of 'economic citizenship' based on the right to work in the occupation of one's choice, where child rearing and household maintenance and the right to earn wages adequate to the support of self and family are included (pp 158–9). Her point of departure is that the achievement of economic citizenship necessitates economic and social autonomy and independence (p 159).

The right to follow the occupation of one's choice was definitely gendered in the Scandinavian countries in the early 20th century. And for married women with a male provider, the right to choose waged work outside the household was strictly limited. Their right to a full-time occupation outside the household was illusionary, and their right to money in marriage limited. 'Economic citizenship', as defined by Kessler-Harris, was therefore far from fulfilled by the marriage reform.

Women's economic independence – subject to women's agency

Are women assigned to secondary citizenship based on their roles as family members and subject to male domination, as argued by Carole Pateman (referred to in Kessler-Harris, 2003, p 161)? Or, are there alternative ways to strengthen married women's economic position and to achieve economic citizenship in Kessler-Harris' terms? If we turn to the women's movement in the 1910s and 1920s, we find three different strategies to increase women's economic independence: the first claims women's right to occupational work, and the other two attach economic rights to care, guaranteed by the state either directly or indirectly by securing family maintenance (Carlsson, 1986, p 257). The first alternative implies economic independence through the fulfilment of civil citizenship in Marshall's terms; the two other possibilities follow Alice Kessler-Harris's strategy, attaching economic rights to care, including child rearing and household maintenance, in order to obtain economic citizenship for women. While the marriage law committees preferred to increase married women's economic independence indirectly by strengthening the obligation to maintenance within the family – though more as an ideal than as praxis – women activists tried to find solutions along all three lines in early 20th-century Scandinavia.

Civil citizenship based on occupational work

The gendered division of work was rarely thoroughly questioned during the early decades of the 20th century. In Norway, only scattered voices were heard defending married women's right to work in an occupation (Melby, 1995).[7]

In the Swedish women's movement there was a stronger defence of women's right to work outside the home than in Norway (Hagemann, 2002). This may partly be due to the fact that the social democratic women's movement grew much stronger in Sweden than in Norway during the first decades of the 20th century. Within the bourgeois women's movement there was also a more radical liberal faction that adopted a more equality-oriented feminism (Manns, 1997, p 178). Also, there are many examples where different women's organisations cooperated in defending women's right to work (see for example Östberg, 1997, pp 172–4; Frangeur, 1998, p 143; Sainsbury, 2001). When the marriage reform was discussed in 1919, the central journal of the bourgeois women's movement, *Hertha*, as well as the social democratic women's journal *Morgonbris*, published articles sharply criticising women who did not take a job after entering into marriage as 'dangerous enemies of feminism'.[8] This was, of course, not the line taken by women's organisations, but it is interesting that the articles, written by a man, were published at all.

In the 1930s the different approaches to women's work in the women's movement, as well as different directions in gender-related policies in general in Norway and Sweden, were accentuated. What had merely seemed to be rhetorical differences – married women's labour force participation was about the same in all the Nordic countries in the 1910s and 1920s – started to become a reality in the 1930s. After that, there was a steady increase in married women working outside the household in Sweden, Denmark and Finland – but not in Norway, where the proportion of married women in the workforce was consistently low until the 1950s (Åmark, 2006; see also Haavet, 1999; Sainsbury, 2001).

Economic rights attached to care: independent cash benefits

The second alternative solution debated among women activists was economic rights attached to caring work carried out in the household, guaranteed by the state. This was a solution that took its point of departure from the gendered division of labour and the fact that the possibilities to engage in occupational work were gendered. The basic assumption of this strategy was that economic independence for married women doing care work in the family necessitated individual economic rights.

The idea that mothers needed to be economically independent to perform the function of motherhood was discussed in the women's movement at the turn of the century. It was a central question in the International Association for Maternal Security and Sexual Reform, established in 1911 (Allen, 1985). Independent economic rights attached to care were also discussed among Norwegian feminists. The controversial question was how they could be realised. The so-called 'Castbergian Children's Acts', adopted in 1915, decided on economic support to unmarried mothers with low income (Blom, 1994). The law prepared the ground for mothers' benefits, and labour party women pushed the case in their local communities. The next step was to include even married mothers. Norske Kvinners Nasjonalråd (the Norwegian Branch of the International Council of Women), encouraged by Katti Anker Møller, another prominent feminist, proposed maternity benefits for all married housewives in cooperation with the well-known liberal politician Johan Castberg.[9]

The idea of a mother's wage is, in a Norwegian context, associated with Katti Anker Møller's name. According to her, it was necessary for mothers to be economically independent. The state should take economic responsibility for all mothers, she claimed, as one element in a total programme to improve the situation for mothers and children. A mother's wage was the obvious consequence of the fact that 'reproduction is the most important issue in politics and social life', she wrote in one of her essays, *Kvindernes fødselspolitik* (*Women's politics of reproduction*) in 1919 (p 5). She equalised housework and paid work and suggested an annual reasonable amount of money per child, ideally to be paid to all mothers, married as well as unmarried. The population issue was of great concern at the turn of the century, and while one of the aims behind the marriage reform was a stable and healthy population, the idea of a mother's wage was, among other things, justified by its supposed contribution to a high birth rate (Møller, 1919, pp 7–9).

Møller's ideas were highly controversial. While women in the Liberal Party were quite supportive at an early stage, the conservatives dismissed her ideas completely. In their eyes, she undermined the marriage institution and threatened monogamy. Marie Michelet, the powerful leader of Norges Husmorforbund (the Norwegian Housewives Organisation), accused Møller of wanting a state-funded matriarchy, encouraging women to prioritise reproduction inside as well as outside marriage as a way of maintenance (*Socialt kristelig tidskrift*, 1919, p 65). The liberal women's movement was caught in a dilemma: they wanted to increase the economic security for housewives, but saw cash benefits as unworthy and unethical (Mohr, 1968, pp 187ff). This shows how the question of cash economy disturbed the 'gendered imagination', taking for granted the heterosexual male provider/female housewife family, with its specific forms of masculinity and femininity. If regulation of cash benefits for housewives and mothers was needed, it was a signal that this family model did not function as a harmonic entity. In a manner of speaking, it shattered the illusion. Women in the Labour Party would be the ones to follow up on Katti Anker Møller's ideas. During the 1920s the mother's wage was transformed into a child benefit, which did not provoke the 'gendered imagination' concerning the family and therefore was less controversial. In 1946, a child benefit for all children, disbursed to mothers, was enacted in Norway.

These matters were debated in Sweden as well. At the turn of the century there was an intense discussion within the Swedish women's movement about the meaning of equality. The internationally well-known feminist Ellen Key accused the established organisations of going too far in their equality ambition and not fully considering that a woman's primary task and duty in society was being a mother. Her ideas influenced the women's movement, but her strong focus on the differences between women and men did not find much support (Manns, 1997, p 109; Bokholm, 2000, pp 286–95). Ellen Key was more of an ideologue than a politician, but she was a member of the International Association for Maternal Security and Sexual Reform. So was the radical feminist and author Frida Stéenhoff, who also founded a Swedish section of the organisation, which existed between 1911 and 1916 (Carlsson Wetterberg, 1998). Frida Stéenhoff was a friend of Katti Anker Møller, but her ideas concerning a mother's wage, or mother's pension as she called it, were slightly different, since she was also eager to defend women's right to work (Stéenhoff, 1903, 1908). She did not accept Ellen Key's idea of a fundamental gender difference. Frida Stéenhoff was a highly controversial figure in the Swedish women's movement, arguing as she did for a more free sexuality and the use of contraceptives, and her ideas about a mother's pension were not seriously discussed.

In contrast to Norway, Sweden implemented hardly any reforms in support of women's rights as mothers during the 1910s and 1920s. The question of a mothers' insurance had been raised in Parliament in 1908, and an official committee was appointed to investigate the issue, but it was not until the 1930s that the first maternity insurance and support for lone mothers were introduced (Abukhanfusa, 1987).

Economic rights attached to care indirectly through marriage

The third (theoretical) solution was family maintenance of women and children. Suggestions for how women's economic position could be improved through marriage were many. One, the proposal advocated by the majority in the marriage law committees discussed above, regulated women's rights to a limited degree. Another idea was a family or breadwinner wage, which was not easily accepted by the women's movement either, since it conflicted with the claim for equal pay for equal work.[10] A more radical idea was to give the person taking care of the household a larger share of the other's income. A moderate proposal in this direction was put forward by Elise Sem, the female member of the Norwegian marriage law committee. She claimed that all means the wife received to cover her personal needs *as well the needs of the household* should become her property (Utkast (N), 1918, p 54). This would empower the wife to take real leadership in the household and to make plans for the future, Sem argued. The wife could save money to the benefit of the family, or she could buy household items to facilitate the housework. The strategy would be to increase the amount of money estimated for the household; the wife would not feel comfortable arguing for her own personal needs, it was said. The two other female members in the Nordic committee, Emilia Broomé from Sweden and Elise Hein from Denmark, shared this view, but the male members of the committee did not support the proposal.[11]

While the suggestions from Norway were quite modest, Swedish women were more proactive. At the initiative of a leading member of the women's movement, a more radical proposal was worked out by the lawyer Georg Stiernstedt in 1915. The essence of the proposal was that all income earned during marriage should be seen as common and be divided into two equal and individually owned parts. This proposal was widely discussed in women's journals and at joint meetings with representatives from the most central women's organisations, sometimes also including social democratic women. In the discussions, Stiernstedt's ideas received a lot of support, at least in theory, as an ideal, but also met opposition. One objection was more tactical in nature, namely, that such a far-reaching reform would never be accepted in Parliament, which was probably true. The most important objection was that the proposal was in opposition to the claim that married women should have the right to dispose of their own income, which had been so central in the women's movement. This objection came from, among others, Anna Sterky, a leading social democratic woman. The lawyer Mathilda Stael von Holstein, who had been engaged in the debate since the marriage reform process started, argued in a similar way, saying that 'there was something repulsive about the idea that another person should have disposal of what oneself has earned through one's work'. It is interesting that Stiernstedt's proposed solution could, on the one hand, be seen as conservative in the sense that it would strengthen the family as an institution and preserve the gendered division of labour, and on the other hand as radical in the sense that it aimed at doing away with the economic power of the husband within the family. This duality explains why the proposal had supporters among conservative as well as among radical liberal women. Ultimately, an agreement could not be reached, and the equal sharing proposal was left out of the women's organisations' joint resolution to the marriage law committee in 1916 (Melby et al, 2006a, ch 6).

As shown above, women activists made efforts along different lines to increase married women's economic independence during the early decades of the 20th century. Claiming civil rights in terms of women's rights to occupational work was a marginal strategy, but more important in Sweden than in Norway. A more vigorous strategy for combining gender division and gender equality in both countries was to attach economic rights to care, either directly or indirectly. In terms of actual national differences in policies, Sweden, in contrast to Norway, hardly implemented any reforms in support of women's rights as mothers during the 1910s and 1920s. So, this far, we can ascertain that in Norway the housewife ideology was more explicit, but so were women's rights as mothers and thereby women's economic security. While in Sweden the principle of gender equality was interpreted more literally, the Norwegian policies went beyond the principle of formal equality to compensate for the gender difference. We will now turn to the rules on custody of children to see if this area can deepen our understanding of the gender-equality ideologies in the two countries.

Parenthood and the discourse of equality

According to the old marriage legislation in Sweden-Finland, Norway and Denmark, the father had custody of the children – including in the event of divorce, if he was not totally unsuited. In Norway the first reform in this area came about in 1859, when mothers in marriage got the same right as fathers to decide on issues concerning their children in everyday life. By this reform, economic custody was distinguished from daily custody. However, the borderline between the two elements of custody has, as Lucy Smith points out, always been blurred (Smith, 1980, p 56). In Sweden the so-called *målsmanskap*, which gave husbands the formal power to decide in all questions concerning the children, persisted until the new Marriage Act of 1920, when rules similar to the Norwegian ones were adopted. For the women's movement equality, meaning joint custody in all respects, was a central claim, but it had to accept this more limited solution.

When it came to custody of children after divorce, the solutions in Norway and Sweden differed. The divorce law adopted in Norway in 1909 stated that the mother had priority in relation to the custody of small children, and this view was maintained through the harmonisation of the Scandinavian family laws during the 1910s and 1920s. Sweden and the other Nordic countries did not follow Norway on this point; rather, the father and mother were made equal in relation to the custody of children after divorce. If they could not agree, the case would be brought to court. Joint custody after divorce was never discussed, and consequently a conflict between mother and father would arise if they both aspired to guardianship. In practice, however, research has shown that the most common solution up until today has been that the mother gets custody (Niskanen, 2000). The difference between Norway and Sweden, then, seems to be formal rather than actual on this point. Nevertheless, the different rules in the two countries seem to confirm the pattern pointed out above, marked by a more pronounced housewife norm combined with an extension of women's rights in Norway. We will here look more closely into the motivations behind these different rules in Norway and Sweden in terms of equality, difference and women's empowerment.

Maternity rights or equal rights

At the beginning of the 20th century there was a strong tendency in Norwegian politics to strengthen the position of mothers, whether married or not. In this ambition the conservatives, the liberals and the social democrats were able to unite. Their motives varied, but all had their origin in anxiety about poverty and increased illegitimacy. The Norwegian divorce law of 1909 gave, as mentioned, priority to the mother as the guardian of small children. Also in 1909 a maternal leave linked to health insurance was introduced, and working-class women also got the right to paid maternal leave and maternal care. Six years later, in 1915, the above-mentioned 'Castbergian Children's Acts' were adopted. A general maternity benefit (relief) not related to paid work and a special pension for lone mothers were now introduced.

A principal aim, central to Johan Castberg's political visions, was that 'the child's best interest' should be the guideline in this kind of legislation. (Ot.prp. nr 8, p 46). When mothers' priority was first introduced in 1909 it aroused some debate, but the proposal can hardly be called controversial. The mother's priority was established in law, but with reference to 'the child's best interest', which meant that even a mother of small children could be deemed unsuited for custody. This regulation was passed down in the Children's Act of 1915, and the notion of mothers' priority for small children was not questioned in the debate in Parliament (Stortingsforhandlinger, bd. 8I, pp 205f). When the Norwegians met the claim for gender neutrality on this point in the Scandinavian Family Committee, they withheld the rule of giving the mother priority for small children.

In 1920 Sweden adopted the model of dividing custody, giving the mother the same right as the father to decide on everyday matters, which had been in operation since 1859 in Norway. In other words, Sweden was late compared to Norway in putting the parents on equal terms in daily care, and Sweden did not follow Norway and many other countries in adopting rules at the beginning of the 20th century that gave the mother priority for (small) children. When the law reform was discussed in Parliament in 1920 no one criticised the fact that the father became sole guardian in more formal and economic matters, but some parliamentary members questioned whether it was at all adequate to give the mother the right to decide in matters concerning children. Some referred to men's and women's supposedly different nature, where a man was seen as more rational and capable of decision making than a woman. But most of the debate revolved around the problem that might arise if the parents did not agree on how to raise their children. The government bill proposed that those cases could be brought to court. Such a rule would be a threat to marriage, it was argued, and counteract the principal aim of the new marriage reform, namely to protect the home, the family and a stable society. In the end the proposal was accepted, but without this rule stating the possibility of letting the court settle disputes between parents.[12]

Concerning custody in the case of divorce, an initiative by the Fredrika-Bremer-Association in 1902 led to the first motion proposing the abolition of fathers' priority for children in case of divorce in Sweden. Instead, the parents should try to reach an agreement on custody, and if they failed the court would decide which parent was best suited to take care of the children (Cederschiöld, 1903, p 70). The motion was rejected but gave rise to a lively and interesting discussion in Parliament, illustrating how new ideas about femininity and motherliness could be used in an argumentation for equality. The liberal Karl Staaff, later prime minister, in his plea for a reform, emphasised the mother's rights and opposed an earlier speaker's statement that paternal love was as strong as maternal love.[13] Unlike in Norway, however, there was apparently no discussion at all in Sweden about giving the mother a principal priority in relation to the custody of small children after divorce. The Marriage Act of 1915, regulating the formation and dissolution of marriages, followed the motion of 1902 and the 1913 proposal of the Swedish Marriage Law Committee, and formally made the parents equal in custody questions after divorce. As in the Norwegian case, the custody decision should be guided by the best interests of the child. If the parents had come to an agreement, the court should decide accordingly only if this agreement did not evidently collide with best interest of the child.[14]

Many countries did, as Norway, adopt rules at this time that gave the mother priority for (small) children (Smith, 1980, p 49). Later on, the tendency has been to base the decision on mothers and fathers as, in principle, equally suited parents. In Norway this was not the case until 1980 (see Chapter Six, this volume). That Norway retains some priority for mothers is what, in a longer comparative perspective, seems exceptional. In England, for example, equality in relation to custody in case of divorce was introduced in 1925, and during the 1920s all the other Nordic countries chose the same path. This is again a clear illustration of our point, that the willingness to compensate for gender difference by ascribing rights to women *as* mothers seems to have been more dominant in Norway.

Along with the strengthening of the married mother's position in Norway went an ambition also to strengthen the position of unmarried mothers and children born out of wedlock. One way to do this was, as mentioned, through economic support from the state; another was by taking measures to get fathers to accept their responsibility, economically by maintenance and inheritance rights and morally by giving the children the right to adopt their father's name. While there was consensus in the discussions about the children's right to maintenance from their fathers, the questions of inheritance and family name were controversial, since this was seen as a threat to the marriage institution. Nevertheless, the 'Castbergian Children's Acts' stated that a child born out of wedlock had the right to inherit from the father as well as to carry his name. The central aim in these laws was to get men to accept their responsibility as fathers and support their illegitimate children. If they did not do so, the new laws also opened up the possibility for public support (Haavet, 2006).

In Sweden we can see the same tendency, during the 1910s, towards strengthening the position of illegitimate children. A special law on children born outside marriage from 1917 secured maintenance for those children, but it did not go as far as giving them the right to inherit and to carry their father's name. Single women's right to public support was not acknowledged in the legislation until the end of the 1930s. However, the differences between the two countries should not be exaggerated; the burden of proof of fatherhood was greater in Norway (Bergman, 2003, p 95f). This focus on disciplining fathers and getting them to accept responsibility for their illegitimate children differs from how these matters were handled in the rest of Europe, where the focus was on women as being those to blame (Elgan, 1994, p 119f; Kulawik, 1999). It is also interesting, as Helena Bergman has pointed out, that, embedded in these reforms, was a gender-specific ideology – also in Sweden, despite a stronger rhetoric of equality in general – a rhetoric stressing women as carers and men as breadwinners (Bergman, 2003, p 56). At this point the question was primarily about control and obligations. Today it is sometimes transformed into or at least influenced by a discourse on a father's right to his illegitimate child.

The question of equality in relation to parenthood is of a different nature than economic matters. While economic means, at least in theory, can be individualised and divided, this is not the case with human beings. Here lies a potential, and more existentially based, conflict of interests. The trend during recent decades in both Sweden and Norway, as shown in Christine Roman's and Trine Annfelt's chapters in this volume, goes towards strengthening the parents' joint responsibility for the children. Maternal leave has also been transformed into a parental leave. At the same time, there is a renewed tendency towards individualism in the discussions in Sweden as well as in Norway about dividing the parental leave into two parts, one for the father and one for the mother.

Concluding remarks

An overall ambition in this book is to discuss and further investigate whether it is reasonable to talk about a Nordic gender model. Our study of the early 20th century Nordic marriage Act reforms confirms that it is relevant to talk of a Nordic model of marriage. With that as a starting point, we have in this chapter focused on the differences between the Nordic countries, more precisely between Norway and Sweden. Our study to a certain degree confirms earlier findings; Norwegian policies are, compared with Swedish, framed by a more pronounced housewife ideology and rhetoric of gender difference. But the housewife norm went together with, and could maybe partly be seen as a means to a gender-equality policy, we argue.

The chapter has stressed the importance of looking at 'gender equality' as a historical concept, changing with time. However, we find that the concept of equality differs not only with historical context, and not only across national borders, but is also dependent on whether the woman had a male provider or not. When gender equality was claimed at the beginning of the 20th century, it was usually based on the assumption of gendered division of labour. This concept of equality prevailed in 'normal' families only, while within the families without a male provider (unmarried women, lone mothers and poor wives), the assumption was that they should/could work outside the home. The heterosexual male provider/female housewife family was set up as a norm, but with exceptions, and then to be overruled by a class-related concept of gender equality based on sameness.

The question of economic independence and what we here call economic citizenship for women serves as an entry into a conceptualisation of equality. This constitutes the core theme in our chapter and is probably the most important issue for women's empowerment and human dignity during the last century. The marriage Acts adopted between 1909 and 1929 realised a kind of dual breadwinner model, though strictly limited, we argue. Women's contribution to the family economy was equalised through joint responsibility for family maintenance and equal status between the two main forms of maintenance. However, married women were not equal to men when it came to economic output and security. The reform thereby expressed the dilemma of modernity: a dilemma between gendered division and equality, between a housewife norm and an equality norm, between family orientation and individualism.

Among the women's organisations there was at the time a vivid debate about how to secure the economic position of married women. Three principally different strategies can be found in the debate. Some, but few, thoroughly questioned the gender division and supported civil citizenship as a strategy for achieving economic citizenship. In other words, only a handful understood the concept of equality to signify that women and men should be equal regarding civil rights/the right to occupational work. A more important strategy was to attach economic rights to care, thereby reducing the importance of civil rights. While in Norway the claim for cash benefit from the state was supported and partly realised, the more favourable strategy among Swedish women activists was to claim the equal sharing of all income in the family. The difference was that of attaching economic rights directly or indirectly to women as mothers. Both strategies nevertheless made efforts to combine family orientation and individualisation for women and made gendered division a prerequisite for equality policies. They were two different ways of trying to make gender equality substantial and not merely rhetorical. As such, they represented important steps towards economic citizenship for married women/mothers.

In the early decades of the 20th century, most married women were housewives, and instruments to facilitate married women's full civil citizenship through their entry into the labour market had not yet been introduced, in Norway or Sweden. In both countries the Nordic marriage model, combining features from a dual breadwinner model and a male breadwinner model, was widely supported. Economic rights were attached to care work; as a family member, the wife was furnished with 'housewife's rights' by defining the commitment of the male breadwinner. Norwegian policies went a step further by addressing individual economic rights for women. In Norway, in contrast to the Swedish case, reforms in support of individual mothers' rights were established early in the 20th century. It seems as if the strong principle of gender equality, interpreted as gender neutrality, in Sweden excluded this solution for securing women's economic citizenship, while, on the contrary, the more pronounced housewife ideology and rhetoric of gender difference in Norway resulted in an extension of women's rights. The willingness to compensate for gender difference through ascription of rights to women as mothers was more dominant in Norway.

The question of parenthood is a key area where gender politics meets family politics. National differences in terms of parenthood and custody of children confirm, to a certain degree, the stronger housewife norm in Norway as compared with Sweden. While the strategy in Norway was in favour of maternity rights beyond the principle of formal gender equality, the equality norm, based on the principle of gender neutrality, prevailed in Sweden. But the national variations were first and foremost rhetorical; in practice, the children usually followed their mother after a divorce, also in Sweden.

Nevertheless, while in Norway the mother had priority for the custody of small children (while in Sweden mother and father were made equal) this was only one element in Norwegian politics to strengthen the position of mothers. Also, the Norwegian solution can be understood as gender-equality politics, but with reference to 'the child's best interest'. In the Swedish case, gender equality meant gender neutrality.

We have seen that there is more than one conceptualisation of equality. It is not quite obvious whose policies were most promising in terms of achieving economic independence. But the question should be raised whether a Norwegian housewife norm was a strategy for gender equality in the way that mothers, independent of marital status, achieved economic rights. The Norwegian case demonstrates how motherhood and strengthened mothers' rights was a strategy for women's citizenship, at least during this period. Nevertheless, this strategy was controversial. The introduction of a cash economy into marriage and the family seems to disturb the gendered perception of the heterosexual male provider/female housewife family as a harmonic entity without conflicts of interests.

Notes

[1] This huge marriage reform also included changes in the rules regulating the formation of marriage as well as the rules related to divorce. The reform was analysed in the project 'The Nordic Marriage Model in a Comparative Perspective', in which we participated with Anu Pylkkänen and Bente Rosenbeck (see Melby et al, 2006a, 2006b).

[2] Lena Sommestad (1997) finds a strong wage-work norm for women in Sweden until the 1930s; see also Lundqvist (Chapter Four, this volume). As recent research has shown, the housewife norm was more of a norm and an ideal among the poorer segments of the population at this time (see eg Plymoth, 2002).

[3] There was, as we know, a gendered division of labour also in the labour market, which we will not discuss in this context.

[4] A right that unmarried women already had obtained.

[5] However, as Zeuthen (2005, p 207) has pointed out, this individualisation presupposes the individual's participation in the labour market; for those dependent on social benefits, the family is still seen as the economic unit.

[6] It is important to remember that women's work, historically, has always been underestimated in statistics (see eg Åmark, 2006).

[7] In her speech to the annual meeting of Norske Kvinners Nasjonalråd (Norwegian branch of the ICW) in 1916, Karen Grude Koht emphasised the importance of education for women and proclaimed that 'there were no strict rules any longer – either one was married or not. Everyone could choose individually.' She encouraged women to prepare for an independent life (Referat, landsmøte i NKN 1916, p 179). This liberal view on married women's work was supported by Fredrikke Mørch, who replaced Gina Krog as editor of *Nylænde*, the journal of the Norwegian women's rights movement (*Nylænde*, 1926, p 131).

[8] The signature ML in *Morgonbris*, 11, 1919, p 9. See also Magnus Lithner in *Hertha*, 1918, nos 15 and 16.

[9] The proposal was printed in *Nylænde* 1 March 1913.

[10] The idea of a breadwinner salary was supported by some, among them members of the women's movement in the Norwegian Labour Party (see Seip, 1981, p 183).

[11] Familjerättskommissionens Møder II Afdeling. Samling i København. November-December 1915.

[12] Riksdagstrycket, FK protokoll 1920 3, nr 35: 60, AK protokoll 1920 3, nr. 41:64.

[13] Riksdagstrycket, AK, Protokoll 1902 2, nr. 26, p 46.

[14] Riksdagstrycket, FK Protokoll 1920 3 nr 35: 60, AK Protokoll 1920 3, nr. 41: 64.

Bibliography

Abukhanfusa, K. (1987) *Piskan och moroten: om könens tilldelning av skyldigheter och rättigheter i det svenska socialförsäkringssystemet 1913–1980*, Stockholm: Carlsson.

Allen, A.T. (1985) 'Mothers of the New Generation: Adele Schreiber, Helene Stöcker, and the evolution of a German idea of motherhood, 1900–1914', *Signs. Journal of Women in Culture and Society*, vol 10, pp 418–38.

Åmark, K. (2006) 'Women's labour force participation in the Nordic countries during the 20th century', in K. Petersen, N.F. Christiansen, K. Petersen, N. Edling and P. Haave (eds) *The Nordic Model: A historical reappraisal*, Copenhagen: Museum Tusculanum.

Bergman, H. (2003) *Att fostra till föräldraskap. Barnavårdsmän, genuspolitik och välfärdsstat 1900–1950*, Stockholm: Arkiv.

Bergman, H. and Hobson, B. (2002) 'Compulsory Fatherhood: The coding of fatherhood in the Swedish welfare state', in B. Hobson (ed) *Making Men into Fathers. Men, masculinities and the social politics of fatherhood*, Cambridge: Cambridge University Press, pp 92–124.

Blom, I. (1994) 'Voluntary motherhood 1900–1930: Theories and politics of a Norwegian feminist in an international perspective', in G. Bock and P. Thane (eds), *Maternity and Gender Policies. Women and the rise of the European welfare states 1880s–1950s*, London and New York: Routledge.

Bokholm, S. (2000) *En kvinnoröst i manssamhället. Agda Montelius 1850–1920*, Stockholm: Stockholmia förlag.

Borchorst, A., Christensen, A.-D. and Raaum, N. (1999) 'Equal Democracies? Conclusions and perspectives', in C. Bergqvist, A. Borchorst, A.-D. Christensen, V. Ramstedt-Silén, N.C. Raaum and A. Styrkárdóttir (eds) *Equal Democracies? Gender and politics in the Nordic countries*, Oslo: Scandinavian University Press, Nordic Council of Ministers, pp 227–89.

Bradley, D. (1996) *Family Law and Political Culture. Scandinavian laws in comparative perspective*, London: Sweet & Maxwell.

Carlsson, C. (1986) *Kvinnosyn och kvinnopolitik. En studie av svensk socialdemokrati 1880–1910*, Lund: Arkiv.

Cederschiöld, M. (1903) 'Den svenska kvinnans rättsliga ställning i familjen och i samhället', *Datgny*, no 3.

Elgan, E. (1994) *Genus och politik. En jämförelse mellan svensk och fransk abort- och prentivmedelspolitik från sekelskiftet till andra världskriget*, Uppsala.

Familjerättskommissionens Møder. II Afdeling. Samling i København. November–December 1915.

Frangeur, R. (1998) *Yrkeskvinna eller makens tjänarinna? Striden om yrkesrätten för gifta kvinnor i mellankrigstidens Sverige*, Lund: Arkiv.

Haavet, I.E. (1999) 'Framveksten av velferdsstatens familiepolitikk i Norge og Sverige', *Tidsskrift for velferdsforskning*, vol 2, 67–84.

Haavet, I.E. (2006) 'Milk, Mothers and Marriage', in N.F. Christiansen, K. Petersen, N. Edling and P. Haave (eds) *The Nordic Model: A historical reappraisal*, Copenhagen: Museum Tusculanum Press, pp 189-214.

Hagemann, G. (2002) 'Citizenship and Social Order: Gender politics in twentieth-century Norway and Sweden', *Women's History Review*, vol 11, pp 417–29.

Hertha (1919) Journal of the Fredrika-Bremer-Association, 15, 16.

Indst.0.XIII. (1909) *Om utfærdigelse av lov angaaende ophævelse av det egteskapelige samliv og opløsning av egteskap*, Stortingsforhandlingene, bd. 6.

Kessler-Harris, A. (2003) 'In Pursuit of Economic Citizenship', *Social Politics*, vol 10, pp 157–75.

Kulawik, T. (1999) 'Maskulinism och välfärdsstatens framväxt i Sverige och Tyskland', *Kvinnovetenskaplig tidskrift*, vol 3, pp 3–17.

Lagberedningen (1918) *Lagberedningens förslag till revision av giftermålsbalken och vissa delar av ärvdabalken IV. Förslag till giftermålsbalk m.m.*, Stockholm.

Manns, U. (1997) *Den sanna frigörelsen. Fredrika-Bremer-Förbundet 1884–1902*, Stockholm/Stehag: Symposion.

Marshall, T.H. (1950) *Citizenship and Social Class*, London: Pluto Press.

Melby, K. (1995) 'Kvinnelighetens strategier. Norges Husmorforbund 1915–1940 og Norges Lærerinneforbund 1912–1940', PhD Dissertation, Trondheim: University of Trondheim.

Melby, K., Pylkkänen, A., Rosenbeck, B. and Carlsson Wetterberg, C. (2000) *The Nordic Model of Marriage and the Welfare State*, Nord 2000: 27, Copenhagen: Nordic Council of Ministers.

Melby, K., Pylkkänen, A., Rosenbeck, B. and Carlsson Wetterberg, C. (2006a) *Inte ett ord om kärlek. Äktenskap och politik i Norden ca. 1850–1930*, Stockholm: Makadam.

Melby, K., Pylkkänen, A., Rosenbeck, B. and Carlsson Wetterberg, C (2006b) 'The Nordic Model of Marriage', *Women's History Review*, vol 15, no 4, pp 651–61.

Mohr, T. (1968) *Katti Anker Møller: en banebryter*, Oslo: Tiden.

Møller, K.A. (1919) *Kvindernes fødselspolitik*, Kristiania: Det norske arbeiderpartis forlag.

Morgonbris (1919) (the Swedish social democratic women's journal), 19.

Niskanen, K. (2000) 'Husbondeväldets röst. Äktenskap, egendom och kön under första delen av 1900-talet', in K. Niskanen, B. Liljewall and M. Sjöberg (eds) *Kvinnor och jord, Arbete och ägande från medeltid till nutid*, Stockholm: Nordiska museets förlag, pp 131-58.

Norske Kvinners Nasjonalråds familielønskomite (1929), Oslo.

Nylænde (various issues).

Östberg, K. (1997) *Efter rösträtten*, Stockholm: Stehag.

Ot.prp.nr.8. (1909) *Om utfærdigelse av lov angaaende ophævelse av det egteskapelige samliv og opløsning av egteskap* (Stortingsforhandlingene, bd. 3).

Plymoth, B. (2002) *Fostrande försörjning. Fattigvård, filantropi och genus i fabriksstaden Norrköping 1872–1914*, Stockholm: Almqvist & Wiksell.

Referat fra landsmøte i Norske Kvinner Nasjonalråd 1916, Norske Kvinners Nasjonalråds arkiv, 3600, nr. 25 B, Universitetsbiblioteket i Oslo.

Riksdagstrycket (Parliamentary publications, Sweden) Första kammaren (FK) och Andra kammarens (AK) protokoll 1920.

Sainsbury, D. (2001) 'Gender and the Making of the Welfare State: Norway and Sweden', *Social Politics*, vol 8, pp 113–43.

Seip, A.-L. (1981) *Om velfersdsstatens framvekst*, Oslo: Scandinavian University Press.

Smith, L. (1980) *Foreldremyndighet og barnerett*, Oslo: Scandinavian University Press.

Socialt kristelig tidskrift (1919).

Sommestad, L. (1997) 'Welfare State Attitudes to the Male Breadwinning System: the United States and Sweden in comparative perspective', *International Review of Social History*, vol 5.

Stéenhoff, F. (1903) *Feminismens moral*, Stockholm: Wahlström & Widstrand.

Stéenhoff, F. (1908) *Penningen och kärleken*, Stockholm: Björck & Börjesson.

Stortingsforhandlinger (1915) Parliamentary publications, Norway.

Utkast (N) (1918) *Utkast til lov om ektefællers formuesforhold. Avgit av de norske delegerte ved det skandinaviske familieretsarbeid 31. august 1918*, trykt som vedlegg til Ot.prp.58 (1926).

Westerhäll-Gisselsson, L. (1985) 'Aktuella spörsmål. Jämställdhetssyftet inom den sociala familjerätten – förr – nu – i framtiden', *Svensk juristtidning*.

Wetterberg, C.C. (1998) 'Equal or Different? That's not the question. Women's political strategies in historical perspective', in D. van der Fehr, A. Jonasdottir and B. Rosenbeck (eds) *Is There a Nordic Feminism? Nordic feminist thought in culture and society*, London: UCL Press, pp 21-43.

Zeuthen, H.E. (2005) 'Rettighetsreformerne siden 1990'erne', in J.H. Petersen and K. Petersen (eds) *13 reformer af den danske velfærdsstat*, Odense: University Press of Southern Denmark, pp 203–15.

THREE

Married women's right to pay taxes: debates on gender, economic citizenship and tax law reform in Denmark, 1945–83

Anna-Birte Ravn

According to our present law, a woman who marries in the technical terms of taxation ceases to be an independent person; she becomes a kind of accessory to her husband. ... Let me just mention my own example. I am a lawyer and my husband is a composer. In spite of that, he is the one who must state my income and capital as well as his own, and he is the one responsible for the truth of the statement. As a lawyer I have to keep books which also contain information on the income of my clients ...; these are documents which according to my professional secrecy I cannot show to others. So, my husband does not have the right to control that the figures I give him are correct; but nevertheless he will get a fine or punishment, if my information is not correct. On the other hand, I cannot ensure that what he writes in the tax form is true ... I have no right to demand to see the completed tax form, nor do I have the right to sign it. (Saunte, 1951)

Edel Saunte specialised in family law and functioned as barrister in the Danish High Courts. She was chair of the Danish Women's Society 1936–41, and she was a member of the Social Democratic Party. When she wrote her 1951 article in the social democratic women's magazine, *Frie Kvinder*, cited above, two official commission reports, appearing in 1948 and 1950, had unanimously recommended the preservation of the gendered tax system. But in spite of Saunte's pointing out the irrationalities and injustices of the system, she did not argue for its total abolition. She advocated individualisation of taxes in regard to legal responsibilities, but preservation of the principle of joint taxation of spouses. The question is, why?

Joint taxation of spouses and the status of the husband as head of the household was part of the first income and capital tax law in Denmark, enacted in 1903. Moreover, a revised tax law in 1922 assigned to the married man the status of family provider – in outright contradiction to the 1925 Marriage Act, which formally equalised spouses and stated the mutual obligation of wife and husband to provide for the family. Even so, the gendered tax system lingered on through the 'Golden Era' of the Danish welfare state (1955–75) and was abolished only in 1983, when a revised tax law formally equalised spouses. How should this apparent contradiction be interpreted? It has been argued that the formal egalitarianism of the 1925 Marriage Act was an important precondition for the emerging Danish welfare state model (Melby et al, 2001). How should we then understand that, in regard to taxation, the 'social contract' of the welfare state was predicated on a 'sexual contract'?

Before 1903, the burden of national taxation lay on land, and the taxable subject was the individual landowner, including married women.[1] The 1903 tax law reform – one of the results of the Liberal farmers taking over government power in 1901 – shifted the burden of taxation from land to income and capital, from countryside to town. The law stated that 'the Head of the Family is taxed of the total Income of the Household' (§7) and 'of the Capital of the Persons belonging to the Household' (§15). So, the married man became the prototype of the national taxpayer, the economic citizen of the nation. He had also long been the prototype of the nation's political citizen. The Danish Constitution of 1849 gave universal and equal suffrage to men only, but not to all men. Excepted from political citizenship were – apart from all women – male servants and poor, criminal, insane and foreign men. The political citizen was a Danish man in charge of a household, who paid everyone, including the state, his due, who had not forfeited his respectability by receiving public assistance or committing a crime, and who was in possession of all his faculties. Since 1849 he had exercised his political citizenship right for the 'common good' on behalf of women, children, servants, etc. With the revised 1915 Constitution women and servants achieved political citizenship, but for women, marriage still meant the loss of economic citizenship as regards the right to pay taxes.

The connection between gender, political citizenship and taxpaying is even more explicit when it comes to local government. From the 1860s and until the 1950s suffrage in local elections and eligibility to local councils depended on the payment of local taxes. From the inception of democracy, local political citizenship in Denmark was conditioned on economic independence, the so-called right of the husband. In fact, one of the most hotly debated issues in Parliament in the years before the 1908 reform of the Local Electoral Law was whether married women who did not pay their own taxes and thus were not economic citizens could be given political citizenship. After more than 20 years of discussion, male parliamentarians of all political affiliations in 1908 decided to give universal and equal suffrage for local councils to all women – in their special capacities as wives, housewives and mothers (Bach, 2003). But married women's possibility of exercising their new political right remained dependent on their husbands' paying local taxes. Up until 1953, married women were not allowed to vote, and up until 1965 they could not be elected to local councils if their husbands had not paid due taxes (Pedersen, 1966, pp 15–16).

The thesis of this chapter is that the economic irrationalities and injustices, the degrading treatment as well as the obvious political discrimination of married women in the tax law system make sense only within a special form of gendered thinking on the relationship between individual, family and state. This gendered habit of mind – or 'gendered imagination'[2] – framed discussions of what was fair and shaped the boundaries of what was politically plausible. It took for granted the heterosexual male provider/female housewife family as the norm of civil society. It favoured a specific form of masculinity, the married man at the head of his household and providing for his family, and a specific form of femininity, the married woman as wife, housewife and mother. And the gendered tax system did not only affect imaginations. By disadvantaging married women's paid work, it also contributed to the material construction and preservation of the heterosexual male provider/female housewife family.

So, while the marriage reforms of the 1920s recognised married women's contribution to welfare through work in the family, the tax law system, constructed in the first decades of the 20th century and lingering on through the formative years and the 'Golden Era' of the Danish welfare state, contributed to keeping married women in 'their place'. If the marriage reforms are read as a new contract between married women and the state, the gendered tax law system could be interpreted as a contract between married men and the state, securing maximum welfare for men and children, but at the expense of married women's status as full citizens.

In the following the factors contributing to preserving the gendered tax law system as well as the factors finally leading to change will be discussed. The chapter follows parliamentary debates and reports from official commissions representing all political parties, as well as women's voices of opposition as they appeared in women's rights movements and among social democratic women in the period 1945–83. The debates will be put in the context of married women's changing labour market participation and the economic consequences of the gendered tax law system for women and for families of different classes. Finally, the Danish case will be compared with similar developments in Sweden and Norway. But first, a short overview of the gendered elements of the Danish tax law system from 1903 until 1983 is given.

Gendered tax legislation in Denmark, 1903–83

From its inception in 1903, modern Danish tax legislation was gendered in several ways. First, the original state tax law of 1903 (Lov af 15. Maj 1903) rested on the premise of the husband as head of the household who was jointly taxed with his wife and dependent children. Since the tax system was progressive and the wife's income was put 'on top' of her husband's, she was more heavily taxed than he was.[3] In regard to local taxation, as distinct from state taxation, legislators did not even bother to mention that married women were not taxable subjects;

the legal interpretation of the 'everybody' in the main paragraph of the law was perfectly clear: 'everybody' did not include married women (Pedersen, 1966, p 14). Separate taxation of spouses – and of children – was introduced in Danish income tax legislation in the late 1960s as part of the Pay-As-You-Earn system (Lov af 31. marts 1967), but formal equality was not achieved until the 1982 Act on Fiscal Equality between Spouses (Lov af 26. Maj 1982). This law made taxation of spouses gender neutral, but did not abolish joint taxation in regard to capital. So, joint taxation of spouses is still part of the Danish tax system.

Second, the 1903 law gave the husband a deduction in income before tax for every child under 15 years. In 1967 child allowances were detached from the tax system and included in social legislation; they were made universal for children under the age of 18 and paid to the mother (Nielsen, 1996).

Third, the second Danish state tax law of 1912 (Lov af 8. Juni 1912) introduced a tax relief in the household income before tax for independently employed wives; this so-called 'wife deduction', granted to the husband, was meant to compensate for increased household expenses resulting from the employment of married women outside the home. The amount was set at a low maximum and could not exceed half of the husband's regular deductions. It was abolished in 1975 (Ligestillingsrådet, 1978, p 19).

Finally, while the tax laws of 1903 and 1912 did not distinguish between providers and non-providers, this distinction was introduced in the 1922 Tax Law (Lov af 10. April 1922), which defined the prototype of the provider as the married man who was taxed jointly with his wife. The marital tax relief was reintroduced in a new form in 1970, when the Pay-As-You-Earn system gave the married couple a double personal allowance, whether both or only one spouse earned an income (i.e. a kind of housewife bonus). Moreover, the personal allowance (as well as debts/deficits) was made transferable between spouses. This system was preserved in the 1982 Act on Fiscal Equality between Spouses – and still exists.

For the married couple the economic consequences were ambiguous and changing over time, but already in the early 1930s the Danish tax system, as well as its Norwegian and Swedish counterparts, led to different net income for married and single persons at the average income level of a worker (Montanari, 1999, p 226). So for married women, including working-class wives, joint taxation of spouses and marital tax relief (housewife bonus) mostly functioned as disincentives to independent employment. On the other hand, the so-called 'wife deduction' was meant to, if not encourage, then at least make easier such employment. The ideal of the full-time housewife and mother lurks in the background, however, and the chronological order of the different gendered elements of Danish tax legislation suggests that this ideal emerged during the first two decades of the 20th century.

Joint taxation of spouses, including deductions in household income for children and independently working wives, may be interpreted as part of the old system of formal gender inequality. The distinction between married men as providers and married women as non-providers is a new phenomenon, however, that goes hand in hand with formal gender equality. In the Danish case, the distinction was introduced exactly at the time of three major victories for gender equality: One was the 1915 Constitution, which gave women the vote; the second was the 1919 Civil Servants Act, which upheld the principle of equal pay irrespective of gender; and the third was the 1925 Marriage Act, which formally equalised spouses and stated the mutual obligation of husband and wife to provide for the family. The 1919 Civil Servants Act, however, was the first example in Danish legislation of the provider/non-provider distinction. The 1922 Tax Law continued this new trend, and it is interesting that, in direct contradiction to the forthcoming marriage law, the husband was defined as the provider irrespective of whether there were children in the family or not. So, the ideal of the full-time housewife and mother dependent on a male breadwinner is a modern phenomenon, competing in Danish tax legislation and discourse of the 20th century with older elements of gender inequality as well as new visions of gender equality.

Debates on gender, economic citizenship and tax legislation

The new income tax law of 1903 was challenged from a gender perspective by the Danish Women's Society[4] at its annual national meeting in 1913. Half a century later, in the report of a government Committee on the Taxation of Spouses, published in 1963, the Society was joined by female trade unionists, and although the opponents of the gendered tax system were in a minority on the committee, the law was changed in 1967.

But how did the opponents argue their case? And how was the system defended by the vast majority of political agents in Parliament and parliamentary and government committees? Did political discourses on gender and taxation radically change during the 20th century, or are they better characterised by continuity?

During the major part of the 20th century, politics in Denmark relied on political alliances and compromises between four political parties, reflecting social contradictions not only between labour and capital, but also between rural and urban interests. Except for a couple of years just after the turn of the century, no political party gained absolute majority in the Danish Parliament during the 20th century.

Taking over government power from the right in 1901, the Liberal Party, representing middle-class farmers, left its decisive stamp on political decisions far beyond its numerical constituency, at least until the Second World War. The Social Democratic Party formed its first government in 1924–26, and from 1929 held government power for the greater part of the period, often in coalition with the Social Liberal Party, which represented small farmers and urban intellectuals. Liberal governments kept returning for shorter periods, however, whereas the Conservatives, reconstituted from the old Right in 1915 to represent not only big farming and capital interests, but also large parts of the urban middle classes, took over government power in coalition with the Liberals for 10 years after 1982. Almost every major reform in the development of the Danish welfare state was a compromise between these four parties.

Opposition to the gendered tax system, 1913–60

The primary organisation of the opposition to the gendered tax system was the Danish Women's Society, which first raised the claim for *separate taxation of spouses* in 1913, and, except for a few years in the early 1950s, separate taxation was the principal policy of the Society as it appeared in numerous resolutions to government and Parliament in the period 1915–60. During the 1930s, when debates on married women's right to work were at their height, the official claims of the Society became more modest; it did not, however, give up the main principles of its tax policy.

The original arguments against joint taxation of spouses were: first, that it was irrational and degrading that women, who before marriage were full economic citizens, would after marriage be treated like underage children; second, that it was an obvious injustice that a married woman would forfeit her right to vote in local elections in the case of her husband's non-payment of taxes; and finally, that joint taxation of spouses put a penalty on marriage and thus threatened the institution of marriage, which the state was supposed to protect and sustain.

The Danish Women's Society also *opposed the marital tax relief,* which defined the husband as provider for a dependent wife. According to the Society, this provision was offensive to the wife, since it underestimated her economic efforts in the household. There was no reason to give a man tax relief because he had married a woman and thus had the work for which he had previously had to pay done for free. Moreover, the marital tax relief favoured married people at the expense of unmarried persons, many of whom also had to maintain a household. The main argument was that *adult persons, women as well as men, had to provide for themselves.* Tax relief for providers should only apply to persons responsible for the provision of children, and *tax relief for children should be raised and made universal.*

So, the basic policy of the Danish Women's Society was that women should be full economic citizens, on a par with men. The weak spot of this policy was that it did not solve the problem of inequality between women, that housewives and so-called 'assistant wives', especially in the large agricultural sector, did not have an income of their own. Moreover, while in the early period housework was considered – and probably in reality *was* – an important contribution to family provision, it lost cultural appreciation – and probably economic importance – over time. Male breadwinner/female housewife families would lose from the implementation of the Society's taxation policy, and this was the basis of opposition also inside the association.[5]

This opposition grew during the interwar years, and it was vehemently pronounced in public when, in 1945, the Society published a pamphlet supporting its tax policy on the grounds that housework was exempted from taxation and thus gave male breadwinner/female housewife families an economic advantage (Dahlsgaard and Schmidt, 1945). The internal opposition reached its peak in the early 1950s, when the Danish Women's Society for the first and only time since 1913 officially deviated from its basic policy of individual taxation of spouses and temporarily accepted the gendered tax system. The explicit reason given for the Society's change of policy was that, according to new economic calculations, joint taxation of spouses in combination with marital tax relief and an adjusted 'wife deduction' resulted in an easier taxation of about 85% of all taxpayers and that only the most wealthy couples would suffer from the system (Biza et al, 1982). Even so, the consequence was that the Society sacrificed gender equality, that is, married women's fundamental citizenship rights, for equality between families of different classes.

In 1947 the Social Democratic Women's Clubs started publication of the magazine *Frie Kvinder*. In the second issue, Inga Dahlsgaard (who together with her husband, both Social Democrats, had written the 1945 pamphlet mentioned above) argued that joint taxation of spouses was not only unfair to wage-earning married women, it was also unjust to married couples where both spouses were engaged in wage work, compared with couples where only the husband earned a taxable income, while the 'income' earned by the wife doing housework was tax free. To calm down her readers, most of whom were Social Democratic housewives, she added that 'presumably' no sensible person would impose taxes on the income in kind produced by housewives, but according to Dahlsgaard, the time had come to equalise married women with other taxpaying citizens, to detach the tax system from the subsistence economy and to include it in the modern money economy (Dahlsgaard, 1947).

The editors of *Frie Kvinder* seem to have agreed, but the issue of taxation was not taken up again in the magazine until Edel Saunte's 1951 article, mentioned in the introduction to this chapter. Why did Saunte, in 1951, abstain from the demand for separate taxation of spouses, for which she had long been a leading spokeswoman? Her argument was crystal clear: joint taxation of spouses was unjust towards married women; but since, especially, more wealthy couples would gain by separate taxation, whereas most working-class families would lose by it, she preferred a more modest reform, involving the preservation of joint taxation but an individualisation of legal responsibilities (Saunte, 1951). In other words: gender equality or justice for married women had to give way to equality between classes.

Occasionally, the opposition of the Danish Women's Society and Social Democratic women was joined by the Danish Women's National Council (DKN).[6] When a request for women's representation in the Tax Law Commission, appointed by the Minister of Finance in 1937, was not granted, the Danish Women's Society and the DKN in 1938 sent a joint application to the Commission, claiming married women's right to pay their share of taxes and thus be released from the legal effects of husbands' non-payment. As a modest result, married women in 1953 gained the right to be acquainted with the completed tax return. They also gained the right, but not the obligation, to sign it; their signature had no consequence for the validity of the completed tax return and implied no obligations in addition to those existing (Lov af 17. december 1952).

Behind this 1953 'victory' was one woman in particular: Kirsten Gloerfelt-Tarp, president of the DKN 1931–46 and elected to Parliament for the Social Liberals in 1945. Trained in national economics, a factory inspector by profession and well acquainted with the conditions of professional as well as working-class women, she was the only person to speak in Parliament before 1960 against the gendered tax system.[7] Like the Social Democrat Edel Saunte, she pointed to its irrationalities and its inconsistencies when compared with marriage legislation, and she demanded an investigation of the system by impartial experts who would listen also to the voice of women's organisations, but – except for the minor change in 1953 – in vain. None of her fellow MPs even bothered to comment – and silence is a very effective weapon.

Defence of the gendered tax system, 1937–60

Gloerfelt-Tarp's strongest attack on the tax law system was directed specifically at the Tax Law Commission of 1937, which consisted of 29 male representatives of all political parties, and whose reports were published in 1948 and 1950 (Betænkning, 1948; Skattelovskommissionens Betænkning, 1950). The reports did comment on the possibility of separate taxation of spouses, but the conclusion was a unanimous recommendation to continue the joint taxation system.

Paradoxically, the Tax Law Commission found its main argument for joint taxation of spouses in the 1925 Marriage Act. *Because* of the mutual obligation of husband and wife to provide, the argument went, the family was an economic unit, and the only 'possible and natural' thing to do was to impose taxes in accordance with the principle of the economic ability of this unit. How the family unit earned its income, whether it was earned by the husband alone or by both spouses, was a private matter of no concern to the public authorities.

The Commission, in its 1948 report, proposed the abolition of the 'wife deduction'. The argument focused on the economic meaning of housework: was housework consumption, and thus a private matter of no interest to the tax authorities? Or was housework actually production, and thus a matter of concern for these authorities? In the latter case, the independent employment of the wife would mean a loss of income that would justify the 'wife deduction'. In order to sustain the recommendation of abolishing the 'wife deduction', the Commission resorted to the technical argument that it would be impossible to estimate the value of housework (the same would be true of the work of 'assistant wives'). Not only did the time spent on housework differ, but women's qualifications as housekeepers were also very different! In its second report of 1950, however, the Commission accepted that the independent employment of married women might cause a rise in household expenses and reintroduced the 'wife deduction' in its recommendations.

The overall conclusion of the Tax Law Commission's reports was that, although in principle the married couple could be taxed either separately or together, joint taxation of spouses seemed to be 'the only technically passable way', since 'in a farming country like Denmark', for a long time to come, the overwhelming proportion of married couples would no doubt be male breadwinner/female housewife or 'assistant wife' families. The Liberal Party influence seems pronounced in these formulations. But the Social Democrats agreed.

The fall – and continuation – of the gendered tax system, 1960–83

Times changed, however. From 1958 the post-war economic boom reached Denmark, resulting in increased demands for labour power and a new status for married women, in parliamentary debates, as 'labour force reserve'.

Since the early 20th century and until 1940, Danish women's labour market participation – including 'assistant wives' mostly working in agriculture – had been slowly increasing. From 1940 until 1960, the percentage of *gainfully* employed women decreased,[8] after which the percentage again started to rise (Åmark, 2006, p 308), this time dramatically. During the 1950s, *married* women's labour market participation decreased, relatively as well as in absolute figures. According to official statistics, in 1950, 262,800 or 26.9% of married women were part of the Danish labour force; in 1960 the corresponding figures were 244,800 or 22.6%. Ten years later, however, in 1970, the figures had more than doubled; by then, 568,000 married women or 49.2% were gainfully employed (Borchorst, 1980, p 202; see also Appendix, Tables 3 and 4).

In the early 1960s, Social Democratic/Social Liberal governments introduced general purchase taxes, combined with reduction of direct income taxes, by raising the threshold and the limit of proportional taxes. These reforms were passed unanimously by the four 'old parties', and although the overall concern of the legislature was with class and not with gender relations, 'gendered imaginations' formed the opposition of especially the Social Democrats and the Socialist People's Party[9] against any fundamental change in the gendered tax system.[10] This way of arguing left the space open for the opposition, the Liberals and the Conservatives, to press the gender question, which they did – without any serious intention of fundamental change, however.

In 1960, Kirsten Gloerfelt-Tarp left Parliament, but her voice on the gendered injustices of tax legislation was taken over by two other female Social Liberal MPs, soon to be joined by a Conservative, and finally, in 1963, the first Social Democratic MP spoke in favour of separate taxation of spouses.[11] These four women MPs explicitly raised the claim for married women's economic citizenship rights. Their male colleagues, however, suggested waiting for the report of the special Committee on Taxation of Spouses, which had been appointed by the Liberal Minister of Finance in 1961.

This Committee was unique in that for the first time in Denmark a woman's organisation, the DKN, had been asked to appoint two members to an official committee on tax issues. Also remarkable was that the Danish Federation of Trade Unions (DsF) appointed a woman as one of its two members, and women thus constituted one-third of the Committee members. The Committee report was published in 1963, disclosing that in this case the alleged capacity of Danish political culture to reach a compromise had failed. A minority of two women – Jytte Christensen,[12] appointed by the DKN to represent wage-earning women, together with Ella Olsen,[13] appointed by the DsF – recommended individual taxation of spouses and a more easy taxation of 'assistant wives', abolition of marital tax relief and 'wife deduction', as well as an increase in child allowances. This position was in full accordance with the basic claims raised by the Danish Women's Society since 1913. What was new, however, was the alliance between the Society and female trade unionists.

In contrast to the reports of the Tax Law Commission of 1937, women's voices were distinct also in the Committee's common evaluation of the consequences of the existing tax legislation. The evaluation included considerations on distributive consequences not only for families (the so-called principle of economic ability), but also for married women as independent individuals (the principle of individuality) (Betænkning, 1963, pp 57–66). Jytte Christensen's and Ella Olsen's main arguments for the minority proposal were, first, that joint taxation of spouses was discriminating against married women and a penalty on marriage, and second, that separate taxation would encourage married women – especially well-educated women, but also women with more moderate earnings – to take up or increase their gainful employment (Betænkning, 1963, pp 72–3, 84–6). Ella Olsen emphasised that even if the economic consequences of the reform proposal were an increase in the tax burden of ordinary families (just as in the early 1950s, as previously mentioned), married women who worked outside the home would *all* benefit from the proposal (Olsen, 1963). The concept of the 'male provider' was out of date, she argued; only children should be provided for by others, whereas *adults had to provide for themselves*, either in the family or in the labour market.

Another minority of three male members of the Committee, including the chairman, reiterated the arguments of the Tax Law Commission of 1937 in arguing for the continuation of joint taxation of spouses combined with an increase in the 'wife deduction', which should also be given to husbands with 'assistant wives'. The majority of the Committee (four members), including the second representative of the DKN appointed to represent housewives, and the male representative of the DsF, did not choose between the two opposing recommendations. In their opinion the choice should not be made by the Committee since it would have to rest on general social and cultural norms and political values (Betænkning, 1963, pp 71–2).

Speaking at a public meeting convened by the DKN after publication of the report, one member of the majority, Professor of Law Bent Christensen, expressed himself in less diplomatic terms. In his opinion, politicians had to choose between two different principles: on the one hand, the principle of equal rights between women and men, and on the other, the political goal of levelling economic differences in society (Christensen, 1963). Leaving little doubt about his personal preferences, Bent Christensen constructed an opposition between class and gender and between economy and culture (formal law). Whereas class, in his phrasing of the argument, was a matter of economic inequality and redistribution, gender inequality was only about formal rights or recognition, and any idea of economic citizenship for married women seemed totally absent from his 'gendered imagination'.

And he was supported by Svend Bache Vognbjerg, the male representative of the DsF, who, according to an internal document, recommended the executive committee of the Federation to propose preservation of joint taxation of spouses and an increase in the 'wife deduction' (Vognbjerg, 1963). His primary argument was consideration for the male provider/female housewife family, which would probably lose from the reform suggested by his colleague Ella Olsen. In his opinion, economic justice and redistribution were a matter of class and family only, not a matter of gender.

The work of the Committee on Taxation of Spouses took place in a context of heated public debate on women's proper place 'outside or inside the home'. In the period 1959–65, Danish newspapers and magazines including *Kvinden og Samfundet*, the periodical of the Danish Women's Society, witnessed a clash between the interests of housewives on one side and wage-earning women on the other. The debates were inspired by contemporary public discussions in Sweden,[14] but they never reached the intensity of the Swedish encounters (Biza et al, 1982, pp 79–108, 138–46). In Denmark, housewives' organisations, which constituted by far the largest women's movement, did not take part in the discussions (Biza et al, 1982, pp 182–230), and it is remarkable that the periodical of the Social Democratic Women's Clubs, *Frie Kvinder*, unanimously supported Ella Olsen's position and recommended the proposal for separate taxation of spouses.

The 1963 committee report on taxation of spouses put the problem back into Parliament, where, besides the political pressure of women parliamentarians of different affiliations, the very clear minority statement of a representative of female trade unionists in alliance with the Danish Women's Society seems to have had an effect. Some months after the publication of the committee report, the Social Democratic Minister of Finance – although vigorously defending the privileges of the male gender and arguing for social justice as a matter of equality between married men, irrespective of the occupation of their wives (Hansen, 1963) – totally reversed his attitude by proposing separate taxation of spouses to be included in a reformed Pay-As-You-Earn tax system.[15]

The reform of the gendered tax system was passed in Parliament in 1967 and did include separate taxation of spouses, but only in relation to married women's earned income. The principle of joint taxation and the husband's status as head of the household[16] in relation to the tax authorities was preserved. A new, all-male government committee, in its 1974 report, recommended that the only exception to separate taxation should be the transferability of unutilised personal allowances, the argument being that in this way an increase in the tax burden of married couples, where one spouse – usually the wife – did not earn an income or had an income below the personal allowance, would be avoided or reduced (Betænkning, 1974). In the end, the 1982 Act on Fiscal Equality between Spouses did pay some tribute to the family unit. The law preserved the transferability between spouses of deficits and debts and of personal allowances.

The Swedish case

In Sweden separate taxation of spouses was enacted in 1970, a few years after the Danish reform. So, as in the Danish case, married couples in Sweden were jointly taxed for most of the 20th century. Demands for separate taxation of spouses were first raised in Sweden in 1904 and thereafter appeared practically annually, but the question of what was problematic about joint taxation was reformulated from the mid-1940s. Whereas in the early years the gendered tax system was debated in the context of population policy, the main argument being that the system involved a penalty on marriage, negatively affecting the marriage rate and thereby the birth rate, joint taxation of spouses was, from the mid-1940s, addressed as primarily a question of married women's labour market participation. According to Viktoria Bergström, however, since the reasoning about solutions to the problem was still framed by 'the natural order of the gender discourse', this new perspective was not in itself sufficient to change Swedish tax legislation (Bergström, 2004, pp 1–3).

Commission reports of 1949, 1951 and 1959 defended the joint taxation of spouses on the grounds that the marital household was the 'natural' taxable unit. The 1949 report stated that it was only fair that spouses pay more than two single income earners with the same income. A married couple's ability to pay was greater, since the domestic work of the wife produced an income in kind that was not taxed. In other words, the investigators behind the 1949 report interpreted joint taxation of spouses as a 'natural' consequence of the modified dual breadwinner model of the 1921 Marriage Act (see Carlsson Wetterberg and Melby, Chapter Two, this volume). That married couples, where both had an income in cash, paid unfairly high taxes was not considered important by the Commission, and married women's labour market participation was understood as a question of social rather than fiscal/economic policy.

While the 1951 Commission report upheld the idea of a married couple's household as an economic unit and that spouses therefore should be taxed jointly, the idea of married women's domestic work as productive was abandoned. The domestic work of a wife could not be distinguished from household work performed by other taxpayers, the new investigators argued. So, the dual breadwinner model was replaced by a single breadwinner model, where married men supported wives who had no income of their own, and since married couples were no longer considered to have greater ability to pay taxes, the general tax deduction for married income earners was doubled, compared to single income earners. In practice, this reduced taxes for married men, and the ensuing split-income[17] reform of the joint income tax system was especially profitable for married couples with only one income. Although the system's negative effect on married women's labour market participation was considered problematic in the 1959 Commission report, this Commission just proposed an extension of the split-income system (Bergström, 2004, pp 5–9), and in 1960 the Swedish Parliament decided almost unanimously to maintain joint taxation of spouses (Florin, 1999, p 111).

Viktoria Bergström's thesis is that only when the challenge to the dominant gender discourse became so strong that 'the natural order lost its degree of naturalness' was the transition from joint to separate taxation possible (Bergström, 2004, p 3). As in Denmark, this happened in Sweden in the early 1960s. The single breadwinner model lasted for less than ten years and was soon to be replaced by a clear-cut dual breadwinner model. According to Christina Florin, the crucial moment of change occurred in 1964, when the leading men of the Swedish wage earners' organisations, including the Swedish Federation of Trade Unions (LO), decided to take a stand for separate taxation of spouses (Florin, 1999, p 114).[18]

Two years before, young female academics had started a newspaper debate on the tax system's unfairness towards wage-earning women. In their opinion, all women should work outside the household, and they saw women's gainful employment as the road to emancipation. Unlike earlier motions from individual citizens on the same point, this time, in the context of a radical 'gender role debate' (see Lundqvist, Chapter Four, and Roman, Chapter Five, this volume) and an economic boom, which accentuated the need for labour supply, the argument was heard. The Social Democratic Labour Party (SAP) put the question of separate taxation of spouses on its agenda in 1964, stressing, however, that the question of class and redistribution had to be solved before a reform could be carried through. Within the Social Democratic Women's Federation, whose members were primarily housewives, the leader and other prominent members, as for instance Alva Myrdal, also endorsed the idea of separate taxation. The immediate result was a heated public debate between housewives of all classes on one side, and a younger generation of wage-earning women on the other.

Even so, within a few years Swedish society witnessed a total change in mentality. The dream of a male breadwinner model, which had been part and parcel of the Social Democratic vision since the early 20th century, vanished into thin air. Other left and centre parties agreed, and so, after a while, did the right. However, to calm down public protest against the reform, the Right Party as well as the Social Democrats, including the Women's Federation, chose 'a strategy of silence'. Christina Florin emphasises the strange fact that even if men, as husbands, gained from the old system of joint taxation, housewives did not find allies among organisations dominated by men. It was the young wage-earning women who gained the support of the press and of men with power. In 1969 the labour shortage became acute in Sweden, and although in the spring of 1970 the Social Democratic government faced a private petition, initiated by a housewife and signed by 63,000 citizens, for the preservation of joint taxation, it did not waver. Married women's contribution to family maintenance through domestic work had become economically irrational, and the reform was enacted later that same year (Florin, 1999; Hirdman, 1998).

In spite of parallel developments in Sweden and Denmark, one important difference between the joint-income tax systems of the two countries stands out.[19] Compared with the Danish system, the gendered impact of joint taxation in Sweden during most of the 20th century was less oppressive towards married women. Even if spouses were taxed jointly, Swedish legislators took the full consequence of the 1921 Marriage Act, which abandoned the husband's guardianship of his wife (see Carlsson Wetterberg and Melby, Chapter Two, this volume), and gave husband and wife the right to fill in their own separate tax returns and pay taxes separately. Swedish income tax law also gave the wife the right to receive the 'wife deduction' to compensate for costs connected with working outside the home (Bergström, 2004, p 4). In contrast to the Danish case, married women in Sweden were thus, from 1921, recognised as economic citizens and persons in their own right. The redistributive effects of the Swedish income tax law system were very much the same as in Denmark, however. Male provider/female housewife families and married men in general gained by joint taxation of spouses, whereas married women working outside the home had to pay disproportionately high taxes.

The Norwegian case

Turning to Norway, an apparent paradox emerges. As described by Christina Carlsson Wetterberg and Kari Melby (Chapter Two, this volume), from the early decades of the 20th century a housewife norm was predominant in Norwegian discourses on gender equality, whereas in Sweden gender neutrality was more pronounced. In practice, from the 1930s onwards this difference materialised in the gainful employment outside the home of relatively more Swedish than Norwegian married women (see Appendix, Tables 3 and 4). But as regards tax legislation, married women in Norway gained the right to separate taxation in 1959,[20] ten years before the Swedish and Danish reforms (Lønnå, 1996, p 166; Blom, 1999, pp 325–6).

Elisabeth Lønnå ascribes this early reform to the work of the Norwegian Women's Society,[21] but in Norway the legacy of path dependence may also have been important. According to Norwegian tax laws of 1911, joint taxation of spouses was the general rule. However, the wife could demand separate taxation of separate property and income. This latter rule was abolished in 1921 (Betænkning, 1963, p 29), and the Norwegian Women's Society immediately started to protest against the new system. The protests were intensified after the Second World War and, contrary to its Danish sister organisation, the Society upheld the demand for separate taxation of spouses through the 1950s. It was opposed by the Norwegian Federation of Housewives, which, however, considered the existing law to be unfair to wage-earning women and argued for a tax deduction on married women's earned income. Working-class women's organisations did not take part in the discussions.

In Parliament the Social Democratic Labour Party, which constituted the majority and held government power, argued that separate taxation of spouses would unduly favour families with two income earners, at the expense of families with only one provider. As in Denmark, the question of class overruled demands for gender equality. All parties agreed that a denial of the family as an economic unit would have severe consequences and that, in accordance with the principle of economic capacity, the family was the proper taxable unit. In the late 1950s, however, the Liberal Party put separate taxation of spouses on its programme, and generally the argument about the need for the labour market participation of married women, especially well-educated women, seems to have been decisive in the reluctant change of opinions within the Norwegian Parliament and government. The tax law of 1959 gave married couples the right to choose between joint and separate taxation of income, and the Norwegian Women's Society, demanding a mandatory separate taxation of spouses, continued to protest, but in vain (Lønnå, 1996, pp 161–6).

The conclusion is that there were important differences between the Scandinavian countries in the ways the tax systems construed married women as economic citizens. Following the tenor of the marriage law reforms in the early 20th century, married women's contribution to family maintenance through work in the household was recognised in the Norwegian and Swedish laws, which ascribed to them the status of economic citizens. The Danish law, however, treated married women as subordinate persons with no rights or obligations in relation to the tax authorities; they were construed as totally dependent on their husbands. The explanation is not obvious, but the preoccupation of the Liberal Party with preserving the 'family farm' and its influence on Danish political culture may be one important reason for this 'Danish exceptionalism'. When it comes to redistribution, however, the tax law systems of the three Scandinavian countries all worked in favour of married men and the male provider/female housewife family and to the detriment of married women's work outside the household. It is worth noting, however, that in spite of – in fact, probably *because* of – a dominant housewife norm, Norway was the first country not only in Scandinavia but in Europe to introduce separate taxation of spouses (Montanari, 1999, p 224).

Conclusion

A main conclusion is that during the period 1945–60 questions of class and redistribution between classes were predominant in Danish tax-legislation discourses and practices. Not only was the opposition to the gendered tax system silenced – gender equality was also constructed as irreconcilable with equality between classes. The heterosexual married couple was represented as a natural economic unit, and in spite of formal inequality of husband and wife in relation to the tax authorities, the distribution of work and economic power within the family was defined as private and therefore of no concern to the state. In spite of a considerable increase in the 'wife deduction' in 1947, married women's gainful employment declined during the 1950s, not only relatively, but also in absolute terms.

In the period after 1960, married women's gainful participation in the labour market started to increase, and so did the earned income of working-class married couples. For the first time, women's voices of opposition to the gendered tax system were included in mainstream political debates. But the hegemonic discourse now constructed gender equality in regard to tax legislation as a matter of formal rights or recognition, and still not as a matter of economic power and redistribution within the family. Since the 1930s the heterosexual male provider/female housewife family had formed the basis of Social Democratic visions for welfare state developments (Melby et al, 2001), and around 1960 this type of family became the object of a renaissance, a 'new romanticism', in the Social Democratic Party (Hansen and Petersen, 2000). The alliance between so-called bourgeois (in fact mostly middle class) and working-class women against the discrimination of married women in the tax law system seems to have been decisive in changing political opinions – at least those of the Social Democrats. Not until the late 1970s, however, did the Social Democratic Party give up the idea of the heterosexual male provider/female housewife family as the basis of the welfare state and the main provider of welfare (Hansen and Petersen, 2000).

Married women's lack of economic (civil) and political rights in the Danish tax law system makes sense only within a 'gendered imagination' that took for granted the heterosexual male provider/female housewife family, and the system itself contributed to constructing and preserving this family type. The apparent contradiction between the recognition of married women as providers in the 1925 Marriage Law and married women's status as provided for by their husbands in the 1922 Tax Law could be interpreted as a mere irrationality of the legislation. More likely, however, both reforms were conscious attempts to reconstruct and modernise Danish society. While the marriage reforms recognised married women as economic citizens contributing welfare in their capacities as wives, housewives and mothers, the tax law system curtailed them to act within these same capacities. If the marriage reforms constituted a new contract between married women and the state, which bestowed upon them new power within the family, the gendered tax law system deprived them of fundamental citizenship rights in society at large. The intention of the Social Democrats may have been to discipline men in order to preserve the heterosexual family as the main provider of welfare as well as reproduction (Melby et al, 2001), but the result was a new contract between married men and the state, securing maximum welfare for men, children and maybe women, but at the expense of married women's status as full citizens. The 'social contract' of the emerging welfare state became predicated on a 'sexual contract'.

Notes

[1] This rule was continued after 1903 as regards tax on real property (Pedersen, 1966, p 13).

[2] The concept 'gendered imagination' is borrowed from Alice Kessler-Harris (2001, pp 5–6).

[3] Even if the wife was not legally responsible for paying taxes, according to the law of 1903, she was obliged to compensate her husband for taxes paid on her income (Pedersen, 1966, p 14).

[4] The Danish Women's Society was established in 1871 and still exists.

[5] On the Society's dilemma between recognising married women's housework and working for economic redistribution between women and men, see Ravn (2005).

[6] The Danish Women's National Council was established in 1899 as an umbrella organisation for various political, professional, religious and other women's organisations.

[7] Folketingets Forhandlinger, 17 and 19 December 1946; 13, 16, and 21 November 1951.

[8] When the agricultural sector is excluded there is quite a steady growth of female gainful employment in the period 1900–60 (Åmark, 2006, p 309; see also Appendix, Table 3).

[9] The Socialist People's Party (SF) was established in 1959 as the result of a split in the Danish Communist Party (DKP).

[10] See, for instance, Folketingets Forhandlinger, 7 March 1961; 6 December 1962.

[11] Folketingets Forhandlinger, 6 December 1962; 12 December 1962; 15 March 1963.

[12] Jytte Christensen was an expert on tax issues and chair of the internal Tax Committee of the Danish Women's Society.

[13] Ella Olsen was secretary to the Federation of Tobacco Workers, and from 1963 president of the Federation.

[14] See below in this chapter and compare Lundqvist and Roman, Chapters Four and Five, this volume.

[15] Folketingets Forhandlinger, 1 October compared with 15 March 1963.

[16] In the original 1967 law the husband was characterised as 'head of the household', and although this appellation was removed in 1968 (Lov af 31. maj 1968), the law still gave him this formal status; he now became the family's 'main person' (Pedersen, 1974, p 11).

[17] The split income or 'splitting system' meant that the aggregate income of the spouses was divided in two and taxed as two equally sized incomes, consequently at a lower rate of progression.

[18] See also Yvonne Hirdman, who argues that within the LO the question of labour market supply was debated as a matter of married women or immigrants, and that at the 1964 congress this question was decided in favour of married women (Hirdman, 1998, pp 191–7).

[19] Another difference was that Swedish local income tax was proportional, whereas in Denmark local as well as state income taxes were progressive. Proportional taxes meant that husbands and wives were taxed at the same tax rate and not – as in Denmark – that the husband's income was taxed at the bottom of the tax rate schedule, while the wife's income was taxed at a higher rate of progression (Bergström, 2004; Betænkning, 1963).

[20] Within another ten years separate taxation was applied also to spouses working in the same enterprise, for example in farming.

[21] Among Norwegian feminists the story goes that when the king and government returned from England after the Second World War, in June 1945, the president of the Norwegian Women's Society, Margarete Bonnevie, greeted them at the quay in the port of Oslo, waving a report she had made on joint taxation of spouses (Lønnå, 1996, p 137).

Bibliography

Åmark, K. (2006) 'Women's Labour Force Participation in the Nordic Countries during the Twentieth Century', in N.F. Christiansen, K. Petersen, N. Edling and P. Haave (eds) *The Nordic Model of Welfare: A historical reappraisal*, Copenhagen: Museum Tusculanum Press, pp 299–333.

Bach, T.K. (2003) 'En Morgengave'. Kvindevalgretsdebatten i Rigsdagen 1886–1908', MA dissertation, Aalborg: Institute of History, Aalborg University.

Bergström, V. (2004) 'Gender and the Swedish Income Tax System in the Post-war Period', paper presented at the European Social Science History Conference, Berlin, 24–7 March.

Betænkning om Beskatningen af Indkomst og Formue m.v. (1948), Afgivet af Skattelovskommissionen, I. Del, Copenhagen: J.H. Schultz A/S.

Betænkning om Ægtefællers Beskatning (1963), Afgivet af det af finansministeren den 8. marts 1961 nedsatte udvalg, Betænkning nr. 327, Copenhagen.

Betænkning fra Udvalget til Forbedring af Kildeskatten om Ægtefællers Beskatning (1974), Betænkning nr. 703, Copenhagen.

Biza, L.C., Lange, B.K. and Lous, E.K. (1982) 'Ude eller hjemme', MA dissertation, Aarhus: Institute of History, Aarhus University.

Blom, I. (1999) 'Brudd og kontinuitet. Fra 1950 mot årtusindskiftet', in I. Blom and S. Sogner (eds) *Med kjønnsperspektiv på norsk historie*, Oslo: Cappelen Akademisk Forlag, pp 299–344.

Borchorst, A. (1980) *Kvinder som arbejdskraftreserve – politisk floskel eller social realitet?*, MA dissertation, Aarhus: Institute of Political Science, Aarhus University.

Christensen, B. (1963) 'Talepapir', *Danske Kvinders Nationalråds Arkiv*, Copenhagen: Rigsarkivet.

Dahlsgaard, I. (1947) 'Skat og ægteskab', *Frie Kvinder*, no 2.

Dahlsgaard, I. and Schmidt, E.I. (1945) *Skat og Ægteskab*, Copenhagen: Dansk Kvindesamfund.

Dansk Kvindesamfunds Arkiv, Aarhus: Kvindehistorisk Samling, State and University Library:

Protokol, skatteudvalget, 1946–63.

Protokol, udvalget for særbeskatning, 1963.

Sagsmateriale, skatteudvalget (DKA, Sag 147; DKA, Sag 26).

Florin, C. (1999) 'Skatten som befriar. Hemmafruar mot yrkeskvinnor i 1960-talets särbeskattningsdebatt', in C. Florin, L. Sommestad and U. Wikander (eds) *Kvinnor mot kvinnor. Om systerskapets svårigheter*, Stockholm: Norstedts Förlag, pp 106–35.

Folketingets Forhandlinger (various years) *Rigsdagstidende*, Copenhagen.

Frie Kvinder (1947–73), Copenhagen: Socialdemokratiske kvinder.

Haavet, I.E. (2006) 'Milk, Mothers and Marriage: Family policy formation in Norway and in neighbouring countries in the twentieth century', in N.F. Christiansen, K. Petersen, N. Edling and P. Haave (eds) *The Nordic Model of Welfare: A historical reappraisal*, Copenhagen: Museum Tusculanum Press, pp 189–214.

Hansen, A.E. and Petersen, K. (2000) 'Mellem arbejde og familie. Arbejderbevægelsens familiepolitik 1945–1980', *Arbejderhistorie. Tidsskrift for historie, kultur og politik*, no 4, pp 33–54.

Hansen, P. (1963) 'En skattereform må også løse sambeskatningsproblemet', *Frie Kvinder*, no 5.

Hirdman, Y. (1998) *Med kluven tunga. LO och genusordningen*, Uddevalla: Atlas.

Kessler-Harris, A. (2001) *In Pursuit of Equity: Women, men, and the quest for economic citizenship in 20th-century America*, New York: Oxford University Press.

Ligestillingsrådet (1978) *Ligestillingsrådets oplæg om skattemæssig ligestilling mellem den gifte kvinde og den gifte mand*, Copenhagen: Ligestillingsrådet.

Lovtidende (various years):

Lov om Indkomst- og Formueskat til Staten af 15. Maj 1903.

Lov om Indkomst- og Formueskat til Staten af 8. Juni 1912.

Lov om Indkomst- og Formueskat til Staten af 10. April 1922.

Lov om visse midlertidige bestemmelser vedrørende påligningen af indkomst- og formueskat til staten, 17. december 1952.

Lov om udskrivning af indkomst- og formueskat til staten for skatteåret 1956–57, 28. marts 1956.

Lov om opkrævning af indkomst- og formueskat for personer m.v. (Kildeskat), 31. marts 1967.

Lov om ændring af lov om opkrævning af indkomst- og formueskat for personer m.v. (Kildeskat), 31. maj 1968.

Lov om ændring af forskellige skattelove (Skattemæssig ligestilling af ægtefæller), 26. maj 1982.

Lønnå, E. (1996) *Stolthet og kvinnekamp. Norsk Kvinnesaksforenings historie fra 1913*, Oslo: Gyldendal.

Melby, K., Rosenbeck, B. and Wetterberg, C.C. (2001) 'Ekteskapslovreform. En forutsetning for velferdsstaten?', in H.R. Christensen, U. Lundberg and K. Petersen (eds) *Frihed, lighed og velfærd*, Rapporter fra Det 24. Nordiske Historikermøde, Aarhus 9.-13. august, Bind 2, pp 191–213.

Montanari, I. (1999) 'Från familjestöd till hemmamakastöd och barnstöd: Ekonomiskt stöd till familjer 1950–1990 i 18 länder', in A. Berge, W. Korpi, J. Palme, S.-Å. Stenberg and K. Åmark (eds) *Välfärdsstat i brytningstid: Historisk-samhällsvetenskapliga studier om genus och klass, ojämlikhet och fattigdom*, Sociologisk Forskning: Supplement, pp 218–52.

Nielsen, H.R. (1996) 'Livets lighed. Lis Groes og familiepolitikken i 1950erne', *Kvinden og Samfundet*, Dansk Kvindesamfund i 125 år, jubilæumsskrift, Copenhagen, pp 25–34.

Ohlander, A.-S. (1989) 'Det osynliga barnet? Kampen om den socialdemokratiska familjepolitiken', in K. Misgeld, K. Molin and K. Åmark (eds) *Socialdemokratins samhälle. SAP och Sverige under 100 år*, Stockholm: Tiden, pp 170–90.

Olsen, E. (1963) 'Hvorfor fortsætte med et forældet forsørgerbegreb?', *Frie kvinder*, no 4.

Pedersen, I.M. (1966) *Forsørgerbegrebet. Studier i familiens retlige problemer*, Betænkning nr. 440, Copenhagen.

Pedersen, I.M. (1974) *Tillægsbetænkning til Forsørgerbegrebet. Studier i familiens retlige problemer*, Betænkning nr. 708, Copenhagen.

Ravn, A.-B. (2005) 'Hverken lighed eller anerkendelse? Kvinder, mænd og skattelovgivning i Danmark', *Kvinder, Køn & Forskning*, no 4, pp 42–55.

Saunte, E. (1951) 'Skattespørgsmålet er stadig aktuelt', *Frie Kvinder*, no 3.

Skattelovskommissionens Betænkning (1950) II. Del, Copenhagen: J.H. Schultz A/S.

Vognbjerg, S.B. (1963) *Betænkning om ægtefællers beskatning m.v.* Notat til formanden, 4. februar, forelagt LO's Forretningsudvalg 8. februar, Copenhagen: ABA, LO's arkiv, kasse 2580.

FOUR

Family policy between science and politics

Åsa Lundqvist

Introduction

Should the state regulate family affairs? If so, how and under what circumstances? These questions have dominated family policy debates over many decades and in most states. In Sweden, many ideas on how 'the family' should be organised have been presented by intellectuals, politicians and experts over time, and reforms of family regulations have emerged since the early 1930s.

This chapter studies the development of Swedish family politics between the 1930s and the early 1970s. My point of departure is that the emergence of Swedish family politics is mainly based on interplay between (i) research on family and gender relations, (ii) government expertise, (iii) social policy, and (iv) labour market regulation (Immergut, 1992; Orloff, 1993; Rueschemeyer and Skocpol, 1996; Daly, 2000). Thus, I will analyse the amalgamation of political ambitions, social reforms, and ideas and suggestions put forward by experts in governmental commissions. The main object is to explore the arguments behind social and family policy proposals between 1930 and 1970, and how they were implemented.[1]

Another aim is to discuss the meaning and understanding of gender behind the expansion of Swedish family politics between 1930 and 1970.[2]

The governmental commission reports in the Swedish political landscape: some methodological reflections

To understand the growth of family policy, some specific features of the Swedish political system, that is the important role of governmental commissions in policy formation in Sweden, must be highlighted.

In Sweden, central ministries are relatively small, due to the fact that policy implementation is the responsibility of independent government boards and agencies. The practice of preparing governmental proposals through ad hoc commissions has also contributed to the limited size of governmental administration. Furthermore, the central role played by ad hoc commissions and independent public agencies in the policy process means that experts and state officials have been very important policy shapers, especially in emerging fields such as family policy.

Historically, these commissions included representatives from almost all political parties, as well as interest groups, civil servants from relevant ministries and agencies, and academic experts. The different representatives were involved already at an early stage of policy formulation. For this reason, the system of ad hoc commissions has been considered a knowledge-producing institution as well as a key institution for consensus building in Swedish politics (Johansson, 1992).

This chapter focuses on the period between 1930 and 1970, a time when the 'Swedish Model' was implemented and social democracy dominated the political arena.[3] This period has also been described as 'the heyday of the state commission system' (Johansson, 1992, p 246).

Government commission reports are used as primary material in this chapter. I have selected reports that illustrate dominating questions and discourses in different periods. Furthermore, the selected reports are analysed as normative texts, anchored in their own time. My aim is to contextualise the different arguments in order to understand how family policy was constructed and how political ambitions and intellectual arguments were intertwined. [4]

The growth of Swedish family politics

The expansion of the social policy field in the 1930s resulted in the growth of a concrete and materialised family policy (originally 'population policy', cf Ohlander, 1992). Family policy was an important part of the modernisation of Swedish society: the family, politicians and intellectuals argued, should be chiselled out and reformed by mapping the population's everyday life in the wake of industrialism.

Family policy, however, emerged alongside many other policy fields, for example economic and labour market policies. During the early 1930s, labour market policy focused mainly on fighting unemployment. In an attempt to decrease unemployment and to alleviate a housing shortage, the construction sector was stimulated. Furthermore, action was taken to regulate the timing of investments and to stabilise aggregate demand (Benner, 1997; Schön, 2000).

In this context, social policy reforms were undertaken in order to change social conditions. Decreasing birth rates made a political response necessary, some claimed. Motives and analyses behind social policy achievements were also intertwined with the latest scientific findings, and this relationship remained strong throughout the period.

However, Swedish family politics also underwent several transformations during the time between 1930 and 1970, and each period contains contradictory patterns: from an early period, strengthening the functionality of the nuclear family and at the same time emphasising equality between men and women; over a more ambivalent period when the dual roles of women are highlighted at the same time as the nuclear family, with a male breadwinner, is emphasised even more than before; to a phase where discourses on gender neutrality dominate. These phases will be addressed below.

The text follows a chronological order: it starts with an analysis of the 1930s and ends in the early 1970s. The first phase includes the period between 1930 and the early 1940s, a time when 'a brand new family' was introduced as a core theme and discourse by politicians. This family type was mapped by academic expertise, mainly through large-scale surveys of social conditions (often published as government commission reports). This 'new family' was characterised by ideas of equality. However, ensuing reforms were based on the conception of differences between women and men. In the second phase – 1940 to 1960 – family policy as a field was stabilised. This was, as we shall see, also a time when both gender difference and gender equality appeared in the debate, not least in relation to family and work. The third phase was dominated by a shift in discourse as well as political praxis, moving beyond a family policy mainly directed at women/mothers towards a policy and discourse embracing a gender-neutral ideal.

'A brand new family': the emergence of modern family politics, 1930–40

A scientific treatment of social policy has not yet been set on trial. But since social politics must transform into social planning, and since social planning must be carried out under rational control, and not just by fumbling policies, the time has come for social science scholars to step out of their isolation. In order to create social change, they must go beyond registration of facts and consistent analysing to raise rational plans for special purposes. (Myrdal, 1944, p 20)

These words are Alva Myrdal's. She was a prominent social democratic intellectual, challenging social scientists in a very direct fashion. Scientific findings should, Myrdal claimed, form the foundation for social policy reforms. However, Alva Myrdal's exhortation illuminates a process that had already begun.

A number of social reforms had been initiated already during the 1930s, mainly to reduce widespread poverty, but also declining birth rates. The reforms were all based on government commission reports, studying social conditions, and suggesting possible reforms to alleviate the social problems.

Inspired by contemporary sociologists such as William Fielding Ogburn, Ernest W. Burgess and Robert Lynd, society was mapped and described as being premised in a fast and exorable transformation. Industrialisation was seen as the cause of a decreasing agricultural population, mainly due to the process of urbanisation. At the same time, the modern division of labour emerged. In this process, the family was described as an institution in crisis by experts in government commission reports (see for example SOU 1936:59; SOU 1938:47). When production was separated from the household, men were detached from domestic work. Earlier so-called family functions, related to, for example, economic relations, childrearing as well as gender relations, had changed dramatically, mainly through new divisions of labour: it was argued among commission experts that the former 'multiple breadwinner model' (the term used in government commission reports) was replaced by new ideals on how to organise the household within families (see for example SOU 1938:47): 'In due course, people got used to the dominating industrial system, stating that the supporting role of the family was transferred to one person: the family father' (p 53).

In theory, women's tasks in the modern family were reduced to maintaining consumption and taking care of the children. In the wake of changing gender relations, increasing tensions between women and men emerged, resulting in decreasing birth rates.

The character of the family had consequently changed, and contemporary experts argued that empirical studies indicated that the family as an institution was in deep crisis.

In this context, the commissions emerged as a crisis-management mechanism. The instructions given to the experts, outlined by the government, aimed to reform existing social and economic conditions, thereby facilitating family formation. To back up this argument, experts put major emphasis on equal conditions between women and men, in the family, in the home and in the labour market, during the 1930s and early 1940s. Ideas of a whole new society emerged from which, as some very influential architects argued, a 'brand new type of family' would arise (Asplund et al, 1931, p 44; SOU 1936:59). In this new and modern family, women would be released from their duties as carers by letting society take over the responsibility for childcare. It was argued that families where both spouses had gainful employment were more content than single-income families, mainly because this situation created a 'conscious sense of community' between family members.

However, even if visions about gender equality were a central argument at the time, many of the experts' suggestions concerned women only. The reason shows in the analysis of the causes behind the crisis of the family and declining birth rates. Declining birth rates were partly explained by the male breadwinner system, where women's role in society was limited to that of carers. In this context, it was argued, women's future satisfaction as women, wives and mothers was in doubt: current social conditions did not provide for women to have a family, mainly because men did not, or could not, take responsibility for family life. Paradoxically, many poor women had to work outside the home to contribute to family maintenance during this period. As a result, medical experts considered most of the caring done by poor mothers to be of low quality.

Due to these factors, women's situation was analysed as problematic and paradoxical, and, as a consequence, the emphasis was directed mainly towards women, who became the primary object of social reforms. In contrast, men as a group were not identified as a target for family policy reforms (see for example SOU 1936:12; SOU 1936:15; SOU 1938:13; SOU 1938:47).

To halt decreasing birth rates and reduce social inequalities, government commissions proposed a number of social reforms, many of which were later implemented: the introduction of antenatal clinics and child-welfare centres, legal prohibitions against dismissal of married or pregnant women from the workplace, means-tested maternity support and, as a peak in reform activity, payment of the universal child allowance directly to the mother (SOU 1929:28; SOU 1936:12; SOU 1936:15; SOU 1938:47; SOU 1946:5; SOU 1946:6; SOU 1946:23; also compare Hirdman, 1989, 1998; Ohlander, 1992; Frangeur, 1998; Bergman, 2003).

Another angle of the debate emphasised the connection between decreasing fertility and what was referred to as the 'rationalisation of sexual patterns' in the population. This turned out to be a complicated and multifaceted issue. While the predominant view was that declining birth rates were an issue of major concern, it was also argued that poor families with many children should not be encouraged to have more children. Instead, birth control should be encouraged for these families, as well as sexual information provided by schools, health institutions and families (SOU 1936:59). It was also argued that abortion should be legalised in certain cases, for example for older women and women who had suffered badly from earlier pregnancies (SOU 1936:12).

Sterilisation was also considered a method of birth control. Experts drawing on contemporary medical, psychological and sociological research argued that women (and later on also men) who suffered from psychological and neurological diseases should not be allowed to have children. The idea of sterilisation as birth control was later introduced (cf Broberg and Roll-Hansen, 1996; see also Melby, 2005 for the 'sterilisation debate' in Norway).

These ideas, presented during the 1930s, mirror the complex relationship between the concepts of equality and difference: equality was emphasised in a more ideological way, that is, in theory it was assumed that in a sophisticated, modern society, all citizens should be equal. However, in practical politics and discussions, differences were emphasised to improve social conditions for selected groups, for example, women and children, and to put forward race-hygiene ideals. Thus, at this early time, the experts' ideas – some of which were later implemented in the political system – made up of a complex mixture of egalitarian ideals, a male breadwinner focus, and even race-hygiene ideals, that is, a politics of eugenics.

Ambivalent family ideals: family policy 1940–60

The social reforms carried out during the 1930s and early 1940s had – together with a stabilisation of labour market relations and international economic developments – led to an unprecedented economic growth and dramatic improvements in social conditions in post-war Sweden (Benner, 1997; Schön, 2000). In this context, state-appointed experts began studying the contemporary social and economic conditions for families with children.

However, it seems as if a shift in the attempt to change social and economic conditions appeared in the early post-war analysis of the family. On the one hand, family policy was no longer targeted only at population growth. Instead, social justice emerged as a dominant theme in the family policy discourse. On the other hand, if the experts in the 1930s discussed how to achieve equal conditions in the home and in the labour market for men and women, experts during the late 1940s and 1950s simultaneously emphasised differences and similarities between men and women. Theories of industrialisation were criticised as being too structural and general in their analysis of social change, missing the centrality of personal relations in the family. Instead, personal relations and consumption patterns in the household became important objects for analysis.

Government commission reports in the 1940s and 1950s combined the analysis of structural aspects such as urbanisation and the entry of modern capitalism with individual and interpersonal factors. Macro and micro-level changes were analysed together. Personal and individual aspects such as sexuality, child rearing and the relationship between women and men were related to labour market conditions and demand management. However, the definition of the 'personal' was rather narrow, mainly covering married women's everyday life. Women were singled out as responsible for the family's well-being. As an example, when the expansion of day care institutions was discussed, the scientific expertise in the commissions emphasised that the mother was the most important adult for a newborn child. 'It is not our attempt to replace the home or take away the children from their mothers and place them in collective institutions' (SOU 1951:15, p 10).

Thus, social expertise was used to legitimise the woman as the 'caring head' of the family, and the man as the provider. This perspective was concretised, for example, in a commission report on family counselling (SOU 1957:33). The background of the report was an ongoing public debate on prevention of abortions. At the time, abortion was seen as a major social problem, linked to increasing divorce rates. It was assumed that a comprehensive study could shed light on this development and also provide advice on how to prevent it.

According to the experts on the commission, there were numerous reasons for the increasing divorce rate among young couples. Again, urbanisation and industrialisation were identified as the main sources of social disruption: 'Urban man seems to be more exposed to nervous diseases, alcoholism, marital conflicts … more than before industrialisation' (SOU 1957:33, p 28).

Experts claimed, however, that industrialisation did not necessarily lead to the disintegration of the family as such. On the contrary, improved living standards expanded the possibilities for free time, which had a positive impact on the family as a whole. Nevertheless, many social problems within the family remained, resulting in increasing divorce rates. Attention was therefore directed towards emotional relations between adults, a significant change in comparison to other commission reports, and the intellectual inspiration came from influential social scientists.

In 1956 Curt Åmark, a psychologist, wrote a paper called 'Familjens kris i modernt samhällsliv' ('The family crisis in modern social life'). Some years earlier, Torgny Segerstedt and Agne Lundqvist, both sociologists at Uppsala University, presented their studies of Huskvarna and Katrineholm in *Människan i industrisamhället* (*Man in industrial society*) (1949). These studies were echoed in the 1957 commission report.

In the analysis of the consequences of industrialisation, technical change created a more complicated individual who was forced to reflect on a growing number of aspects of life, which resulted in a great deal of uncertainty within the population. At the same time, the family, which Segerstedt described as the 'heart of society', was still a central institution in people's lives. Even if the stability of the family was threatened by the anomic consequences of industrial society, its integrative function remained important.

Segerstedt's study represented a classical structural–functionalist analysis of social change, which was incorporated in the mainstream scientific and political discourse: industrialisation – and the growth of modern society – had led to the emergence of a differentiated society. At the same time, societal patterns were harmonised and individuals became more and more dependent on each other.

Following this analysis, the 1957 annual report on family counselling argued that a major problem for modern families was the clash between traditional family values and a more democratic family organisation. In contrast to patriarchal family organisation, a modern marriage was based on the autonomy of men and women (and children). An effect was that both men and women became ambivalent in their new roles. On the one hand, the emotional uncertainty of men increased when they were no longer automatically family heads. On the other hand, women were expected to be more active and autonomous in the family, although most women had a childhood characterised by subordination within the traditional patriarchal family. This, the commission claimed, resulted in an ambivalent and uncertain identity. Moreover, a growing proportion of women were financially independent and this enabled them to leave unsatisfying marriages (which was paradoxical, since financial independence for women was seen as a way of strengthening the bonds between spouses). At this stage, the contradiction between the two roles of women – as mothers (and responsible for the home) and as employees and participants in the labour market – was also fast becoming an issue of concern, and it became increasingly important during the 1950s (and will be described shortly).

All in all, the 1957 commission report assumed that industrialisation had brought the traditional family form into a crisis where both women and men were alienated from their traditional roles and in search of a new family structure. Moreover, it was argued that the 'constant talk about divorce results in notions where individuals end up thinking that divorce is the only solution, especially when conflicts arise' (SOU 1957:33, p 30). This discourse (the 'constant talk') about divorce and social problems in families was seen as a major problem that had to be changed, mainly by offering professional counselling to families in crisis. In other words, both emotional problems and material needs should be subject to social reforms and public intervention: the growth of the social insurance system and social services in general should be complemented by public counselling for emotional problems.

To facilitate women's entry into the labour market, a discussion of the preconditions for gender equality had begun, exemplified in, for example, the discussion on 'women's two roles', which emerged in both the academic literature and government commission reports (SOU 1951:15; SOU 1952:38; Myrdal and Klein, 1957).

The problem of 'women's two roles', first highlighted by the women of the labour movement, was widely studied by academic researchers during the 1950s and 1960s. Research on the obstacles women faced in the labour market was commissioned by the state.

However, the analysis of how to interpret women's lives was still very much the same as before. One example is Alva Myrdal's and Viola Klein's book *Women's two roles* (1957), whose main argument was based on the assumption that women's situation (as mothers and workers) was problematic and therefore should be the focal object of social reforms.

It was, in other words, a highly ambivalent period, where both gender differences and gender similarities were highlighted. One explanation of the duality between difference and equality was that gender equality was seen as a necessity, due to the shortages on the labour market. Social policy, for example the introduction of public family counselling, the expansion of day care, the introduction of means-tested 'home helps' and vacations for housewives, aimed to support both employed women and women working in the household (cf SOU 1951:15; SOU 1952:19; SOU 1952:38; SOU 1954:4 and SOU 1955:29; Hirdman, 1998).

Ideological adaptation and the emergence of a gender-neutral family policy, 1960–70

Alongside an increasing academic interest in intimate relations between men and women, studies of women's lives in the home and in the labour market increased dramatically at the end of the 1950s and the beginning of the 1960s. This period also marks a new phase in the family policy field, where an ideological adaptation with different motives marks commission reports as well as practical politics.

Prevailing views on women as the 'caring head' of the family were questioned, not least in the 'sex role debate' (Dahlström et al, 1962; Acker et al, 1992). In the wake of this debate, the stay-at-home housewife/male breadwinner model was increasingly undermined when the ideological critique was combined with the structural demands for more labour power and housewives were seen as a potential labour reserve.

In addition, the labour movement became radicalised towards the end of the 1960s and one aspect was the introduction of gender equality as an overarching political goal. Of course, the development did not occur overnight: it had begun more than a decade earlier.

The long period of economic growth and the increasing labour shortages during the 1960s led to a search for new sources of labour power: married women and housewives, together with immigrants, became an increasingly important labour market 'reserve army' in the 1950s and 1960s. The growing role of women in the labour market led to an intense debate over the issue of 'equal pay' for women and men: despite labour shortages and a booming economy, women earned on average 30% less than men, and this was a highly controversial issue in the labour movement (Hirdman, 1998, p 400). In this context, 'women's double roles' as mothers and workers were emphasised even further. However, the perspective on gender relations presented in, for example, Myrdal and Klein's book (1957) led to dramatic changes in the coming years.

In 1961, Eva Moberg, a pioneer in the women's movement, wrote 'Kvinnans villkorliga frigivning' ('Women's conditional release'). She argued that the social framework for gender relations had to change in order to establish gender equality between men and women. Both men and women had leading roles in this process: as human beings and as parents. Women's ability to give birth was not to be confused with the ability to care: caring for and raising children were tasks to be performed by father and mother. If this was realised, women and men would be equals in the labour market.

A year later, a government commission report, *Långtidsutredningen* (*Long Term Survey*) was published. The report, written by government experts, argued that economic growth was in danger because of labour shortages, and urged young mothers to enter the labour market.

The debate was further intensified with the publication of an anthology called *Kvinnors liv och arbete* (*Women's Life and Work*) (Baude et al, 1962). This book marked the beginning of Scandinavian 'sex role research'. It had major influence in the emerging debate on sex roles, a concept which, by this time, had been established in the social science discourse. In the book, Swedish and Norwegian sociologists discussed women's situation in the labour market and in the educational system. Researchers from pedagogics and psychology discussed the differences between women and men in socialisation and personality development.

The debate was an impetus for a transformation in family politics and a change in the discourse on women and men, families and labour market participants, the role of the state in regulating family affairs and the socialisation patterns. It has been argued that the 'sex role debate' forced the coalition of politicians and experts in the government commissions to incorporate these new ideas into the family policy field (Acker et al, 1992).

However, it was not until the late 1960s that a more gender-neutral discourse and policy praxis replaced traditional family policy in practical policy. Instead, different ideas were brought forward by experts in an attempt to solve 'women's double roles'. In the mid-1960s, government commissions argued that the dilemma created by the double role of women could be solved by an expansion of public day care. At the same time, the commissions introduced the concept of 'freedom of choice', which highlighted women's rights to combine gainful employment and motherhood.

> Making freedom of choice complete includes giving economic security to all families, regardless of how many children they have, and even if they become larger than the 'normal family'. It also means that women don't have to choose between children and having a job, but that they can fulfil themselves as a women and individuals (SOU 1964:36, p 26).

The concept of 'freedom of choice' had a great impact on family policy debates, especially with the growing number of women in gainful employment. However, instead of analysing the division of labour in households, the attention was directed towards the day care system.

Nevertheless, social reforms during this period were entirely directed towards individuals, but with an emphasis on women and children. One important step towards establishing a gender-neutral family policy was, however, introduced at the Social Democratic Party (SAP) congress in 1969, where the first *Equality report* (*Jämlikhetsrapporten*) was discussed and later accepted by the congress. The ensuing recommendation for the labour movement was to embrace equality as a leading ideological theme. All policy fields should be included: labour market policy, social policy, housing policy, educational policy, consumer policy, legal policy and wage and tax policies. The goal was a classless society (SAP/LO, 1969).

In this all-embracing ambition, family policy should aim to abolish traditional 'sex roles'. Not only should the roles of men and women be transformed, but traditional views on femininity and masculinity should also be challenged.

Moreover, they argued that with true equality, the focal object for social reforms must be the adult individual. The individual becomes his or her own breadwinner, and society must treat all individuals equally. Thus, the authors suggested a revision of family laws (inheritance, marriage and so on), social and labour market policy, and the tax system (where they advocated individual taxation) (cf Florin, 1999).

From this point of view it was argued that all social insurances should be gender neutral, based on individual incomes. 'Adjustments within the system should be neutral regarding gender, marital status and form of social life' (SAP/LO, 1969, p 103). However, the nuclear family still played an important role in the report, again as a source of stability in a changing world. But it was a different nuclear family that was discussed, a family consisting of autonomous individuals. All in all, the family is, the report argued, a stable unit, and as such important for society – but it consists of independent individuals. The ambition to create equality within the family was linked to the objective of avoiding gender discrimination in the welfare system. The vision was, as mentioned, the classless society where women and men would live under equal conditions. This required a reformulation of social policy systems based on the division between male breadwinners and female carers.

In the wake of the intense debates of the 1960s, several family policy reforms were implemented, all related to gender neutrality. Social insurance and the tax system were modified. In 1970 the so-called housewife insurance was extended to men working at home and, a year later, individual taxation was introduced, labelled the 'greatest equality reform ever' (Florin, 1999) (for the debate in Denmark, see Chapter Three in this volume), and maternity insurance was replaced with a gender-neutral parental insurance in 1974 (Bergman and Hobson, 2002; Klinth, 2002).

Concluding remarks

It has been argued that political ambitions regarding gender equality during the first half of the 20th century were for equality based on gender differences (Melby, 2001). As this chapter shows, the differences were initially defined as natural and outside the boundaries of political intervention. On the other hand, they were seen as a social science problem, where the rise of modernity and industrial society undermined the traditional roles of women and men, calling for a radical change in the notion of 'family'. These contradictory views on the family and on gender differences were reflected in social and family policy reforms thereafter.

The dominant discourse in the first period discussed in this chapter (1930–40) stressed the functions of the nuclear family as a source of stability in the volatility that followed industrialisation. The content was based on macro-sociological theories on industrialisation and its social consequences. Family policy (or population policy, as it was called at the time) was a curious mixture of egalitarianism, a male breadwinner focus and eugenics ideals. As a result, egalitarianism was conditional: poor and old women, women with many children as well as mentally ill men and women were all constructed as different from 'normality'. Reforms enacted during this period were also directed mainly towards women. This early period was, in other words, marked by contradictory assumptions based on both equality and differences. At the same time the private sphere became a matter for public debate: in particular, women's role in the home and as mothers was highlighted. The debate expanded and intensified in the post-war period.

During the second phase (1940–60), dramatic improvements in social conditions and the stabilisation in the labour market transformed family policy ideals and practice. The concepts of equality and difference were altered. On the one hand, women were seen as the 'natural' carers. Thus, experts legitimised women as the 'caring head' of the family while the men's role was identified as income provider ('breadwinner'). The unity was cracking, though. Other experts stressed the dual roles of women. This partial modification of the discourse had a material foundation when women's participation in the labour market became increasingly important. This group of experts argued that women's participation rate in the labour market had to increase as a response to coming labour shortages, and that the responsibility for childcare had to be more widely distributed as a consequence.

The policy went further during the third period (the 1960s), when 'justice' as a key concept was accompanied by the concept of 'equality' as a main theme in family policy. This period was marked by growing labour shortages, radicalisation of the labour movement, and the rise of a discourse on gender relations in which women and men were seen as socially constructed categories. These factors in combination created, and were created by, the coalition of experts and politicians. Together, ideological and material changes brought family policy into a phase dominated by gender neutrality, which replaced the former emphasis on women as the focus of social reforms and placed the focus on both women and men.

The analysis of the development of family policy must include many interacting aspects, such as the development of the labour market, social policy reforms, the interplay between social organisations and the state, and the role of social science expertise. It is complicated, if not impossible, to establish a driving force in these change processes. One can argue that the changing assumptions in social theory are very much a flexible companion to the development on the labour market. Simultaneously, interest groups such as women's organisations or trade unions at times opposed this relationship, resulting in a shift in family policy arguments. Nevertheless, one aspect seems to stand out more clearly than others: the politicians' faith in scientific expertise was a crucial factor in the making of early Swedish family politics.

Notes

[1] The period 1970–2000 is analysed by Christine Roman (see Chapter Five in this volume). Together, we have studied family policy and its construction and transformation of the Swedish family concept from the 1930s to the turn of the millennium.

[2] I am aware that many actors were involved in this process (Carlsson, 1986; Wikander, 1994; Karlsson, 1996; Florin and Kvarnström, 2001) and of the influence of different organisations on the outcomes of policy suggestions (Sainsbury, 1996, 2001; Hobson, 2002). However, my contribution to this particular research field is based on an institutionalist perspective, highlighting the interplay between government experts, social policy goals and labour market regulation.

[3] The 'Swedish Model' refers to a theoretical and empirical concept covering the ambition to modernise Swedish society in the post-war period. This modernisation process included reforms of labour market relations, regulation of fluctuations in the market and equalised social conditions, including reforms of gender and family relations (Magnusson, 1996).

[4] For an in-depth analysis of family policy development from 1970 and onwards, see Christine Roman, Chapter Five in this volume.

Bibliography

Acker, J., Baude, A., Björnberg, U., Dahlström, E., Forsberg, G., Gonäs, L., Holter, H. and Nilsson, H. (eds) (1992) *Kvinnors och mäns liv och arbete*, Stockholm: SNS förlag.

Åmark, C. (1956) 'Familjens kris i modernt samhällsliv', unpublished paper.

Asplund, G. (1931) *Acceptera*, Stockholm: Tiden.

Baude, A., Brūn-Gulbrandsen, S., Dahlström, E., Holmberg, P., Liljeström, R., Thorsell, S., Thyberg, S. and Tiller, P.O. (eds) (1962) *Kvinnors liv och arbete. Svenska och norska studier av ett aktuellt samhällsproblem*, Stockholm: Studieförbundet näringsliv och samhälle.

Benner, M. (1997) *The Politics of Growth. Economic regulation in Sweden 1930–1994*, Lund: Arkiv.

Bergman, H. (2003) *Att fostra till föräldraskap. Barnavårdsmän, genuspolitik och välfärdsstat 1900–1950*, Stockholm: Acta Universitatis Stockholmiensis: Almqvist & Wiksell International.

Bergman, H. and Hobson, B. (2002) 'Compulsory Fatherhood: The coding of fatherhood in the Swedish welfare state', in B. Hobson (ed) *Making Men into Fathers. Men, masculinities and the social politics of fatherhood*, Cambridge: Cambridge University Press, pp 92–125.

Broberg, G. and Roll-Hansen, N.-H. (eds) (1996) *Eugenics and the Welfare State: Sterilisation policy in Denmark, Sweden, Norway, and Finland*, East Lansing: Michigan State University Press.

Carlsson, C. (1986) *Kvinnosyn och kvinnopolitik. En studie av svensk socialdemokrati 1880–1910*, Lund: Arkiv.

Daly, M. (2000) *The Gender Division of Welfare. The impact of the British and German welfare states*, Cambridge: Cambridge University Press.

Florin, C. (1999) 'Skatten som befriar. Hemmafruar mot yrkeskvinnor i 1960-talets särbeskattningsdebatt', in C. Florin, L. Sommestad and U. Wileander (eds) *Kvinnor mot kvinnor. Om systerskapets svårigheter*, Stockholm: Norstedts, pp 106-36.

Florin, C. and Kvarnström, L. (2001) *Kvinnor på gränsen till medborgarskap*, Stockholm: Atlas.

Frangeur, R. (1998) *Yrkeskvinna eller makens tjänarinna. Striden om yrkesrätten för gifta kvinnor i mellankrigstidens Sverige*, Lund: Arkiv.

Hirdman, Y. (1989) *Att lägga livet till rätta. Studier i svensk folkhemspolitik*, Stockholm: Carlssons.

Hirdman, Y. (1998) *Med kluven tunga. LO och genusordningen*, Stockholm: Atlas.

Hobson, B. (ed) (2002) *Making Men into Fathers. Men, masculinities and the social politics of fatherhood*, Cambridge: Cambridge University Press.

Immergut, E. (1992) *Health Politics: Interests and institutions in Western Europe*, Cambridge: Cambridge University Press.

Johansson, J. (1992) *Det statliga kommittéväsendet: kunskap, kontroll, konsensus*, Stockholm: Stockholm University.

Karlsson, G. (1996) *Från broderskap till systerskap. Det socialdemokratiska kvinnoförbundets kamp för inflytande och makt i SAP*, Lund: Arkiv.

Klinth, R. (2002) *Göra pappa med barn. Den svenska pappapolitiken, 1960–95*, Umeå: Boréa förlag.

Magnusson, L. (1996) *Sveriges ekonomiska historia*, Stockholm: Tiden Athena.

Melby, K. (2001) 'The Nordic Model of Marriage', in K. Ståhlberg (ed) *Social Sciences. The Nordic countries and Europe II*, Copenhagen: Nord 2001:23.

Melby, K. (2005) 'Husmortid 1900–1950', in I. Blom and S. Sogner (eds) *Med kjønnsperspektiv på norsk historie. Fra vikingtid til 2000-årsskiftet*, Oslo: Cappelen Akademisk Forlag, pp 255-331.

Moberg, E. (1961) 'Kvinnans villkorliga frigivning', *Unga Liberaler*.

Myrdal, A. (1944) *Folk och familj*, Stockholm: KF:s Bokförlag.

Myrdal, A. and Klein, V. (1957) *Kvinnans dubbla roller*, Stockholm: Barnängens förlag.

Ohlander, A.-S. (1992) 'The Invisible Child? The struggle for a social democratic family policy in Sweden, 1900–1960', in K. Misgeld, K. Molin and K. Åmark (eds) *Creating Social Democracy: A century of the Social Democratic Labour Party in Sweden*, Pennslyvania: PA: Pennsylvania State University Press, pp 213-37.

Orloff, A. (1993) *The Politics of Pensions. A comparative analysis of Britain, Canada and the United States, 1880–1940*, Wisconsin: University of Wisconsin Press.

Rueschemeyer, D. and Skocpol, T. (eds) (1996) *States, Social Knowledge, and the Origins of Modern Social Policies*, Princeton, NJ: Princeton University Press.

Sainsbury. D. (1996) *Gender, Equality and Welfare States*, Cambridge: Cambridge University Press.

Sainsbury. D. (2001) 'Gender and the Making of Welfare States: Norway and Sweden', *Social Politics*, vol 8, pp 112–43.

SAP/LO (1969) *Jämlikhet. Första rapport från SAP LO:s arbetsgrupp för jämlikhetsfrågor*, Borås: Prisma.

Schön, L. (2000) *En modern svensk ekonomisk historia. Tillväxt och omvandling under två sekel*, Stockholm: SNS förlag.

Segerstedt, T. and Lundqvist, A. (1949) *Människan i industrisamhället. Arbetslivet*, Stockholm: SNS förlag.

SOU 1929:28. *Betänkande angående moderskapsskydd.*

SOU 1936:12. *Betänkande angående förlossningsvården och barnmorskeväsendet samt förebyggande mödra- och barnavård. Avgivet av befolkningskommittén.*

SOU 1936:15. *Betänkande angående moderskapspenning och mödrahjälp.*

SOU 1936:59. *Betänkande i sexualfrågan. Avgivet av befolkningskommittén.*

SOU 1938:13. *Betänkande angående förvärvsarbetande kvinnors rättsliga ställning vid äktenskap och barnsbörd. Avgivet av befolkningskommittén.*

SOU 1938:47. *Betänkande ang. gift kvinnas förvärvsarbete m.m. Avgivet av kvinnoarbetskommitténs betänkande.*

SOU 1946:5. *Betänkande om barnkostnadernas fördelning med förslag angående allmänna barnbidrag m.m. Avgivet av 1941 års befolkningsutredning.*

SOU 1946:6. *Betänkande om barnkostnadernas fördelning med förslag angående allmänna barnbidrag m.m. Avgivet av 1941 års befolkningsutredning. Bilagor.*

SOU 1946:23. *Socialvårdskommitténs betänkande XII: Utredning och förslag angående moderskapsbidrag.*

SOU 1947:46. *Betänkande angående familjeliv och hemarbete. Avgivet av utredningen för hem- och familjefrågor.*

SOU 1951:15. *Daghem och förskolor. Betänkande om barnstugor och barntillsyn.*

SOU 1952:19. *Semester åt husmödrar, lantbrukare m.fl.*

SOU 1952:38. *Hemhjälp. Bostadskollektiva kommitténs betänkande.*

SOU 1954:4. *Moderskapsförsäkring mm.*

SOU 1955:29. *Samhället och barnfamiljerna. 1954 års familjeutredning.*

SOU 1957:33. *Allmän familjerådgivning.*

SOU 1961:38. *Stöd åt barnaföderskor.*

SOU 1964:36. *Ökat stöd till barnfamiljer.*

Wikander, U. (ed) (1994) *Det evigt kvinnliga. En historia om förändring,* Stockholm: Tidens förlag.

FIVE

Academic discourse, social policy and the construction of new families

Christine Roman

Introduction

From the late 1960s, Swedish family and gender equality politics has strongly emphasised individualised marriage ties, autonomy and economic independence. The explicit political objective has been to construct institutional means for creating a society 'where every adult individual takes responsibility for herself or himself, without being dependent on other family members' (SOU 1972:41, p 58). Family law has been reformed accordingly, and social rights and entitlements have increasingly become tied to the individual. This institutionalised individualism (cf Beck and Beck-Gernsheim, 2002, p 23) has promoted processes of individualisation and defamilialisation (cf Orloff, 1993; Lister, 2003). The aim of the present chapter is to shed some light on the discursive framework that has shaped this policy.[1] To be more precise, I discuss issues specifically dealing with gender relations, and in particular questions concerning economic independence, paid work, childcare and fatherhood. Focus is on the interplay between academic discourse and political regulations of family structure and gender relations, the assumption being that the social sciences have played an important mediating role between the so-called sex-role movements and the women's movements on the one hand, and the Swedish welfare state, on the other hand. Using Nancy Fraser's concept of 'bridge discourse', it is proposed that sociology and gender studies in particular have taken on this role. In addition, it is suggested that the juridical discourse has functioned as a bridge discourse for groups of men claiming rights to child custody after divorce.

The chapter is organised in the following way. A brief presentation of Nancy Fraser's theory of need struggles in welfare states follows this introduction. The section includes a short discussion about the empirical material. The three subsequent sections contain the empirical analysis. The first of these focuses on the political discourse on family and gender relations in Sweden in the 1970s. I describe the discursive shift that took place and argue that the social sciences, and in particular sex-role theory, played an important role in this process. The section that follows argues that a second discursive shift took place in the 1980s when the concept of 'sex roles' to an increasing extent was replaced by conceptions emphasising power relations between genders. Ambiguities in the development of Swedish gender-equality policy are discussed in the subsequent section, where it is suggested that the concept of 'gender equality' has increasingly become a discursive resource for men to strengthen their rights as fathers (cf Trine Annfelt, Chapter Six in this volume). The final section contains some concluding remarks.

Family politics and the struggle over needs

According to Nancy Fraser (1989, ch 8), talk about needs is institutionalised as a major vocabulary in contemporary welfare states. It concerns questions such as who should provide for citizens' needs (the state? the family? the market?), how should the needs of various groups of people be decided upon, and, in case of conflict, who should be the ones to decide. Fraser thus emphasises that, apart from very general needs such as food and shelter, needs are not simply given; they involve interpretation. This 'politics of need interpretation' has to do with the struggle to establish or deny that a need is a matter of legitimate political concern, the struggle to define that need and determine what would satisfy it, and the struggle over the satisfaction of the need (to secure or withhold provision). Discourse on needs hence functions as a medium for the making and contesting of political claims, and 'appears as a site of struggle where groups with unequal discursive (and non-discursive) resources compete to establish as hegemonic their respective interpretations of legitimate social needs' (Fraser, 1989, p 166).

Following Fraser, I recognise three major kinds of need discourse in welfare states: (i) oppositional discourse, (ii) reprivatising discourse and (iii) expert discourse. Oppositional discourse arises when earlier privatised needs are politicised by social movements. That is, oppositional forms of need talk challenge the established boundaries that separate, for example, 'domestic' from 'political'. One example is the successful struggle by the women's movement to transform wife battering from a 'personal' problem to a public matter. Reprivatisation discourse emerges in response to oppositional discourse. It defends established boundaries between 'public' and 'private' and thereby contests the politicisation of a certain need. In Sweden, a contemporary political debate about the possible use of quotas in parental insurance can serve to illustrate an ongoing struggle between politicisation and reprivatisation. Expert need discourse is closely connected to institutions of knowledge production and utilisation, such as universities, professional associations etc. It translates sufficiently politicised needs into objects of potential state intervention. Sometimes social movements manage to co-opt or create critical expert-discourse publics. Expert discourse can then become a 'bridge discourse' that functions as a mediator between social movements and the state. However, because of its bridge role, the rhetoric of expert discourse tends to be administrative and is likely to represent needs in abstraction from class, gender and ethnicity (Fraser, 1989, p 174).

It is my assumption that the social sciences have functioned as 'bridge discourses' in the Swedish political context. To be more precise, I assert that: (i) in the late 1960s and the 1970s the Scandinavian sociological discourse on 'sex roles' mediated between the state and various groups of people challenging prevailing conceptions of gender and the gendered division of work, (ii) in the 1980s and 1990s some versions of feminist theory played a similar bridging role in relation to the growing women's movement, and that (iii) the social sciences, and above all the juridical discourse, have played a mediating role between the state and groups of men claiming rights as fathers. In addition, I argue that sociological sex-role theory and feminist theory, respectively, played important roles in the discursive shifts that took place in Swedish family politics between the late 1960s and the turn of the millennium. The first shift is traced to the late 1960s, when questions of gender equality increasingly replaced questions of equality between social classes in family politics, and when individuals, rather than the nuclear family as such, became the objects of reform. A second shift took place in the 1980s, when critical discourses about power relations between genders increasingly influenced governmental commission reports and policy documents. However, different, and sometimes opposed, ideas have influenced Swedish family and gender-equality policy. Discourses emphasising fathers' rights from a gender-equality perspective are cases in point.

The empirical base for my analysis consists mainly of written documents such as government commission reports and government bills. It includes material on gendered relations associated both with work in the home and the labour market, and material associated with bodily integrity. In Chapter Four in this volume, Åsa Lundqvist explains the importance of government commissions in the Swedish political system as well as the close relationship between the social sciences and politics in 'the Swedish model'. Suffice it to say that while government commissions lost some of their former status in the mid-1970s, they nevertheless continue to play an important role in policy formation and legislative processes. By explicitly or implicitly diagnosing social and political problems they create discursive frameworks for politics (cf Bacchi, 1999). Not only are government commissions appointed early on in the policy process, but also the subsequent analyses and propositions are published as official reports and circulated for consideration to the parties concerned. Eventually, the collected points of view form the basis for a government bill. Government commissions appointed to deal with family issues have frequently included sociologists and other social scientists. Consequently, social researchers have substantially influenced the discourses that have shaped family policy. Below I will demonstrate this interplay between academic discourse and family politics from the 1970s to the turn of the millennium.

Engineering the gender-neutral family

The nuclear family was still accepted as a necessary unit for adults and children in the 1940s and 1950s. While experts and politicians did call attention to women's 'double roles' as workers and mothers, they simultaneously asserted that mothers are irreplaceable for small children. In other words, the male breadwinner type of family was not seriously questioned. Things looked quite different a decade later, however, when constraining aspects of men and women's different roles within and outside the family were increasingly attended to. The subsequent debates in newspapers and books about women's place in society divided both people and parties (for example, Backberger, 1966; Baude, 1992; Moberg, 1992(1961); Florin, 1999). This so-called sex-role debate, in which sociological sex-role research was significant, contributed to an ideological change in approaches to 'the family'. Not only did sex-role researchers strongly oppose any tendency to confuse women's reproductive capacity and the care for children, but also the gendered division of work between the family and the labour market was increasingly questioned (see also Lundqvist, Chapter Four in this volume.)

This new ideological and theoretical landscape engendered a shift in the political discourse. As mentioned above, gender equality increasingly superseded questions of equality between social classes. The emergence of a concept that distinguishes between gender equality (*jämställdhet*) and equality between social classes (*jämlikhet*) is in itself suggestive. The individual, rather than the nuclear family as such, became the object of reform, and the idea that women ought to work outside the home eventually became the norm. As a result, questions related to women's paid work became important political objectives of reform. One of the overarching political themes throughout the 1970s was to produce incentives for women to become wage earners and to create the necessary institutional conditions to make this possible. Another objective was to construct a politics of fatherhood, to make it more attractive for men to take care of their children. The conceptual changes are reflected in, for example, the tax reform of 1971, the parental insurance of 1974, and in the divorce act of 1974. Several large reforms, resting on the principle of gender neutrality, were agreed upon and gender equality was institutionalised (cf Hirdman, 1998).[2]

The following paragraphs discuss in some detail the interaction between academic and political discourse on two political issues identified as crucial in the 1970s: (i) to adapt family law and the social insurance system to changing family patterns and (ii) to create the institutional means necessary to transform male breadwinner families into dual earner families.

Gender neutrality

In the 1960s, legislation on marriage and the family presupposed a clear gendered division of work. The husband was expected to take on the breadwinner role and the wife to shoulder responsibilities for childcare and domestic duties. Rising female labour market participation (see Appendix, Tables 3 and 4), increasing divorce rates, and the expansion of social rights and benefits had, however, generated a growing gap between actual family patterns and the rules regulating marriage. In order to close this gap, the government appointed a commission to suggest changes in rules regulating the relations between spouses, between ex-spouses, and between parents and children before and after divorce (SOU 1972:41). The directives to the commission prescribed that the reformed family law was to be founded on the principle of gender equality. To be more precise, the directives stated that propositions should be founded on the assumptions that: (i) spouses are independent, autonomous persons within marriage, (ii) marriage is a consensual union between independent persons, (iii) the question of guilt is irrelevant in case of divorce, (iv) shared custody of children should be granted to non-married fathers and (v) rules should, as far as possible, be neutral in relation to different types of families. In addition, it was made clear that new rules should serve as an instrument for reforms, that is, the aim was to promote 'the creation of a society where every adult person can take care of himself or herself, without being dependent on relatives, and where equality between men and women is a reality' (SOU 1972:41, p 58). In other words, the political objective was to further processes of individualisation and defamilialisation.

The analyses carried out by the 1972 commission were in line with the original instructions. Hence, it proposed several changes in family law to construct gender-neutral and individualised marriage rules. Eventually the institution of marriage was transformed into a consensual union, where each party should support themselves and share domestic duties (Romanus, 1992, p 30).

A peculiar mixture of sociological structural–functionalist theory of family change and Scandinavian critical sex-role research guided the analyses carried out by the commission (which worked for ten years). It is thus significant that an entire chapter of the principal report is devoted to a description and analysis of the family's 'loss of functions' during industrialisation. The commission accordingly retold the well-known sociological story about the transformation of a 'multifunctional family' into a companionate family based on emotional ties.[3] However, it also applied theories advanced by Swedish sex-role researchers during the 1960s, which emphasised the importance of gender equality, female labour market participation, and economic independence. In this way sex-role research provided a theoretical ground for the political efforts to construct a new type of gender-neutral family.

It is thus noteworthy that commission experts pointed out not only that 'the family' had lost many of its former 'functions', but also regretted that too many needs were still taken care of by families. For example, it was argued that processes of family change were slowed down by the increasing production of household appliances, which presumably conserved some services in the home that might otherwise be performed outside the home. In addition, it was underlined that the lack of public childcare stopped women from getting paid jobs (SOU 1972:41, p 45). In other words, gender equality was not seen as compatible with the ideal of mothers as housewives (cf Carlsson Wetterberg and Melby, Chapter Two in this volume).

Several government commissions were appointed to analyse widows' pensions and husbands' obligations to pay maintenance to ex-wives. The task was to review rules in order to decide whether gender differences in regulations were justified. The commissions' discussions illustrate the ways in which the double task of closing the conceived gap between rules and reality and creating further incentives for women to become wage earners was dealt with. Posed in a characteristic gender-neutral language, the commission reports thus concluded that maintenance obligations between spouses after the dissolution of marriage must not exist. Moreover, they proposed that the widow's pension was to be successively replaced by a gender-neutral system that is 'better adjusted to existing and *expected* family patterns' (SOU 1971:19, p 52, emphasis added; see also SOU 1977:37, p 47; SOU 1981:62). The explicit motive for the proposed changes was that gender differences in the rules were due to the fact that the existing pension system was constructed in the 1940s and 1950s, when the male breadwinner family was still the dominant type. The commission's judgement was that dual earner families had progressively replaced the above-mentioned type of family (SOU 1971:19, p 42). It also established that women were not to be considered dependent on their husbands. Each adult person should instead be regarded as an independent individual with the rights and obligations to take care of his or her own maintenance. This principle of gender neutrality actually implied that women lost some of the specific rights that originated from their domestic role.

The politicisation of childcare

As mentioned above, oppositional discourse arises when social movements politicise earlier privatised needs. The 1970s discussions about childcare are one example of this process. In the late 1960s, most young children were taken care of by their mothers in their homes. No more than 2% of children were offered a place in public kindergartens in the late 1960s (Jonson, 2004, p 100). In the 1970s childcare had become 'political' in both the discourse sense of the word, that is, actors on several discursive arenas constructed it as 'political', and in the sense that it was handled directly in the official governmental system (cf Fraser, 1989, p 166). Moreover, it was conceived of as a general political issue concerning men as well as women. This indicates a break with earlier political discourse, which constructed childcare as a 'women's question'. That is, while childcare used to be conceived of as a question about women's freedom to choose between being a housewife and being gainfully employed, not only mothers, but also fathers were now seen as responsible for taking care of children (cf Lindvert, 2002, p 122).

In addition, interpretations of children's needs changed. In the 1950s and early 1960s commission experts and politicians had mainly discussed public childcare in terms of labour market needs, and as a way of counterbalancing social differences between children (Jonson, 2004, p 101). In contrast to this, subsequent commissions attached much weight to pedagogical aspects, children's needs and gender equality. One central argument put forward by governmental commissions in the 1970s was that public childcare is in the best interest of the child. To be more precise, both experts and politicians asserted that the male breadwinner type of family is not necessarily beneficial to the child (SOU 1975:30; SOU 1979:57). The former truth that small children need to have their mothers at home was thus dismissed as a myth. In fact, that 'truth' was reversed when commissions claimed that the child's psychological development actually suffers from spending too much time at home with an isolated mother. The concept of 'quality time' was introduced, indicating that the quality of the mother–child relation is more important than the number of hours spent together. Hence, while mothers were constructed as vital to their children in the 1940s and 1950s, new experts wanted to unmask this belief as a myth (see Lundqvist, Chapter Four in this volume). Public childcare was also construed as a 'love resource' for children, that is, by receiving care and love from well-educated preschool teachers, children were not solely dependent on parents. In addition, public childcare institutions were thought of as having the potential to create more democratic individuals, as well as to develop the potentials of the individual child.

To strengthen their arguments, commission members recurrently referred to sociological and social-psychological research. Politicians were thus assured that the assumption that a strict gendered division of roles constrains the child's psychological development rested on 'new scientific findings' and was supported by 'sex role research' (SOU 1979:57; SOU 1981:25, p 16). The new discourse on children's needs consequently challenged hegemonic ideas about relations between parents and children, as well as between genders.

The expansion of public childcare was seen as a necessity. It was not, however, considered sufficient to solve problems related to mothers' increasing employment. Further measures were suggested to facilitate parents' dual roles as workers and carers. One important government commission thus proposed that the existing mother's leave should be transformed into an extended, gender-neutral parental insurance (SOU 1972:34). One interpretation made by the committee was that parents have a need to stay at home with small babies and sick children. Another argument referred to children's needs. However, it was also strongly emphasised that financial state support must not counteract women's employment. Hence, the commission went to great lengths to discuss how to reconcile parental leave with gender equality. Most importantly, the commission considered sharing the leave between parents to be essential in this respect, and consequently underlined that rules must not prevent fathers from staying at home with their children. In addition, it asserted that sharing is in the best interests of the child. Referring to sociological sex-role research that implied that too much influence from mothers is to the detriment of children, the conclusion was that it is important to facilitate close relationships between fathers and their children (SOU 1972:34, p 224).

The 1972 commission's proposal to put fathers on a par with mothers, that is, that fathers were expected to take care of small children, marks an important ideological shift in conceptions of fatherhood. From that time on, the conflict between working life and family life was constructed as a problem concerning both men and women. Just a few years earlier, compensation for mothers only was given topical interest in political discussions (Karlsson, 1996, pp 267–8).

To sum up: sociological research was indeed important in the formation of the Swedish gender-equality discourse. It helped to interpret and mediate need claims from various political groups fighting to abolish housewifery, and to construct a policy aimed at the transformation of breadwinner families into dual earner families. Previously privatised needs, such as childcare, were thus transformed into legitimate political concerns, and established boundaries between 'the private' and 'the political' were challenged. However, the interpretation of needs was, to a large extent, gender neutral. They were framed as children's needs, parents' needs or 'everybody's need' for gender equality. Differences in men's and women's living conditions were thus largely ignored. In the decades to come, this gender-neutral discourse was, however, to be forcefully challenged.

Gendering family discourse

Family sociologists' assumption that everyone benefits from relaxing rigid sex roles was increasingly abandoned in the 1970s. Perspectives focusing on power and conflicting interests between men and women gained ground, that is, that men might have a vested interest in the reproduction of existing gender arrangements. This shift in theoretical perspectives was, of course, largely due to the impact of the women's movement and the ensuing growing field of gender studies. The sex-role theories developed in the 1960s were increasingly succeeded by theories emphasising structural characteristics of the gender system. This change also signified a break with structural–functionalist theories of the family (Roman, 2004, p 121).

The new ways of understanding gender inequalities soon affected the political discourse. Two government commission reports published in 1979 and 1982 mark this break with the earlier discursive framework. The commission that authored the reports was appointed by the government to analyse gender equality and to develop a more comprehensive view on the question (SOU 1979:89; SOU 1982:18). The result turned out to be a highly critical assessment of the gender-equality policy pursued in the 1970s. The commission established that this policy had not been very successful from women's point of view. Studies carried out by the commission had revealed that women still shouldered the responsibility for the family and the household, to the detriment of their position in working life and their overall life situation. The optimism that had characterised earlier governmental commission reports was thus turned into scepticism in the beginning of the 1980s. In addition, the commission criticised the gender–neutral reforms implemented in the 1970s for presuming that spouses equally support themselves, when in reality women had not reached an economic level equivalent to that of men.

The shifting understandings of gender may be partly explained by changes in family structure. Whereas the political objective in the late 1960s and 1970s was to transform male breadwinner families into dual earner families, this task was to a large extent accomplished something like a decade later. The task set out for the 1980 commissions was thus evaluative, that is, to analyse under what circumstances changes had been realised, and to what extent gender equality had really been achieved.

The influence from feminist theory and gender research is quite obvious in the two above-mentioned reports. It is, for example, strongly underlined that women's unpaid work in the household is both socially and economically important. This understanding is very much in line with feminist discussions at the time, such as the Marxist–feminist domestic labour debate and sociological analyses of the importance of housework (cf Oakley, 1974; Molyneux 1979). *Women's* needs are given prominence in these reports, and for the first time men's liability for remaining inequalities is brought to the fore. The commission thus emphasised that men had shirked responsibilities for housework and childcare, thereby leaving women with double workloads. Moreover, men as a group were held accountable for women's inferior position in the labour market, because they had failed to take an active part in childcare and domestic work in the private sphere.

In a follow-up report from 1983, the expression 'the in principle-man' was coined to describe discrepancies between attitudes and practices among Swedish men (DsA 1983:2). The study had revealed that although most Swedish men displayed positive attitudes towards parental leave, the majority did not take the opportunity to stay at home with their children. Opportunities to go on parental leave and shorten working hours were mainly taken by women.

Changes in theoretical perspectives were accompanied by a shift in focus from gendered division of work in the family to gender segregation in working life. What is more, the gender-segregated labour market was identified as the most important issue for achieving gender equality. In keeping with this, the measures proposed by the 1982 commission almost exclusively focused on working life (SOU 1982:18). The same is true for other government commission reports that were published in the 1980s. They analyse gender divisions in working life, whereas gender relations in families are largely neglected. Interestingly, this shift in Swedish gender-equality policy parallels the route taken by Swedish gender research. That is, the attention to family relations that had characterised gender research in the 1970s was increasingly superseded by an interest in gender relations in workplaces. This correspondence may be interpreted as a testimony to the close relation between gender research and Swedish gender-equality politics.

In the following decade Swedish gender-equality policy was subjected to further critique, this time articulated by a government commission exclusively made up of researchers, the first of its kind (SOU 1990:44). In one of the chapters in the principal report, historian Yvonne Hirdman presented her gender system theory, which soon became quite influential in political circles. Following this theory, gender inequality is reproduced by two inherent 'logics' in the gender system: the male norm and gender segregation. According to Hirdman's critical appraisal, Swedish gender-equality policy had contributed to the reproduction of the gender system by transferring women from the home to the female-dominated public sector, where they had become subordinated to a male norm and male control (SOU 1990:44, p 93).

Yet another critical assessment was provided by a government commission appointed to describe and analyse the distribution of economic power and economic resources between men and women in Sweden (SOU 1998:6). The subtitle of its principal report clearly reveals the critical approach taken on *The myth about the rational working life and the gender-equal Sweden.* The report is based on 13 separate research reports analysing the gender distribution of economic resources and power in the labour market, families and the welfare state. Taken together, the reports demonstrate that, at the turn of the millennium, Sweden was still an unequal society where women earned and owned less than men, had lower status and less power, and took on much more responsibility for childcare and housework.

To summarise, the study suggests that at the turn of the century, the previous focus on sex roles had given way to a perspective highlighting power relations between men and women. This new perspective was advanced by feminist researchers, in a way similar to the promotion of sex-role theory by sociologists (cf Klinth, 2002). That is to say, whereas sociological sex-role theory functioned as a bridge discourse in the 1970s, (some versions of) feminist theory took on that role in the following two decades. One important difference must be pointed out, however. The 1970s signify the decade when gender equality was institutionalised in Sweden and when government commission reports laid the ground for costly welfare state reforms. Partly due to reduced economic growth and increasing state budget deficit, this was not the case in the following decades. Hence, the commissions appointed in the 1980s and 1990s actually proposed few measures to increase gender equality. In this sense, I find it correct to conclude that the relation between academic discourse and politics went through a change after the 1970s. Whereas in the 1970s social scientists took on the role of 'social engineers', they were increasingly assigned the function of 'critical voices' in the following decades.

The described changes do not, however, imply that academic discourse lost its impact on political discourse. On the contrary, feminist research has clearly contributed to changing the ways gender equality is understood. It is thus illustrative that a fairly recent official letter from the government proclaims that gender equality is 'a question about breaking the existing social structure that tells us that men are the norm and women are the exception, that men are superior and women are inferior, that men have much power, and women have little power' (Regeringens skrivelse 1999/2000:24, p 5). This statement is obviously influenced by the gender system theory elaborated by Yvonne Hirdman. The effect of Hirdman's theory is also revealed in the former Social Democrat government's plan of action, when it reports that the gender system theory has been used as a tool in Swedish gender-equality policy since 1993 (Regeringens skrivelse 2002/03:140). Hence, at the end of the 20th century political discourse increasingly used a feminist vocabulary. What is more, the majority of Swedish political parties called themselves feminist and had feminist perspectives written into their programmes (cf Dahlerup, 2004).

The impact of feminist discourse is also clearly revealed in political discussions about male violence against women. This issue used to be marginalised in Swedish gender-equality policy, which focused mainly on questions about the gender redistribution of economic resources. However, in the 1990s men's violence against women was identified as a central political problem. Furthermore, it was discussed in terms of gender and power (cf Wendt Höjer, 2002). It is thus significant that the directive to a commission appointed in 1993 was to analyse men's violence against women from 'a woman's perspective' (SOU 1995:60, p 3, *Kvinnofrid*). The impact of feminist theories about male violence is obvious in the resulting report. Hence, domestic violence is explained by reference to the historical power relation between men and women, ideas about male superiority and men's right to control women. Furthermore, it is interpreted as a manifestation of a male sexuality that is oriented to conquest and domination, and to proving masculinity.[4]

Changing conceptions of fatherhood

However, the impact of feminist discourse on official Swedish gender-equality policy is far from unambiguous. Constructions of the father–child relation might serve to illuminate the ways in which different discourses have contributed to shaping this policy.

As indicated above, sociological theory played an important role in the shifting ideological construction of fatherhood that occurred in the 1970s. To take just one example, the 1972 Commission constructed 'the fatherless society' as a new problem, that is, that fathers' absence from the home might negatively affect children's (read boys') psychological development (SOU 1972:41). This 'theory of compensatory masculinity' had been much discussed in sociology and assigned a place in family sociology textbooks. Decision makers could thus be convinced that gender-equality policy rested on solid scientific ground. Eventually it was apparent, however, that the objective to transform men into caregivers was not easily attained. Few fathers seemed willing to take on more responsibility for childcare and domestic duties. As a result, politicians were increasingly criticised for paying lip-service to the aim of transforming men into caring fathers, when in reality little had been done to bring men to change their behaviour. The construction of the parental insurance was considered a case in point. While on a discursive level the reform created opportunities for men to become caring fathers, it had in practice contributed to reproducing gender differences in men's and women's lives. Few men had actually taken the opportunity to stay at home with their children (cf Widerberg, 1981, 1986; Landby Eduards, 1986).[5]

During the last decade or so, efforts have been made to close the mentioned gap between rhetoric and practice. As a matter of fact, Swedish politics towards men as fathers was recently described as the most regulatory and interventionist in the world (Hobson and Morgan, 2002). The parental insurance is once again a case in point. Presently, two months are earmarked for fathers, so-called 'daddy months'. When he introduced the first 'daddy month' in 1994, the responsible (and liberal) minister actually used feminist gender system theory to strengthen his argument. He claimed that decisions about sharing or not sharing the parental leave are not entirely to be considered a private question, the reason being that gender divisions in families are part of a larger gender system characterised by men's structural and symbolic superiority (Klinth, 2002, p 332). This attempt to politicise childcare has, however, been strongly contested by other actors. A heated debate is going on between those advocating more 'daddy months' and those advocating that such matters should be decided upon in the private sphere.

Child custody

Connected to the above-mentioned ideas about the importance of fathers to their children are ideas about the importance of shared custody. Hence, fathers' rights to child custody have continually been strengthened since the 1970s. Non-married men were granted the opportunity to have custody in 1973, and in 1977 joint custody after divorce was made possible (Proposition 1975/76). Since few divorced parents took advantage of this opportunity – only 145 couples applied for joint custody in 1977 (SOU 1995:79, p 48) – it was affirmed as a norm six years later. That is, a court decision was no longer necessary. During the 1990s fathers' rights to child custody were further strengthened, partly due to the successful claim-making by various groups of men. In 1993, for example, a group of non-expert, middle-class men was appointed by the government to formulate a public opinion to increase men's engagement as parents and identify possible barriers that prevent fathers from sharing the parental leave with mothers. The report published by this so-called 'daddy group' (*Pappagruppen*) stirred much attention and public debate (DS 1995:2). The assumption was not only that children need their fathers and that fathers are important role models for boys, but also that the fact that mothers are more often assigned custody of children in the case of conflict implies discrimination against men as fathers. At about the same time, a government commission was appointed to analyse questions about child custody and the relationship between parents and children after divorce. Its point of departure was, firstly, that it is essential for the child to have close contact with its father and, secondly, that conflicts over custody are to be settled exclusively according to the principle of 'the best interest of the child'. The conclusion drawn by the commission was both that shared custody after divorce should be used more often, and that the court should have the authority not only to rule in favour of shared custody in cases of conflict, but also to decide whether the child should live with the father or mother (SOU 1995:79). Changes were realised with the so-called custody reform in 1998.

To sum up, this study suggests that Swedish family and gender-equality policy was far from unequivocal during the period investigated. While feminist perspectives on gender equality have had an impact on political discourse, biological fathers have also gained new rights by drawing on discourses on gender equality and children's needs. It is telling that Sweden is now labelled the most men-friendly country in the world (Hobson, 2004). In Chapter Six, Trine Annfelt demonstrates that in Norway the concepts of 'gender equality' and 'the best interest of the child' have increasingly been used as discursive resources to strengthen fathers' rights after divorce. A similar conclusion can be drawn in the Swedish case. Not only has the discourse about fathers' importance for their children become hegemonic, but also concurrently with increased state intervention in post-divorce families, men as fathers have benefited more and more from the discourse on gender equality (cf Eriksson, 2004). It is here suggested that the juridical discourse has played a crucial role in the process, that is, that it has functioned as a mediator between the state and groups of men claiming rights as fathers in questions of child custody.

Concluding remarks

This chapter discusses the impact of academic discourse on family and gender-equality policy, and the ways in which certain available discourses were adopted by policy. The analyses demonstrate, firstly, that academic discourse played an important mediating role between the Swedish welfare state and social movements that challenged established boundaries between the private and the public. Secondly, they point out the significance of the social sciences in the discursive shifts in family and gender-equality politics during the investigated period, as well as the new truths about gender relations and the parent–child relationship that were established in the process. Thirdly, ambiguities in the Swedish gender-equality policy are revealed by bringing to the fore new rights gained by biological fathers. Considering male violence against women, the new child custody rules may even serve to reproduce power relations between men and women. However, at this point it seems appropriate to point out that while this chapter deals with the impact of academic discourse on political discourse, I have not had the opportunity to elaborate on the question of the possible impact of policy upon research. This side of the story, hence, remains to be told in some other context.

Notes

[1] This chapter is part of a research project funded by the Swedish Council of Research. This project studies the construction and transformation of the Swedish family concept from the 1930s to the turn of the millennium. Åsa Lundqvist (see Chapter Four in this volume) investigates the years in between the 1930s and 1970s.

[2] Other important reforms that were enacted in the 1970s were the right to free abortion (1975), the obligation of every municipality to have a plan for the expansion of public childcare (1976), and the right to reduced working hours for parents with small children (1979).

[3] Considering the interplay between politics and the social sciences, it is interesting that the introductory chapter in the report is almost identical with a chapter in a Swedish university textbook on family sociology from 1965. What is more, the textbook chapter is written by sociologist Jan Trost, who was also appointed as one of the experts in the commission mentioned (Trost, 1965). The sociological 'loss-of-function theory' guided descriptions of changing family patterns till the end of the 1970s.

[4] The commission also goes to great lengths to describe the theory of 'the normalisation of violence' elaborated by feminist sociologist Eva Lundgren.

[5] Fathers used only 5% and 7% of the insurance days in 1980 and 1990 respectively (*På tal om kvinnor och män*, 2004, p 38).

Bibliography

Bacchi, C. (1999) *Women, Policy and Politics. The construction of policy problems*, London: Sage.

Backberger, B. (1966) *Det förkrympta kvinnoidealet*, Stockholm: Albert Bonniers förlag.

Baude, A. (1992) 'Inledning', in J. Acker, A, Baude, U. Björnberg, E. Dahlström, G. Forsberg, L. Gonäs, H. Holter and A. Nilsson (eds) *Visionen om jämställdhet*, Stockholm: SNS, pp 9-15.

Beck, U. and Beck-Gernsheim, E. (2002) *Individualization*, London: Sage Publications.

Dahlerup, D. (2004) 'Feministisk partipolitik? Om skillnader i dansk och svensk jämställdhetsdebatt', in C. Florin and C. Berqvist (eds) *Framtiden i samtiden. Könsrelationer i förändring i Sverige och omvärlden*, Stockholm: Institutet för framtidsstudier, pp 234–63.

DS 1995:2. Stockholm: Fritzes.

DsA 1983:2. Stockholm: LiberFörlag/Allmänna förlag.

Eriksson, M. (2004) *I skuggan av Pappa. Familjerätten och hanteringen av fäders våld*, Diss. Stehag: Förlags AB Gondolin.

Florin, C. (1999) 'Skatten som befriar. Hemmafruar mot yrkeskvinnor i 1960-talets särbeskattningsdebatt', in C. Florin, L. Sommestad and U. Wileander (eds) *Kvinnor mot kvinnor Om systerskapets svårigheter*, Stockholm: Norstedts, pp 106-35.

Fraser, N. (1989) *Unruly Practices. Power, discourse and gender in contemporary social theory*, Cambridge: Polity Press.

Hirdman, Y. (1998) *Med kluven tunga. LO och genusordningen*, Uddevalla: Atlas.

Hobson, B. (2004) 'Pappavänligt samhälle', in C. Florin and C. Berqvist (eds) *Framtiden i samtiden. Könsrelationer i förändring i Sverige och omvärlden*, Stockholm: Institutet för framtidsstudier, pp 84-105.

Hobson, B. and Morgan, D. (2002) 'Introduction', in B. Hobson (ed) *Making Men into Fathers. Men, masculinities and the social politics of fatherhood*, New York: Cambridge, pp 1-2.

Jonson, J.O. (2004) 'Förskola för fördelade?', in M. Bygren, M. Gähler and M. Nermo (eds) *Familj och arbete – vardagsliv i förändring*, Stockholm: SNS förlag, pp 90-121.

Karlsson, G. (1996) *Från broderskap till systerskap. Det socialdemokratiska kvinnoförbundets kamp för inflytande och makt i SAP*, Lund: Arkiv.

Klinth, R. (2002) *Göra pappa med barn. Den svenska pappapolitiken 1960–95*, Umeå: Borea.

Landby Eduards, M. (1986) 'Kön, stat och jämställdhetspolitik', *Kvinnovetenskaplig tidskrift*, vol 7, no 3, pp 4–15.

Lindvert, J. (2002) *Feminism som politik. Sverige och Australien 1960–1990*, Umeå: Borea.

Lister, R. (2003/1997) *Citizenship. Feminist perspectives*, New York: New York University Press.

Moberg, E. (1992) 'Kvinnans villkorliga frigivning', in A. Baude (ed) *Visionen om jämställdhet*, Stockholm: SNS Förlag, pp 194-207 (originally published in *Unga liberaler*, 1961).

Molyneux, M. (1979) 'Beyond the Domestic Labour Debate', *New Left Review*, vol 116, pp 3–27.

Oakley, A. (1974) *The Sociology of Housework*, New York: Pantheon Books.

Orloff, A. (1993) 'Gender and the social rights of citizenship: The comparative analysis of gender relations and welfare states', *American Sociological Review*, vol 58, pp 303–28.

Proposition 1975/76: 170. *Lag om ändring i föräldrabalken.*

På tal om kvinnor och män. En lathund för jämställdhet (2004). Stockholm: SCB.

Regeringens skrivelse 1999/2000:24. *Jämställdhetspolitiken inför 2000-talet.*

Regeringens skrivelse 2002/03:140. *Jämt och ständigt – Regeringens jämställdhetspolitik med handlingsplan för mandatperioden.*

Roman, C. (2004) *Familjen i det moderna. Sociologiska sanningar och feministisk kritik*, Malmö: Liber.

Romanus, G. (1992) 'Ett nätverk för jämställdhet', in A. Baude (ed) *Visionen om jämställdhet*, Stockholm: SNS Förlag, pp 24-38.

SOU 1971:19. *Pensionsfrågor mm. Betänkande avgivet av Pensionsförsäkringskommittén.*

SOU 1972:34. *Familjestöd. Betänkande avgivet av Familjepolitiska kommittén.*

SOU 1972:41. *Familj och äktenskap 1. Betänkande avgivet av Familjesakkunniga.*

SOU 1975:30. *Barnens livsmiljö del 1. Socialdepartementet. Betänkande från Barnmiljöutredningen.*

SOU 1977:37. *Underhåll till barn och frånskilda. Delbetänkande avgivet av Familjesakkunniga.*

SOU 1979:57. *Barnomsorg – behov, efterfråga, planeringsunderlag. Betänkande avgivet av Planeringsgruppen för barnomsorg.*

SOU 1979:89. *Kvinnors arbete. Om hemarbetande kvinnors situation, kvinnors försörjning, barns omsorg och mäns delaktighet i det oavlönade hemarbetet. En rapport från Jämställdhetskommittén.*

SOU 1981:25. *Bra daghem för små barn. Socialdepartementet.*

SOU 1981:62. *Familjepension. Sammanfattning av SOU 1981:61. Betänkande avgivet av Pensionskommittén.*

SOU 1982:18. *Förvärvsarbete och föräldraskap. Åtgärdsförslag från Jämställdhetskommittén. Betänkande avgivet av Jämställdhetskommittén.*

SOU 1990:44. *Demokrati och makt i Sverige. Maktutredningens huvudrapport. Betänkande avgivet av Maktutredningen.*

SOU 1995:60. *Kvinnofrid. Huvudbetänkande avgivet av Kvinnovåldskommissionen.*

SOU 1995:79. *Vårdnad, boende och umgänge. Betänkande avgivet av Vårdnadstvistutredningen.*

SOU 1998:6. *Ty makten är din ... Myten om det rationella arbetslivet och det jämställda Sverige. Betänkande avgivet av Kvinnomaktutredningen.*

Trost, J. (1965) 'Allmänt om familjen', in G. Karlsson and J. Trost (eds) *Familjen i samhället*, Stockholm: Svenska bokförlaget/Norstedts, pp 5-27.

Wendt Höjer, M. (2002) *Rädslans politik. Våld och sexualitet i den svenska demokratin*, Malmö: Liber.

Widerberg, K. (1981) 'Sverige – gammalt patriarkat i ny förklädnad', *Kvinnovetenskaplig tidskrift*, vol 2, no 3, pp 6-25.

Widerberg, K. (1986) 'Har kvinnoforskning med jämställdhetspolitik att göra?', *Kvinnovetenskaplig tidskrift*, vol 7, no 3, pp 36–47.

Part Two
Current challenges: competing discourses on gender equality

SIX

The 'new father': gender equality as discursive resource for family policies

Trine Annfelt

Introduction

The Norwegian Law on Children and Parents (hereafter the Children's Law) was passed in 1981. It replaced a body of laws from 1956 and introduced new ways of thinking about the family. Among other things, the law changed the parents' rights to their children, revoking the mother's automatic right to the custody of young children after divorce. About 2000 the parents' rights to their children were again discussed in the political decision-making bodies. Again the discussion sprang from a concern about parents' rights. Did the Children's Law still incorrectly prioritise mothers' rights over fathers'?

This chapter focuses on the discursive strategies applied in the political debates on this question. It explores what was a natural and plausible way of thinking about the child's interests and about the cooperation, responsibilities and sharing of rights between the parents at two different points in time. The data is sourced from parliamentary debates, political documents and committee reports about the introduction of the Children's Law and about some propositions and amendments to the law around 2000.[1] Both in the 1980s and around 2000 the overriding rule for the development of family policies was that 'the child's best interest' must prevail. This concept was used to legitimise various suggestions, whether they concerned changes or amendments to the law, or arguments for retaining the status quo. In addition to an argumentation of the child's best interest, gender equality was the most-used semantic resource in the discussions on mothers' and fathers' rights after relationship break-ups. One of the main findings is that between 1980 and 2000 gender equality lost importance as a discursive resource for women and gained importance for men.[2]

From presumption for the mother to equal rights with equal responsibilities

The automatic right of custody of young children to their mothers was removed when the Children's Law was introduced.[3] The argument presented both by the

Ministry and by MPs was that not only was giving preference to mothers over fathers *not* in the best interest of the child, it also violated the principle of equal rights for both parents. Custody and care of the child and parents' responsibilities and rights should be determined by the public. The Committee for the Children's Law Reform expressed its view as follows: 'The Panel suggests that ... the general rule giving mothers preferential rights to young children is removed, as this rule not only violates the principle that "the child's best interest" must be the determinant, but also violates the principle regarding parents' equal rights to the child' (NOU 1977:35, p 63). However, fundamental changes were not expected, as the parents' roles in most marriages still were such that 'the mother has the main responsibility for the young children, which would normally ensure that she is in a stronger position in an argument regarding custody as the child is normally bonded more strongly to her' (Ot. Prop. Nr. 62, 1979–80, p 28). While this view still should not result in a rule for preferential rights for the mother, this was because it would have to be used even 'when the child is equally or more strongly bonded to the father ie as a result of parents having equally shared the responsibilities for the child' (Ot. Prop. Nr. 62, 1979–80, p 28). Members of Parliament agreed with this view, as they considered it important that the letter of the law be formulated in such a way that it functioned fairly for fathers when they, in time, came to share responsibility for the child on an equal basis with mothers.

The tenet of a concept, when applied, actualises a set of structuring effects (Neumann, 2001). The effects that 'equality' brings forth are tied to initiatives for fairness for the underprivileged party.[4] With regard to gender, we know our expectations for equality have, in most instances, been aimed at women. Women have been the main focus of both equality legislation and the apparatus needed for its application. This was particularly noticeable towards the end of the 1970s and throughout the 1980s (Stortingsmelding nr. 70, 1991–92). Even society's more general discussions on equality saw increased fairness for women as the main goal. Øvrelid (1996), with reference to a survey on men's opinions from the mid-1980s, points to strong and commonly internalised norms that men should have positive feelings about equality. The connection to gender was not between equality and men, and men were not the aim of strategies and initiatives for equality. Fairness was not seen as a disadvantage to them. The connection was that men should feel good about women being given equal status. This in turn could, for instance, mean favouritism of women as, in a sense, they would be given special, positive treatment.

My point is that during this period two competing applications for the concept 'equality' can be identified. One application produced a connection between equality, fairness and women as the secondary gender. The other application discoursed equality as a benefit in itself. In discussions on gender the second application was used only marginally. However, the understanding of equality as a benefit in itself was very much present as a discursive resource that could easily be actualised for men. The Children's Law committee, the Ministry of Justice and the Norwegian Odelsting[5] could and in effect did do this. They actualised a discourse on equality that served as a resource of power that strengthened the fathers' position in the question of child custody. The fact that the political powers, without much public resistance, *could* actualise an argument for equality for this purpose is tied to the acknowledgement that equality is beneficial in itself.[6] *That* they did so can be viewed as one of many contributions that strengthen the position of precisely this discourse on gender equality. That just *they* did so is interesting to note, proportional to the displacements in the power–knowledge relations that produce gender: knowledge tells what is for real. In this instance, we are told firstly, that fathers are underprivileged, therefore initiatives for fairness for them must be taken; secondly, we are told that fathers, in time, will become as deserving of custody of the children as are mothers. The understandings behind this concept of equality destabilise the prevalent understanding of gender by producing a connection between equality, fairness and men.

Both parents are allocated rights to access/parental responsibility for their children

In 1999 MPs of the most right-wing party in Norway, the Progress Party (Fremskrittspartiet), put forward suggestions for changes to the law on access rights and parental responsibilities. The changes were aimed at strengthening the father's position at the time of separation, initially by making joint parental responsibility and split residence (for the child) the basis of the law. The amendments were also proposed to preserve access for the non-resident parent by limiting the right to move (abroad) of the parent with whom the child lived permanently.[7]

The MPs pointed to children's need for close contact with both parents, and the fact that more than 200,000 children grow up in homes where the parents do not live together, mostly in homes where the father is absent. They argued that recent research had shown that children's need for regular contact with both parents is greater and more basic than previously thought, and that research had shown how very important it is for children that they are ensured good and regular contact with both parents, and how seriously a child can be damaged by being denied such contact. They wrote: 'We note an increasing amount of violence among children and youth, much of this can be seen as a direct result of fathers being sidelined in the daily care of the young' (Dokument nr. 8:44, 1998–99). The law must offer stronger protection against sabotage of access rights and also indicate stronger sanctions against the parent who prevents access. Another basic problem with the Children's Law was a parent's 'right to relocate with the children': 'To a large degree this precluded contact between the child and the other parent, as for instance expensive travel costs combined with poor economy make access very difficult for the non-resident parent.'.

The suggestions were discussed in the parliamentary Family, Culture and Administration Committee and in the Odelsting (22 February 2001). The discussions identify the perceived similarities and differences, at the time, in the discourse on what is best for the child and in the discourse on gender. Below I will show the construction of the representations of mothers and fathers and the correlation between these around 2000, and contrast them with similar constructions in the documents of the 1980s. What do the MPs now see as true and natural? What is now reasonable and possible to talk about, and how? What do we now need to do something about, and why?

From the committee's unanimous remarks it appears that what 'everybody' agreed upon was that:

> as a rule, after the parents separate, it is in the child's best interest to maintain contact and spend time with both parents. ... The committee therefore thinks men must to a larger degree be given equal rights with women for custody of the children so as to ensure good contact with both parents (Innst. O. nr. 44, 2000–2001, p 1 of 5).

In the Odelsting the Christian Democrat (Kristelig Folkeparti) MP stressed that modern fathers shoulder more of the responsibility for children than before. In her view, therefore, '[in] most cases it is very much in the child's best interest to have as much and as close contact with both parents as possible. At the same time it is important to recognise that in certain situations contact with only one of the parents is in the child's best interest' (Odelsting, 22 February 2001, p 2 of 6). She agreed with the Progress Party that there was a problem in the Children's Law, namely that one parent could sometimes sabotage, without consequences, agreements made regarding time with or access to the child. The MP did not wish to introduce an amendment that denied a parent with whom the child lived permanently the right to relocate, but she commented that many who had access experienced that:

> the parent with whom the child lives permanently relocates to another part of the country without trying to reach an amended agreement with the other parent to cover the new situation, or evaluating what is in the best interest of the child, whether it is to relocate with one parent to another part of the country or not (Odelsting, 22 February 2001, p 2 of 6).

The minister herself (from the Labour Party, Arbeiderpartiet) agreed with the proposers that there had been changes in society since the Children's Law had been passed: 'We see a development towards more women participating in the workforce, while more fathers than before perform the role of caregiver in the home.' Many parents wrote to her 'and are desperately unhappy that they no longer can have the relationship with their children that they desire.' Others wrote and told of parents who 'do not care about their children, who cut all contact, pay no maintenance or who use violence' (Odelsting, 22 February 2001, p 4 of 6). The minister emphasised that the law should serve the child in the best possible way, that it was important that it should facilitate extensive cooperation between the parents after separation and that, for the child, good contact with both parents was important: 'That fathers assume greater responsibilities for the care, both within or without the family, benefits mother and child', she said.

During the same debate, the MP from the Centre Party (Senterpartiet) commented that the proposal from the Progress Party made it possible to order the parents to share custody. The good results seen when the child lived as much with one parent as with the other all came about from voluntary agreements, not about cases of conflict that had come before the courts. Because of this she would 'caution against making use of the experiences gained from voluntary agreements too easy'. It made her 'a bit worried' that the minister was 'very, very – twice "very" – pleased with the Progress Party's commitment to these things' (Odelsting, 22 February 2001, p 4 of 6). This MP was happy that the rules on maintenance, shared time and custody were on the agenda. As for lowering the level of conflict at separation, she herself believed more in amending the maintenance rules. 'So I am probably one of those [people] considered rather old-fashioned. I believe that in any conflict it is important that the child remains with one parent, and I believe that overall it is better that the mother is granted custody' (Odelsting, 22 February 2001, p 3 of 6).

When the rule for a general presumption in favour of the mother was removed, with the introduction of the Children's Law (1981), the ministry and the MPs of the Odelsting generally looked at two 'truths' or knowledge logics for parenthood: the first that it was in the best interest of the child that the mother was granted custody at the time of separation and that the father was granted access. The reason was the presumption that, in practice, the mother would spend most time caring for and being with the children and therefore the children would become more attached to her. Some MPs also argued for a natural mother–child relationship. The logic was that the mother was more important to the child, if one had to prioritise one parent. The second was that it was fairer that the mother was granted custody of the children because normally she spent most time nurturing the children, and she to a greater degree, or even alone, had to give up some of her time in paid work to care for the children. One can conclude from the documents from around 1980 that it was taken for granted that, if nothing else argued against it, the mother was both the most important and the most entitled.

In 2002 the Odelsting MPs took different logics for granted. The greatest difference is that the father is constantly talked about as *more important* and that the power relationship between the father as a category and the mother as a category has changed. The representation of the father as more important (than we previously knew or were prepared to acknowledge?) is clearly manifested in the Progress Party's political thrust. The father is seen as important not because of the time and care he has invested in the child: it is the father figure as such that is seen as important. The representatives fully or partly support the Progress Party's description of reality and at the same time agree on the increased importance of the father figure – generally an increased importance of men in a child's life – and also that the father's position must be strengthened relative to the mother's.

Christine Roman (Chapter 5, this volume) reports a similar change in Sweden, where the discourse about the importance of the father has become hegemonic. She finds that with increased state intervention in families after divorce men, as fathers, have increasingly benefited from the discourse on gender equality.

Representation–producing work

The parliamentary debates indicate that the representation of the father as more important has become hegemonic. The Centre Party's contribution to the debate is particularly interesting, as their MP resisted this representation and posited that when there is a conflict between the parents at separation it is better for the children that the mother has custody. A hegemonic representation provides the framework for what and how one can say or not say something about a phenomenon, what must happen to be disqualified, to be taken seriously, or even to be listened to, and so on. This becomes apparent from the MP's wording. First she moderates all her critical statements by using a diminutive. Next she supports the mutual production of opinions by signalling support for the amendments to the systems for maintenance. To signal support for a theme that is coupled to the main theme can be interpreted as a strategy for maintaining the integrity of the actual context. Finally, her initiative relegates her to a position of 'old-fashioned', hardly a position with which a leading politician voluntarily identifies. When looking at the debate on the introduction of the Children's Law, it is very clear that this MP could have asserted her current viewpoint without any problem, which of course means that at that time the hegemonic representations of mother and father were different.

Carabine (2001) gives examples of how the production of hegemonic representations occurs and how they are maintained. One of the discursive resources in the production and maintenance of what at all times appears 'natural' is the silence that arises when a theme loses legitimacy. Can this explain the rather veiled statements made by the MP of the Christian Party and by the minister? They both confirm the current representation of the father as more important. But the Christian Party's MP also says that it is important to acknowledge that sometimes it is in the child's best interest to maintain contact with only one of the parents. However, she gives no examples, nor does she elaborate any further. The minister talks of parents who sever maintenance and use violence. But she does not give these shirking and/or violent parents any gender, and she mentions nothing about the possible consequences of such behaviour in relation to the main theme of the debate, namely 'equal rights to time with/custody of their children'. She only specifies gender when she talks about the fathers, 'who much more than before perform nurturing tasks within the home' (Odelsting, 22 February

2001, p 4 of 6); her remarks concerning severance of contact or use of violence do not specify gender. As mentioned, she also 'appreciates very, very much' the stand the Progress Party has taken to ensure the rights of the father. In this she is supported unanimously by the parliamentary committee.

Discursive effects

The notion of fathers that men through the ages have been subjected to is, within social constructionism, understood contextually. It is true for everybody that the way we see ourselves and the world is restricted by what is available in the discursive formations that make up the framework for our existence and life history. Davies puts it this way:

> Correct membership of the social order entails being able to read situations correctly such that what is obvious for everyone else is also obvious for you. It involves knowing how to be positioned and how to position yourself as a member of the group who knows and takes for granted what other people know and take for granted in a number of different settings (2000, p 22).

To learn to desire what is available is central to Davies' understanding of the formation and maintenance of subjects. Due to changes in the hegemonic representations, the discursive resources available to the participants in their subjectivity processes change. As for real live fathers, this means that changes in the hegemonic representations bring about a probability that today more men become fathers who are important in the role of nurturer in the child's life. The involvement of the father is met with enthusiasm and is anticipated by other people and by the fathers themselves. The awareness that subjects at any time are a result of the process of subjectification that runs simultaneously throughout the *individual* life cycle also points out that the structuring opportunities that the new representations entail do not, of course, affect all lives in the same way. Not all men (women) turn out to be nurturing fathers (mothers) (Brantsæther, 2001; Mellberg, 2002; Skjørten, 2005).

The enclosures to White Paper no. 29 (Stortingsmelding nr. 29 2002–2003) *About the Family – the Commitments of Life together and Parenthood* give us numbers and explain different aspects of the joint lives of mothers and fathers and parenthood around 1980 and 2000. For parents with children of child-benefit age, the report shows that, around 2000, the fathers spent more time nurturing children than they did in 1980. However, the report still concludes that 'fathers are to a much lesser degree than the mothers the child's most important nurturer' (Stortingsmelding no. 29, p 95). As far as how parents share the housework, Kitterød (Stortingsmelding no. 29, p 87) still finds that it varies greatly among parents of young children, but less so than in 1980. The mothers of small children still spend considerably more time on everyday housework than do the fathers. As for time invested in paid employment, Kitterød and Kjeldstad (Stortingsmelding no. 29, p 89) find the differences are 'formidable when one looks at how many hours on average per week mothers and fathers active in the workforce actually work'. However, fathers' long working hours have been reduced, and the researchers view this as indicative that having children has had a small, but noticeable, influence on men's working habits during the last 10 years.

According to Lilleaas (2003), something happens to the division of labour when a young and highly educated couple have a second child. Although they may agree on the need to share the nurturing and the housework, many lapse into the patterns they grew up with. In Lilleaas' words, they work together in creating asymmetry. The fathers in her study maintained the amount of time they had had for rest and training/sport, and the time they spent with the children was often spent on play or sport. The amount of time the fathers spent with the children was that part of the family responsibility they took up without being nagged about it by the mothers. The mothers, to a much greater degree, sacrificed their own interests. When he looked after the children, she did the housework.

Fathers who have obtained a good access arrangement, that is, the children live with the father on a regular basis and they spend a lot of time together, are the most satisfied with their arrangement, and the mothers in the main appreciate that fathers and children have lots of time together (Stortingsmelding no. 29, p 98).[8] Seven out of ten fathers believe the child would have wished for more time with them, and almost 60% would like a different arrangement for custody and access. Close to 90% of children are living with their mothers and this has hardly changed since the 1980s. At the time of mediation about 40% of parents are in serious conflict over sharing the children, but most parents manage to agree on where the children will live and how much time each parent will have with the children. Research has not been able to show any significant advantage or disadvantage as regards joint custody/split residence (for the child), and no particular disadvantages to any other type of living arrangement.

In summary, the amount of time the fathers spend with their children has increased, and increasingly they take it for granted that they will spend this time together. Still, the father spends less time with the children than does the mother, and he spends it differently. This becomes apparent when we look at how parents share the total time spent on nurturing, housework, rest, sports and work outside the home. An increased level of conflict after separation indicates that in any case, fathers now see themselves as equally important to and equally deserving of the children. That fathers, on average, spend more time with their children than before, that 60% of fathers wish for a different care arrangement and that seven out of ten fathers believe the children want more time with them, can be understood this way. Earlier, we saw that MPs also share this view in general.

Is it possible that our modern hegemonic representations of the father have become the frame of reference for court decisions in child-sharing cases where there are allegations of violence (Skjørten, 2002; Stortingsmelding no. 29, p 101)?

During the period 1998–2000 violence was mentioned in court in 30 cases that went before the high court. In nine of the cases there were allegations of violence against the mother. In six of the cases the courts based their decision on the fact that this had happened, but in only one case did the court place particular importance on the father's violence in its consideration of the parents' nurturing abilities. In these nine cases the courts granted custody to the mother in five cases and to the father in four cases. In 11 cases it was alleged that the father had used violence against the children. In three of these cases, the decision on permanent residence was based on the violence. In the remaining cases the decisions were based on other circumstances. The mother gained custody of the children in seven and the father in four of the cases. Ten cases mentioned sexual interference. It was the mother who suspected the father, but it was not only her allegations and suspicions that were considered: in several cases kindergartens were concerned as well and the child welfare authorities were asked to investigate. Half the cases concerned children aged four years or younger. In only one of these cases did the allegation of interference affect the court's decision on where the child would reside. In half of the cases the courts granted custody to the mother, and in the other half to the father.

Are the representations of 'mother' changing?

To under-communicate variations in a category, not to give validity to variation through a continuous production of statements and practices is, according to Carabine, one of the conditions that constitutes 'truth'. The debate of the 1980s on the introduction of the Children's Law barely showed evidence of attempts to point to the variations within the categories for father and mother. The few attempts only point to variations among fathers. The assumption that fathers vary is indicated by the many MPs who more or less directly pointed out that in some families the father participated only a little in nurturing, while in other families parental responsibilities were carried out as a joint project. It is also indicated by one MP who wanted restricted visiting rights for violent fathers. In other words, there are participating and non-participating fathers, important and less important fathers. The mother category is, however, presented as homogeneous. Her attachment to and nurture of the child is taken for granted. While the suggestion for removing the presumption for mothers is broadly supported, it still shows that something is afoot. Mothers are presented as an unquestionable good, but not only mothers are considered the best nurturer for the child.

Also around the year 2000 the obvious belief that all mothers are important to their children is fully confirmed and maintained. However, the representation of the mother is destabilised from other points. Around 1980 what several MPs were concerned with was that access to the child could be realised for the parent with whom the child did not live. Some MPs pointed out that, when necessary, one would have to consider practical issues such as geographical distances, working conditions and so on when the right to access was implemented. Others pointed to the parents' economic situation: expenses in connection with travel for access should be made tax deductible. The MPs were also concerned with the need for both partners to maintain a reasonable standard of living.

An MP from the Labour Party linked the implementation of the right to access to the parents' actions:

> The right to access is today often poorly utilised, or in the worst cases it is opposed by one of the parents. This happens either because the parent without custody fails his/her responsibilities or because the parent with whom the child lives denies the other parent visiting or caring opportunities (Odelsting no. 13 1981, p 200).

It is this connection between making access possible and the mother's and the father's actions and intentions that appears more visible around 2000. The connection appears also to have taken on a somewhat different characteristic than in the MP's speech. She presents the possibility that either parent could fail. Some parents do not utilise their opportunities (to be with the child) and others oppose their partner's right to spend time with the child. The latter is 'the worst case' scenario. To oppose access now becomes even worse than failing in one's parental responsibilities. At the same time, the choice of the words 'in the worst case' indicates that even though this is bad, it does not happen often.

Around 2000 the corresponding problems were presented as follows: 'The parent who only has access is often exposed to the boycott and sabotage of the arranged visiting or access appointments by the other parent' (Dokument nr. 8: 44 (1998–99), p 2 of 6). The logic the proposers formulated from this was that 'the law must protect better against sabotage of access and must implement stronger sanctions against the one who opposes access' (Dokument nr. 8: 44 (1998–99), p 2 of 6). In the Odelsting debate the MP from the Christian Democratic Party added a corresponding element to the process of changing the representations of mother and father: it is a problem that access arrangements are sabotaged without consequences. The MP also commented that many parents with access rights experience the problem that the other parent moves *away* with the child. (Odelsting, 22 February 2001, p 2 of 6). The Progress Party took this the furthest: 'One of the most basic problems in the Norwegian Children's Law is the free right to relocate – the right to move away with the children' (Innst. O. no. 44 2000–2001, p 5 of 5). First, the right to relocate is defined as moving away *with* the children and not *from* the children; second, the obvious point, that both mothers and fathers relocate equally often, is not mentioned (Stortingsmelding nr. 29, 2002–2003, p 22). In the same debate the Progress Party mentioned all the communications about 'how impossible it is for children growing up without contact with one of their parents. The majority of these communications of course come from fathers.' In the debate on the new rules for maintenance, the Conservative Party criticised the old rules because they 'do not encourage the one responsible for the maintenance, in most cases the fathers, to spend time with the child' (Odelstinget, 6 June 2001, p 8 of 14). Here, the father becomes the person who needs to be encouraged to spend time with the children, and simultaneously a victim of the lack of such encouragement. Or from the same debate, as it was clearly stated by the Progress Party: 'By stipulating children's equal time with either parent, one will also prevent one parent from becoming sidelined and therefore *unable to fight any further* for contact with the children, which is of course a considerable loss to the children' (emphasised by the MP) (Odelstinget, 6 June 2001, p 8 of 14).

First and foremost the Progress Party, but also the other MPs, skewed the description of reality. Around 1980, as shown earlier, the implementation of access rights was mainly presented as a practical and economic problem. It was also a problem that one party, mostly the mother, could oppose the other parent's right to time with the children, while the other party, mostly the father, would not utilise this right. All these themes are still discussed in the documents, and images of the father and the mother in these discussions, of course – considering the short period of time elapsed – remain unchanged to a great degree. At the same time, new representations of the mother and the father are emerging. In summary, I would like to point out that the mother is emerging as a problem, the father as a victim. I see little or nothing of this in the debates from the 1980s. It is *she* who now *very often* subjects the father to boycotts of his right to and time with the children, while he needs the protection of the law so that sanctions against her can be implemented. She has also become a problem for the children, who have an *impossible time growing up* (Odelstinget, 6 June 2001, p 8 of 14) – they lack time with their father because the mother sabotages his right to access and because she moves away with them.

As the earlier examples show, the Progress Party was behind the statements that most clearly define the mother as a problem and the father as her victim. It is reasonable to interpret their evidence as information on ongoing changes in the discourse on mothers and fathers. As the MPs of the Progress Party repeatedly pointed out, they are the leaders on family politics. In other words, they manifest a discursive position authorised to speak with strength. Their leading role shows that they are among the first allowed to speak forcefully from an overriding conviction. 'I will not fail to remind you that the proposal submitted on the whole includes changes that are in accordance with the Progress Party's proposal from 1996', said one of the representatives in the Odelsting during the debate on the rules for maintenance (Odelstinget, 6 June 2001, p 5 of 14). And, as we saw earlier, a minister from the Labour Party, which normally made a point of distancing itself from the Progress Party, declared herself 'very, very happy' with their initiative in the debate on equal rights to access and parental responsibilities.

The power–knowledge relationships are strong, 'positive' forces within the social processes (Foucault, 1979). When new 'truths' about the father and the mother are established and gain validity, new areas of action are concurrently made legitimate for them, over time and for better or worse. This is shown very concretely when new understandings become operational through changes to the law and, as a consequence, mesh very strongly with social processes through the implementation of the law. The court decisions in child custody cases mentioned earlier serve as an example.

Equality as a power resource before and now

I have pointed to the power resource embedded in the concept of equality. Not least, the introduction of the law on gender equality in 1978 and the apparatus around this prove this concept as an effective political resource. In the 1970s to 1980s it was possible to activate this resource primarily for the benefit of women. What 'everybody' agreed on was that women were the unequal gender, which of course was fair enough. This situation has changed: in the semantic struggle about the relationship between the genders the linking of equality–fairness–women has lost legitimacy. According to Skjeie and Teigen (2003), gender equality has the duty to yield. In Norway young men now constitute the group that is most negative towards equality.

I have shown that an argument on equality, at the time of the introduction of the Children's Law, was actualised in favour of men. At the same time, the actual division of work in the home and with the children and the assumption that this created strong emotional ties to the mother would ensure that her first right to the children would remain until the time of equal sharing. Around 2000 there was a new representation of the father, just as, for sure, there were many 'new' fathers in real life, compared with the 1980s. The research results I have referred to are a good indication that the understanding many men have of themselves as good nurturers has become the norm, and for many men this certainly is also deeply felt. Finally, some real fathers may of course have become the most important thing in their children's lives. The *representation* of the father has obviously changed, and it appears to be both a quantitative and a qualitative difference. As there was only one representation of mothers in the 1980s, there seems to be only one representation of fathers today.[9] I call this representation 'father as more important' (than before) and it seems to have affected both men's subjectivity processes and how men and women today see reality, including the understandings of reality that the MPs share and that consequently influence the politics they formulate. The representation of 'father as more important' is a discursive resource that can be actualised so that men can be shown as unequally treated and thus establish and legitimise the linking of equality–fairness–men. There is always more than one possible representation of a category, which in turn exposes it to struggle. As for the linkage between the concept of equality and gender, it appears that when this concept is linked to women it has become less legitimate, while it has gained legitimacy when linked to men.

The hegemonic representation of the father today makes the father not only important to his children, but indispensable, and perhaps at least as important as the mother. The parliamentary debate pointed to research as a witness to his being indispensable, and the parliamentary committee followed this up by emphasising that the father is indispensable as a role model to his children. Brandth and Kvande (1995) show that the mother sees the father as maybe more important than herself. As mentioned, we also see that the father invests less time in his children than the mother does and that men, when they become fathers, spend more time at work and give up fewer interests than women do. The new representation of the father as more important is a discursive resource that can be and is actualised in order to justify this. This can be described as an element in the reinforcement of the gender hierarchy by which his rights to a possible sharing of the children are achieved at less cost to him in the form of loss of time, interests and experience from the working life.

Notes

[1] The political documents are Norwegian Official Reports (NOU), White Papers (*Stortingsmeldinger*), ministerial letters of hearings, hearing reports, committee reports and parliamentary debates.

[2] During the same period, biologism has also gained importance as a discursive resource for fathers' rights. Around 2000 the politicians debated fathers' rights, arguing that all children have a natural need to know and bond with their biological father, whether they have previously lived together with him or not (Annfelt, 2005).

[3] This removal was greatly requested in the public debate, but gained thorough support in the hearing reports, in the ministry, the committee of justice and the Odelsting (see below) (NOU:1977:35; Ot.Prop.Nr. 62 (1979–80)).

[4] The *concept* 'equality' holds someone as 'the first' and someone else as 'the other'. To use the concept implies both ranking the categories in question and marking them as different (Sarup, 1993). Around 1980 women were positioned in the discourse as 'the other', who must be given equal status so as to obtain more fairness in society.

[5] Odelstinget is the larger division of the Norwegian Parliament.

[6] According to the chairman of the committee of justice, Olsen-Hagen (from the Labour Party), the Bill had spurred extensive debate and the viewpoints had varied from 'those who thought the Bill would sap the marriage instead of strengthening it, over those who expressed satisfaction with the idea of giving fathers equal status, to those who asserted

that the Bill deprived women of one of the few privileges they had' (from the discussions in the Odelsting, 16 March 1981, p 192).

[7] Split residence (for the child) is still not the basis of the law. The argument is that this arrangement would be too demanding for parents experiencing a deep conflict related to the relationship break-up (Stortingsmelding no. 29 (2002–2003)). The right to relocate has been changed. If the parents have joint legal custody, the parent living permanently with the child cannot move abroad without the consent of the other parent.

[8] This seems to be the situation in other European countries as well. In an interview with Lord Filkin when he was in charge of family policy (in England), he says that only 2% of separated fathers return to court because their ex-partner has frustrated a contact order, and twice as many parents with residence, mainly mothers, as separated fathers wanted their partner's contact with children to increase (*The Guardian*, 28 October 2004, p 12).

[9] This seems to go for Sweden as well, so long as the father is white. Ericcson (2004, 2005) shows how the representation 'violent father' and the representation of the ethnic non-Swedish father have become fused, leaving the representation of the ethnic Swedish father gender equal and nurturing.

Bibliography

Andenæs, A. (2005) 'Neutral Claims – Gendered Meanings: Parenthood and developmental psychology in a modern welfare state', *Feminism and Psychology*, vol 2, pp 211–28.

Annfelt, T. (2005) 'På vei mot sædens rett? Om endringer i politiske diskurser om farskap', *Tidsskrift for kjønnsforskning*, vol 2, pp 40–56.

Brandth, B. and Kvande, E. (1995) 'Maskulinitet og barneomsorg', *Kvinneforskning*, vol 1, pp 86–95.

Brandth, B. and Kvande, E. (1996) 'Nye fedre i likestilte familier', in B. Brandth and K. Moxnes (eds) *Familie for tiden. Stabilitet og forandring*, Oslo: Tano Aschehaug, pp 161-77.

Brantsæther, M. (2001) *Møter med menn dømt for seksuelle overgrep mot barn*, Oslo: Universitetet i Oslo, Institutt for sosiologi og samfunnsgeografi.

Carabine, J. (2001) 'Unmarried Motherhood 1830–1990: A genealogical analysis', in M. Wetherell, S. Taylor and S.J. Yates (eds) *Discourse as Data. A guide for analysis*, London: Sage, pp 267-311.

Davies, B. (2000) *A body of writing 1990–1999*, Oxford: AltaMira Press.

Dokument nr. 8:44, 1998-99, in *Stortingsforhandlinger 1998-1999*, vol 56.

Ericcson, M. (2004) *I skuggan av Pappa. Familjerätten och handteringen av Fäders vold*, Stehag: Förlags AB Gondolin.

Ericcson, M. (2005) 'Den onda och den normala fadersmakten? Fäders vold i svensk offentlig politikk', *Tidsskrift for kjønnsforskning*, vol 2, pp 56–73.

Foucault, M. (1979) *The History of Sexuality, Volume 1*, London: Allan Lane.

Innst. O. nr. 44, 2000-01, in *Stortingsforhandlinger 2000–2001*, vol 6b.

Lilleaas, U.-B. (2003) *Fra en kropp i ustand til kroppen i det moderne*, Oslo: Universitetet i Oslo, Institutt for sosiologi og samfunnsgeografi.

Mellberg, N. (2002) *När det overkliga blir verklighet*, Umeå: Boréa Bokförlag.

Neumann, I.B. (2001) *Norge – en kritikk*, Oslo: Pax Forlag.

NOU 1977:35. *Lov om barn og foreldre.*

Ot.prp.no.62, 1979-80, in *Stortingsforhandlinger 1979–1980*, vol 4c.

Odelstingsforhandlinger 22. Februar 2001, in *Stortlingsforhandlinger 2000–2001*, vol 7b.

Øvrelid, B. (1996) 'Notid og framtid: Dei små forteljingane, dei lokale sanningane og det postmoderne', in H. Holter (ed) *Hun og han. Kjønn i forskning og politikk*, Oslo: Pax Forlag.

Sarup, M. (1993) *An introductory guide to post-structuralism and postmodernism*, New York: Harvester/Wheatsheaf.

Skjeie, H. and Teigen, M. (2003) *Menn i mellom*, Oslo: Gyldendal Norsk Forlag.

Skjørten, K. (2005) *Samlivsbrudd og barnefordeling*, Oslo: Gyldendal Akademisk.

Stortingsmelding nr. 70 (1991–92). *Likestillingspolitikk for 1990-åra.*

Stortingsmelding nr. 29 (2002–2003). *Om familien. forpliktende samliv og foreldreskap.*

SEVEN

From powerful to powerless fathers: gender equality in Danish family policies on parenthood

Charlotte Andersen and Anna-Birte Ravn

Introduction

From the late 1960s to the mid-1990s Danish family policies on parenthood underwent radical change. The change can be described in terms of equality – as equalising children born out of wedlock with children born in marriage or as equalising unmarried fathers with married fathers and with unmarried mothers. This is not the whole story, however. Beneath this process of equalisation a profoundly new perception of fatherhood and of the position of fathers vis-à-vis mothers evolved: in the 1960s political debates on parenthood constructed unmarried mothers as weak and unmarried fathers as powerful, but in the 1990s this construction was turned upside down. The unmarried father was now portrayed as a victim of discrimination, as the gender most in need of equality. And whereas, in contrast to the mother, the father of the 1960s was primarily a socio-economic and not a socio-emotional or biological figure, the main characteristic of the 'new father' of the 1990s (see Annfelt, Chapter Six) was his biological sex.

This chapter analyses the changes in Danish family legislation on custody and visiting rights in respect of children after divorce or partnership break-up, focusing on political discourses on fatherhood and motherhood, gender and equality. The primary sources are parliamentary documents that disclose a clear shift of opinion both within the bourgeois parties[1] and within the parties on the left in Parliament.[2] In the 1960s and 1970s the greatest defenders of the rights of unmarried mothers were parties on the left, but by the 1980s the bourgeois parties came to provide the strongest defence of single mothers' rights against fathers' claims to children born out of wedlock. And whereas through the 1980s the preservation of the institution of marriage and the heterosexual family was the primary objective of the bourgeois parties, by the 1990s all political parties agreed that the first obligation of Parliament was to ensure a child's right to both parents, whether the parents were formally married or not.

From the late 1960s the hegemony of the heterosexual family started to dissolve, and the foundation of the Nordic marriage laws of the 1920s (see Carlsson Wetterberg and Melby, Chapter Two) began to quake. New family patterns and living arrangements – fewer marriages, more divorces, more partnerships – resulted in more children born out of wedlock or raised by one parent or a second parent other than the biological parent, and the period 1969–95 saw four successive changes in Danish family legislation regarding custody rules and regulations on visiting rights. The laws on contract and dissolution of marriage and on majority rights were changed in 1969, 1978, 1985 and 1995.[3]

Changing laws on parenthood

According to the Danish marriage laws of the 1920s, both parents were obliged to provide for the child and both had the right to daily care and everyday decisions in marriage, while the father remained sole guardian in economic matters. After divorce, however, parents were placed equally in regard to custody rights, with the exception of the mother's priority for children under the age of two (Lov om Umyndighed og Værgemaal, 1922). The father was obliged to pay maintenance, and also in most cases alimony. A new law in 1957 gave full custody rights to married mothers on a par with fathers (Lov nr. 17 af 6. februar 1957). Unmarried mothers were obliged to provide for their children and had full custody rights, but the father had to support the child through payment of maintenance.[4] Moreover, from 1937 'illegitimate' children in Denmark had the right to inherit from their father and to carry his name.

In 1969, the Danish Parliament first decided that an unmarried father should be able to attain visiting rights provided that he had had 'close or frequent contact' with the child. Second, the priority of mothers' custody of children under the age of two in case of divorce was abolished (Lov nr. 257 af 4. juni 1969). While the original law proposal of 1968 (Forslag til lov, 3. oktober 1968) retained this provision, although in a new formulation,[5] it was removed during the negotiations (to be discussed later), and the 1969 law was enacted without reference to mothers' priority for small children.

In 1978 a new custody law opened the possibility that unmarried fathers could gain custody of the child. In the child's best interest and despite protests from the mother, a court decision could transfer custody rights to the father, provided that the parents had had a 'marriage-like' partnership for a longer period of time, that is, that the father had had strong and lasting connections with the child (Lov nr. 244 af 8. juni 1978).

By the mid-1980s, inspired by developments in the other Scandinavian countries, the concept of 'parents' joint custody' was introduced in Danish family legislation. While the intention of earlier laws had been to ensure that the parent who did not have custody could maintain contact with the child, the main purpose of the new law of 1985 was to 'ensure the child's relations to both parents'. From

1986 cohabiting couples could decide to share joint custody of their child, and irrespective of the former character of their relationship parents could voluntarily decide to share custody after divorce or partnership break-up. The only condition for this decision to be legally effective was that it was sanctioned by the county authorities. Moreover, despite the intention to focus on the child's rights, the law of 1985 expanded the rights of the unmarried father in two other respects: first, the reservations of the 1969 law concerning unmarried fathers' visiting rights – that they should have had close or frequent contact with the child – were repealed. Second, while, according to the 1978 law, transfer of custody rights to the unmarried father by court decision could only take place if it was absolutely necessary in the interest of the child, the 1985 law opened up a liberalisation on this point (Lov nr. 230 af 6. juni 1985). The overall result of the 1985 law was that unmarried fathers were equalised with formerly married fathers in regard to visiting rights and custody of children.

Finally, the 1995 Custody and Visiting Rights Act gave the unmarried father (almost) the same rights as the unmarried mother. Indeed, it could be argued that the unmarried father got more rights than the mother – or rather, the same rights for less. First, while the mother (unless she had voluntarily agreed to joint custody) retained custody rights in partnership relations, the father got an equal right to custody of the child on partnership break-up.[6] One reason given for this change was that it would prevent mothers from refusing to sign a voluntary contract with their partner on joint custody.[7] Second, the unmarried father's visiting rights were extended. Even if the parents had never lived together or had lived in a partnership for only a short period of time, county authorities could assign visiting rights to the father. The rational argument behind this new provision was that children's right to see their fathers should not depend on the parents' relations. Third, the 1995 law stated that if one parent (in practice usually the mother) obstructed the other parent's (usually the father's) visiting rights that would be a ground for court decisions transferring custody rights to the other parent (Lov nr. 387 af 14. juni 1995).[8] The overall purpose that gave meaning to these changes was the shared conviction among politicians that a child needs and therefore has the right to 'both parents', that is, two parents of different sex. In other words, children who had never seen their father were supposed to need him because of his biological sex.

While the reforms of the 1970s and the 1980s were brought forward by the left-wing parties, including the Social Democratic Party, and contested by the bourgeois Liberal and Conservative Parties, the laws of the 1960s and 1990s were enacted by consensus among parliamentarians of all political affiliations.[9]

The following sections discuss the changing perceptions of fatherhood and motherhood, marriage and partnership, parents' rights and obligations, gender and equality, voiced by Danish MPs in the period 1969–95 and lying behind the successive alterations in Danish family law.

Changing concepts of fatherhood and motherhood

When in 1968 a Liberal/Conservative/Social-Liberal government first proposed that unmarried fathers should have visiting rights in relation to their children, all members of Parliament, from the Conservative to the Left-Socialist Party, approved. They also agreed when a Liberal MP[10] suggested that, in order to treat married couples equally in case of divorce, the mother's priority for children under the age of two should be abolished. However, no equality of result was envisaged by the new law. Unmarried fathers were portrayed in the debate as generally not interested in their children, and the amendment to allow visiting rights to unmarried fathers was meant only to cover the exceptions, when the father had lived together with the mother and child for a long period and had had close and frequent contact with the child – in other words, when the parents had had a 'marriage-like' relationship. Similarly, the abolition of mothers' priority for custody of young children was meant to cover only very rare cases, when it was in the best interests of the child to live with the father. The mother was seen as the natural carer and thus the parent with whom children under the age of two should normally stay (Folketingets forhandlinger, 24.05.1968, 17.10.1968, 21.05.1969).

While no real changes were envisaged as a consequence of the 1969 law, by the 1990s the intention of some politicians was to achieve equality of result in regard to custody of children. In the early 1990s the Social Democrats and other parties in opposition to the Liberal/Conservative government proposed a parliamentary decision that included the securing of gender equalisation of custody grants – in other words, the Social Democrats advocated rules that would give fathers and mothers 50% each of the custody rights (Forslag til folketingsbeslutning (B87), 1991–92; (B15), 1992–93).[11] What had happened to the images of fathers and mothers in the less than 30 years since the first amendment to the custody and visiting rights law?

The premises of the 1969 law were that married and unmarried fathers were fundamentally different. Whereas the former were presumed to love and care for their children, the latter were supposed to be indifferent – at least in the overwhelming number of cases. In the mid-1990s all biological fathers – even those who had never lived with, maybe never seen, their children – were presumed to love and need them and, perhaps more important, all children were supposed to need their fathers. The debates of the 1960s took for granted that, in contrast to fathers, all mothers, married and unmarried, were natural carers of their children, and although this picture was not fundamentally shaken by the 1990s, it had been scratched. Appearing in scattered remarks of MPs since the 1960s, the image of divorced and unmarried mothers as sabotaging the visiting rights of fathers gained general recognition in the 1990s – to the point that it was included in the 1995 law as one reason for transferring custody rights to the father (Folketingets forhandlinger, 07.03.1995).

Ending the hegemony of the institution of marriage

The Liberal Party's suggestion in 1969 to abolish the mother's priority for young children can be best understood as an endeavour to protect marriage as the foundation of an orderly society. If unmarried fathers were given rights, however small, to their children it would threaten the institution of marriage, and fully equalising husband and wife in cases of divorce would, on this understanding, make marriage the better option for men.[12] In general, the defence of the institution of marriage came from the Liberal and Conservative parties.[13] It peaked in the 1980s – and then almost totally disappeared in the 1990s.[14]

The law of 1985 that introduced voluntary joint custody in partnership relations and on divorce and break-up of partnership was proposed by the left opposition, including the Social Democrats[15] and opposed by the Conservative/Liberal government. The Conservative minister of justice feared that the law would result in fewer marriages, and advised cohabiting couples to marry. The speaker of the Liberal Party regretted that the concept of the nuclear family, which should be the foundation of Danish society, was being blurred, and she emphasised that the institution of marriage gave fathers all the rights they wanted. In arguing for the precedence of marriage over partnership relations, speakers from the Liberal and Conservative parties argued that the state should not intrude in the family (*sic!*) or tell people how to live their lives. In other words, marriage was represented as the 'natural' family life. Moreover, bourgeois speakers argued that marriage provided the best protection for women and children. Under the proposed law, unmarried women would lose exclusive rights to their children, and as the weaker party in socio-economic respects they could be exposed to pressure from men, who were normally in a stronger position. Children risked having to endure two divorces: first, when the parents divorced, and second, if the agreement on joint custody did not hold. In partnership relations fathers had no obligations; therefore it was entirely unfair to equalise married and unmarried fathers (Folketingets forhandlinger, 16.10.1984, 21.05.1985).

In the 1990s the battle of the bourgeois parties for the preservation of the institution of marriage as the foundation of society seems to have been lost. Debating the law proposal of 1995, the Conservative speaker rejoiced in the success of the 1985 law on voluntary joint custody (which his party had then opposed) and fully supported strengthening the legal status of unmarried fathers. Now the consensus-building mantra proclaimed by speakers of all political affiliations[16] was that the child needed both a father and a mother (Folketingets forhandlinger, 07.03.1995).

Rights and obligations – responsibilities to provide and to care

In spite of all allusions to the child's right to both parents, custody rights and visiting rights that are bestowed on the parent not having custody of the child

– most often the father – are parents' rights, not the child's. The child does not have visiting rights, the right to visit his or her father or mother; rather, the parent's visiting rights are a child's obligation. In the words of a Left Socialist MP in 1984, the proposed law did not change the fact that children could be forced to visit a parent against their will, but parents could not be forced to have their child visit them against their will (Folketingets forhandlinger, 16.10.1984, sp. 567). This fundamental point puts the question of custody and visiting rights into the realm of gender equality, of parents' rights and obligations – no matter how much politicians talked about the rights of the child and denied the question of gender equality any status in the debates.

The changes in the law from 1969 to 1995 meant that unmarried fathers, who thus far had only had obligations, successively attained more and more rights in regard to their children; and to parliamentarians over the years these changes came to seem only just and fair. Unmarried fathers were obliged to provide, therefore they should also have equal rights to custody, or at least visiting rights. The question of care for children was widely missing from the debates, but when it was touched upon, opponents pointed to mothers' responsibilities and fathers' failing interest in taking care of their children, while proponents argued that increasing numbers of fathers did take care of their children and that reforms would promote the fathers' caring interests.

In 1968–69 only the speaker for the Social Liberal Party mentioned the theme of caring, asserting that, generally speaking, the divorced parent who had given up custody rights would feel morally responsible for the child and have 'a desire for tenderness and care' (Folketingets forhandlinger, 24.05.1968, sp. 3642). In the debates on the 1978 law – proposed by the Social Democratic government – the speaker of the Left Socialist Party suggested that the possibility of transferring custody rights to the unmarried father by court decision should hinge upon the 'indispensable condition that the father has had at least the same close contact with the child as the mother' (Folketingets forhandlinger, 31.05.1978, sp. 11654). This amendment to the government proposal constructed socio–emotional caring as *the* decisive factor, superior to economic provision, and was meant to prevent fathers from getting custody rights because of their generally better economic positions. The speaker warned, in favour of equal opportunities, that promoting formal gender equality on the basis of real inequality might very well have the effect of cementing inequalities. The law was enacted without this amendment.

By the 1980s the speaker of the Left Socialist Party believed that parents' joint custody would result in both parents (read: also the father) becoming more interested in raising their children. While the bourgeois parties in the 1980s constructed mothers as primary carers and therefore as 'deserving' custody of their children, speakers of the left pressing for reform argued that a change of family politics was necessary, because in the real world families' life patterns had changed. Women had gained greater independence from men, and more fathers felt greater responsibility for their children, the speaker for the Socialist People's

Party asserted. Her main point was that the parent who gave up custody rights also lost a sense of responsibility for the child. It was the intention to preserve the commitments and responsibilities for care of both parents that justified the new law (Folketingets forhandlinger, 24.05.1985, sp. 10540, 10560–2).

In the 1990s, however, speakers for the Liberal and Conservative parties also wanted to promote intimate relations between father and child. The Conservatives for instance wanted to support the alleged positive development in family patterns that had resulted in 'ever more fathers being interested in the upbringing of their children and becoming emotionally attached to them on a par with mothers' (Folketingets forhandlinger, 07.03.1995, sp. 3610). The unspoken premise that women were still the primary carers of children did not count as an argument. The legislature wanted to promote a 'universal caregiver model' by giving men rights that, in the long term, were supposed to turn them into caregivers on a par with women. In other words, in regard to caring, men were given new rights without immediate obligations.

During the entire period covered in this chapter the discourse in Parliament on the emotional processes of caring – in contrast to economic processes of providing – were connected to biological sex, not to social gender. Even if from the 1970s the left started to argue that fathers could learn to care, and by the 1990s the bourgeois parties agreed, since contact and care were not conditions for attaining new rights, it was the fathers' biological sex that made them important for the child.

Gender, class and equality

In 1968–69, while all political parties accepted the proposed law, two different constructions of reality competed in parliamentary discourses, marking a split not between the bourgeois parties and the parties on the left, but between male and female representatives. Several female speakers painted a picture of modern gender relations that involved the joint responsibility of husband and wife to provide and to care for their children. Most male speakers stuck to what the most ardent proponents of the law proposal described as a representation of the past, a male breadwinner/female housewife family. As in the debates over change of the gendered tax law system that had taken place in the early 1960s (see Ravn, Chapter Three) female MPs seemed to press for change against the more conservative opinions of their male colleagues. This is not the whole picture, however.

The strongest opposition to the 1969 law that abolished the mother's priority for young children came from a female representative of the socialist left. While the male Conservative minister of justice argued for the proposal, mainly referring to women's 'natural' capacity for care of small children, the female MP warned against equalising women and men without taking into consideration that in society at large they were not equal. She argued against the construction of modern gender relations made by what she described as upper-class women, and feared that fathers would use their stronger economic and social position to put pressure on mothers to give up their children on divorce (Folketingets forhandlinger, 21.05.1969, sp. 6820–6).

Ten years later, in 1978, objections to changing the family law to the benefit of fathers again came from the extreme left, whereas the extreme right-wing Progress Party initiated the change and wanted to go much further than the law, which was proposed by the Social Democratic government and supported by the Socialist People's and the Social Liberal parties.[17] The discussions in 1978 between the extreme left-wing and the extreme right-wing parties were framed by a discourse on power and discrimination: were men discriminated against by the existing rules that made motherhood and primary responsibility for reproduction a power base for women, as maintained by the female speaker of the Progress Party? Or was it, rather, that women, especially single mothers, were economically and legally vulnerable in the face of men's power over production, as emphasised by the Communist and the Left Socialist parties (Folketingets forhandlinger, 14.03.1978, 31.05.1978)? In both cases power relations between men and women were described as a zero-sum game.

The debate over power and discrimination reached its height in the 1980s, but now the roles of the left-wing and the bourgeois political parties of the 1960s and 1970s were turned upside down. In 1985 the Liberal and Conservative parties, arguing for the precedence of marriage over partnership relations, and supported by the Christian People's Party, ardently defended the unmarried mother against any attack on her legitimate right to custody of her child. Commenting on the statement that women used their right to children as a power resource against men, the Conservative minister of justice proclaimed that he did not want to deprive women of that resource. Since men had had ample dominance through the centuries, women's stronger position now could cause no great harm. Echoing the extreme left of the 1970s, the Conservative minister saw no positive contribution to gender equality in depriving women of a privilege and giving it to men instead. On the contrary, both he and the female speaker for the Liberal Party were anxious that the unmarried mother would have to live in constant insecurity and fear of a better-off father demanding custody rights over the child (Folketingets forhandlinger, 16.10.1984, sp. 557–8; 24.05.1985. sp. 10536, 10557–9). On the other hand, in 1985 the Left Socialists gave up their earlier position and sided with the Social Democrats, the Socialist People's Party and the Social Liberals in support of parents' joint custody rights.

Compared with parliamentary debates of the 1960s, 1970s and 1980s, when the proposed law on custody and visiting rights was debated in 1995 the question of gendered power relations was turned upside down, and allusions to the weaker position of mothers in society at large were totally absent. All political parties agreed that the best interest of the child should be the focus and that the fundamental issue was the child's right to both parents, which made it a responsibility and obligation of parents to cooperate in caring for the child. Most speakers explicitly argued that the issue was *not* the parents' rights, but nevertheless the discussions in Parliament focused on strengthening the father's rights. The formally gender-neutral debate on sabotage of visiting rights concealed the fact that what was at stake was the right of the unmarried father, who perhaps had never lived with his child, to have the child visit him, and possibly to gain custody rights of the child, in spite of protests from the mother. By the 1990s the picture of the unmarried mother using her power to deny visiting rights to the powerless, discriminated-against father – a picture that in the 1970s was painted only by the extreme right wing – had turned into common knowledge and won the day. In the debates, the possibility of fathers abusing their visiting rights by not showing up or just forgetting the agreement was hardly mentioned. Only the speaker for the Socialist People's Party remarked that some mothers might want to protect the child against 'bad visits' with the father (Folketingets forhandlinger, 07.03.1995, p 3611) – in other words that the child and the father could have opposing interests. These remarks met no response, however; they were just silenced.

Changing realities?

In 2003 about two-thirds of Danish parents had joint custody of children in partnership relations and after partnership break-up or divorce. The possibility of joint custody that was opened up by the 1985 law was utilised by increasing numbers of parents.[18] However, the meaning of joint custody was more symbolic than substantial. Since, by 2003, just under 90% of children in single breadwinner families lived with a single mother, and a little more than 10% with a single father, there was no equality of result in regard to daily care, and this pattern had not changed since around 1980. On the other hand, the period 1980–2003 showed a marked rise in children visiting the parent with whom they did not live. While in 1980, 55% of children had contact with the other parent at least every fortnight, the equivalent figure in 1990 was 72%, and in 2003 it was 79% (Ottosen, 2004b, pp 12–14). In 13% of divorces or partnership break-ups the child did not visit the other parent. This 2003 figure had not changed over 20–25 years, and the main reason was that the other parent did not claim visiting rights (Ottosen, 2004b, p 7).

In the overwhelming number of cases of divorce or break-up parents agreed on how to 'share' the children, but the question of visiting rights caused trouble in about one-third of the cases. A recent investigation based on case records of 75 of the most problematic cases decided upon by Danish county authorities in the years up to 2003 showed that most of the families involved were socially marginalised and exposed. The most frequent cause of conflict was that the parent with visiting rights was an alcoholic or drug addict, mentally ill or involved in crime, often in some combination. One-third of the cases was 'just' about the extent and the details of the visiting rights, but in another third the conflict arose because of violence against the mother and/or the child(ren). The theme of conflict turned on what kind of contact could or should be established between a child and a father who had been absent for a long time or had never had close contact with the child. The county authorities decided on 'normal' visiting rights in 40% of the 75 cases. In 20% of the cases the visiting rights became restricted or supervised, and in the last 40% they were abolished. The investigation also showed that the children involved were not always given the status of legal subjects whom the authorities listened to and took seriously (Ottosen, 2004a).

Conclusions – a 'universal-caregiver model'?

Christina Carlsson Wetterberg and Kari Melby (Chapter Two) characterise the Nordic model of marriage as a modified dual or 'universal-breadwinner model'.[19] When the model developed into a staunch universal-breadwinner model from the 1960s, the question of reproduction and especially of care for children under age attracted the attention of families and politicians of all political affiliations. As shown by Anette Borchorst (Chapter One) the Nordic welfare states, especially the Danish, took over some responsibility for childcare by adopting laws on universal day-care institutions. The bulk of caring responsibilities still rested with the family, however, and although investigations show that during the period 1969–95 Danish fathers contributed increasingly to caring and household chores, mothers still have the primary responsibility and perform most of these tasks (Bonke, 1995). Despite new laws on parental leave (see Chapter One), mothers also are the ones who most often and for longer periods stay at home to take care of babies. A thoroughly gender-segregated labour market and lower pay for women is one consequence of this inequality with regard to care of children.

The analysis in this chapter shows that, in the early period covered, most political parties tried to balance the rights and obligations of parents with regard to custody and visiting rights of children against the gendered inequalities in reproduction as well as production, constructing the unmarried or divorced mother as the weaker party who deserved protection against the more powerful father. By the end of the period, however, this picture had been turned on its head. Now the unmarried or divorced father needed the welfare state's protection against the powerful mother who tried to deny him the right to his child. Allusions to gender inequalities in society at large were absent from the debates in the 1990s, and mothers' greater responsibility for care was turned into a disadvantage when it was constructed as a power base used by women to oppress and discriminate against men. In other words, the reference to the best interest of the child, and especially the child's right to both parents, was used to silence some discourses on gender equality, while others were legitimated. As Trine Annfelt notes in the Norwegian case (see Chapter Six), the vision of gender equality increasingly became a discursive resource for men, not for women.

By fully equalising mothers and fathers in regard to child custody and visiting rights, some politicians in the 1990s hoped to further a 'universal-caregiver model'[20] and thus to broaden the responsibilities for childcare in the family. Just as women, since the 1960s, had become breadwinners on a par with men, men should be encouraged to become caregivers on a par with women. And the fact that during the period 1969–95 more men did accept more caring responsibilities was used in the parliamentary debates as a solid reason for equalising fathers with mothers. While women's capacity for care was a constant representation of the period, men were increasingly constructed as the mobile gender whose ability to care could be furthered by equal rights. But as the figures mentioned above indicate, by the end of the 20th century the Danish MPs' political ambitions still seem to have found their limits.

Notes

[1] The main bourgeois parties in Denmark in the 20th century were the Liberal Party, the Conservative Party, and the Social Liberal Party. For long periods the Social Liberals formed an alliance with the Social Democratic Party. In 1973 three new parties joined the bourgeois side in Parliament, among them the small Christian People's Party, and the extreme right-wing Progress Party, which became the second largest in Parliament, surpassed only by the Social Democrats.

[2] The Social Democratic Party constituted the bulk of the left in the Danish Parliament in the 20th century. A small Communist Party was the only rival until 1960, when the Socialist People's Party (a split-off from the Communist Party) appeared for the first time, followed in 1968 by the small extreme left-wing Left Socialist Party (a split-off from the Socialist People's Party).

[3] The Children's Act of 2001 introduced a so-called pater-est rule in Danish family legislation, which meant that joint custody of children would continue after divorce or partnership break-up, unless one or both parents requested abolishment (Ottosen, 2004b, p 13). In the autumn of 2006 all political parties agreed on a new 'Responsibility of Parents Act' to be legislated in 2007. The main novelty of this law is that it makes joint custody of children the rule. The mantra behind the law is that a child has the right to two parents, and deviations from the rule are only possible when it is in the best interests of the child, for instance in cases of violence or drug abuse by one parent (*Information*, 21.02.2007).

[4] These obligations of unmarried fathers in the Scandinavian countries dated back to the late 19th century.

[5] The formulation of the 1922 law read: 'Only in very special circumstances, however, should children under the age of two be taken away from the mother' (Lov om Umyndighed og Værgemaal, 1922). The law proposal of 1968 suggested the following reformulation: 'As a rule custody of children under the age of two should be ascribed to the mother' (Forslag til Lov, 3. oktober 1968).

[6] In the same way that the marriage Acts since the 1920s gave married women equality on divorce (the right to half the assets and equal right to children), this 1995 law gave unmarried men equal right to children by dissolution of partnership.

[7] According to the 1995 law, voluntary agreements on joint custody had just to be registered, not sanctioned, by the county authorities.

[8] This change had already been proposed in a Parliament decision in 1984, but was not included in the 1985 law.

[9] Only individual MPs from different parties disagreed.

[10] This MP, as well as most of the other speakers in Parliament in 1968–69, was female. The Danish Women's Society recommended that mothers' priority for young children should not be included in the law. Over the years more male speakers came to represent their parties in parliamentary debates on family legislation.

[11] The parliamentary decision called on the government to propose a revision of the custody Act with the intention of, for example, 'securing equalisation between the genders in the granting of custody rights' (Forslag til folketingsbeslutning (B87), 1991–92; (B15), 1992–93).

[12] A parallel can be drawn with the marriage laws of the 1920s, which by giving married women equality intended to make marriage an attractive option for women (see Carlsson Wetterberg and Melby, Chapter Two).

[13] The small Christian Party that appeared in Parliament for the first time in 1973 also defended the institution of marriage and consequently opposed all amendments to the marriage laws. On the other hand, the extreme right-wing Progress Party, which was also represented in Parliament from 1973 and constituted about one-fifth of MPs, vigorously argued for new rights for unmarried fathers.

[14] The only MP to defend the institution of marriage in 1995 was a female member of the Socialist People's Party.

[15] Apart from the Social Democratic Party, the Socialist People's Party, the Left Socialists and the Social Liberals stood behind the 1985 law. However, individual MPs of these parties disagreed.

[16] Only individual members of the Liberal Party opposed the 1995 law.

[17] From the outset the Liberal and Conservative parties reacted positively to the proposal, but in the end they chose to oppose it, presumably for party-political reasons. The Danish

Communist Party and the Left Socialist Party objected to the proposal, while the female speaker for the Progress Party asserted that the existing rules discriminated against men. The party suggested fully equalising marriage and partnership in regard to parents' rights and obligations.

[18] The figure had risen from about 40% around 1990, no doubt furthered by the Children's Act of 2001 (see note 3).

[19] The concept of 'universal-breadwinner model' refers to Nancy Fraser (1997, p 51) and characterises a welfare-state model that enables women to support themselves and their families through their own wage earnings.

[20] The term 'universal-caregiver model' refers to a welfare-state model where men do 'their fair share of carework', where, in other words, women's current life patterns are the norm for everyone (Fraser, 1997, pp 60–1)

Bibliography

Bonke, J. (1995) *Arbejde, tid og køn – i udvalgte lande*, Copenhagen: The Danish National Institute of Social Research.

Folketingets forhandlinger, 24.05.1968, *Folketingstidende*, 1967–68, sp. 3628–58.

Folketingets forhandlinger, 17.10.1968, *Folketingstidende*, 1968–69, sp. 613–80.

Folketingets forhandlinger, 21.05.1969, *Folketingstidende*, 1968–69, sp. 6798–6839.

Folketingets forhandlinger, 14.03.1978, *Folketingstidende*, 1977–78, sp. 7460–8.

Folketingets forhandlinger, 31.05.1978, *Folketingstidende*, 1977–78, sp. 11654–68.

Folketingets forhandlinger, 16.10.1984, *Folketingstidende*, 1984–85, sp. 552–74.

Folketingets forhandlinger, 21.05.1985, *Folketingstidende*, 1984–85, sp. 10175–84.

Folketingets forhandlinger, 24.05.1985, *Folketingstidende*, 1984–85, sp. 10532–66.

Folketingets forhandlinger, 08.05.1992, *Folketingstidende*, 1991–92, sp. 9847–65.

Folketingets forhandlinger, 20.11.1992, *Folketingstidende*, 1992–93, sp. 2304–21.

Folketingets forhandlinger, 07.03.1995, *Folketingstidende*, 1994–95. pp 3608–20.

Forslag til folketingsbeslutning om revision af myndighedsloven (B87), *Folketingstidende*, 1991–92, Tillæg A, sp. 6589–96.

Forslag til folketingsbeslutning om revision af myndighedsloven (B15), *Folketingstidende*, 1992–93, Tillæg A, sp. 3285–86.

Forslag til Lov om ændring af myndighedsloven (Forældremyndighed og samkvemsret). 3. oktober 1968. *Folketingstidende*, 1968–69, Tillæg A, sp. 835–930.

Fraser, N. (1997) 'After the Family Wage', in N. Fraser, *Justice Interruptus: Critical reflections on the 'postsocialist' condition*, London: Routledge, pp 41–66.

Information, 'Flertal for at stille fraskilte fædre bedre', 21.02.2007.

Lov om Umyndighed og Værgemaal, 1922, *Rigsdagstidenden*, 1921–22, Tillæg C, sp. 1993–2014, 2725–6.

Lov om ændringer i myndighedsloven. Lov nr. 17 af 6. februar 1957. *Folketingstidende*, 1956–57, Tillæg C, sp. 81–4.

Lov om ændring af myndighedsloven. (Forældremyndighed og samkvemsret). Lov nr. 257 af 4. juni 1969. *Folketingstidende*, Tillæg C, sp. 799–800.

Lov om ændring af myndighedsloven og retsplejeloven. (Forældremyndighed m.v. over børn uden for ægteskab). Lov nr. 244 af 8. juni 1978. *Folketingstidende*, Tillæg C, sp. 781–2.

Lov om ændring af myndighedsloven m.v. Lov nr. 230 af 6. juni 1985. *Folketingstidende*, Tillæg C, sp. 489–98.

Lov om forældremyndighed og samvær. Lov nr. 387 af 14. juni 1995. *Folketingstidende*, Tillæg C, pp 587–91.

Ottosen, M.H. (2004a) *Samvær til barnets bedste? Om regler og praksis på samværsområdet*, Copenhagen: The Danish National Institute of Social Research.

Ottosen, M.H. (2004b) *Samvær og børns trivsel*, Copenhagen: The Danish National Institute of Social Research.

EIGHT

Dilemmas of citizenship: tensions between gender equality and cultural diversity in the Danish welfare state

Birte Siim

The multicultural challenge to gender equality

Feminist scholarship has asked important questions about multiculturalism and gender equality and about the relation between women's rights and respect for cultural diversity. The objective of this chapter is to discuss the challenges from migration and multiculturalism in the context of the Nordic welfare states by looking at the tensions between gender equality and respect for diversity. The focus is on the gendered conflicts and tensions between gender and ethnicity in the Danish approach to citizenship.

The problem of multiculturalism and gender equality has only recently been addressed in the Nordic countries (Mørck, 2002; Siim, 2003; Andreassen, 2005). One inspiration is the debate sparkled by Susan Moller Okin's challenging article (1999), 'Is Multiculturalism Bad for Women?', in which Okin explored the tensions between group rights and women's rights and claimed that multiculturalism has been gender blind. The article raised an important debate about multiculturalism and feminism and about the relation between gender equality and respect for cultural diversity (Kymlicka, 1999; Parekh, 1999). Okin's article has been interpreted both as a useful feminist critique of multicultural approaches to group rights that often rate principles of racial equality above those of gender equality (Phillips, 2005) and as a simplistic and universalistic approach to citizenship and multiculturalism that fails to address the contextual nature of rights, family, religion and the public–private divide (Benhabib, 2002). Okin has recently addressed her critics and restated her position, emphasising that she is not against multiculturalism or group rights. What she proposes is that the majority has a special responsibility to women in minority groups whose oppression may be exacerbated by granting group rights and therefore the female members of patriarchal minority groups need to be consulted in debates about group rights (2005, pp 74–5).

Okin's article has raised an important debate about the role of culture and religion and about the voice of women in minority cultures. The article emphasises the negative role of religion and patriarchal oppression in minority cultures and it can be criticised for being insensitive to minority cultures. After 9/11 there has been a strong political trend to make culture and religion the cause of women's oppression and to treat minority women as passive victims of their culture (Siim, 2003). Against this background it is important to emphasise that issues related to gender equality, multiculturalism and women's rights are contextual and should be explored through transnational analysis. Research indicates that the meaning that family and religion have in women's lives is influenced by the interaction between the dominant majority and minority cultures.

The chapter explores the intersections of gender and ethnicity from a citizenship perspective (Siim, 2003) and looks at the interrelations between political institutions, discourses and 'lived citizenship'.[1] The focus is on how minorities experience policies, norms and discourses in their daily lives, including norms about democracy, family, gender equality and masculinity/femininity, how minority women use their rights and how they experience policies, discourses and norms of equality and diversity in their daily lives.

The first section introduces the citizenship frame and discusses the challenges coming from globalisation and migration to the Nordic welfare and gender models characterised by universal social rights, participatory democracy and so-called women-friendly policies (Hernes, 1987). The second section focuses on the specific tensions between gender equality and diversity in the Danish approach to migration and integration, and discusses the barriers to and potentials for including minority women in society. The third section explores the Danish approach to integration by looking at 'lived citizenship', focusing on the voices, identities and practices of politically active migrant women. The conclusion sums up the challenges to gender equality and multiculturalism in the Nordic context and argues that feminist research needs to discuss to what extent the dominant gender-equality model and discourse tend to exclude, marginalise and assimilate minority perspectives on gender relations.

Nordic approaches to welfare, citizenship and gender

This section discusses the challenges from globalisation and migration to the Nordic welfare and gender models characterised by universal social citizenship, participatory democracy and so-called women-friendly policies (Hernes, 1987). The citizenship frame focuses on social, political and civil rights and addresses processes of inclusion and exclusion of individuals and social groups in society. As an institutional framework, citizenship differentiates three aspects: status, which refers to individual rights and obligations; participation, which refers to citizens' voice in democratic politics; and belonging, which may refer to national, individual and collective identities (Lister, 2003). T.H. Marshall's classic model of citizenship (1949) was closely linked to the nation-state and it is necessary to add a new transnational dimension in order to address migration (Lister et al, 2007).

Citizenship is contextual (Siim, 2000) and situated. It is expressed in 'spaces and places' (Lister, 2003) and the citizenship frame has been an inspiration for comparative studies of welfare-state/social politics, political participation and belonging (Lister et al, 2007). The studies focus on the interrelations of class and gender, and recently there have been attempts to include ethnicity and migration (Koopmans and Stratham, 2000; Koopmans et al, 2005).

Globalisation presents new challenges for Nordic welfare research to address the issue of migration. The countries are perceived as belonging to the same model of welfare, citizenship and gender (Hernes, 1987), but they have adopted different approaches towards migration and integration. Sweden's official multiculturalism is often contrasted to Danish assimilation policies (Hedetoft et al, 2006). A recent report from the Nordic Council of Ministers about the implications of migration concludes that, despite policy differences, the key problem in all the Nordic welfare states is 'failed integration' (Brochmann and Hagelund, 2005). The present marginalisation of migrants and refugees from Third World countries in the labour market, in politics and in society challenges the Nordic model, which is based upon strong traditions of social rights and gender equality. The new inequalities based on 'race'/ethnicities indicate that citizenship research needs to explore the different logics connected to class, gender and ethnicity (see Lister et al, 2007).

There is no systematic research about the intersection of gender and ethnicity in Scandinavia, and migration research tends to be gender blind, while Nordic gender research is often blind to ethnicity and race. Feminist research has recently started to explore the potentials and barriers of the so-called 'women-friendly' Scandinavian welfare states to include the cultural diversity of women (de los Reyes et al, 2003).

Feminist scholarship has analysed both similarities and differences in the Nordic approaches to gender equality by looking at public politics, political discourses and social movements (Bergqvist et al, 1999). In spite of differences in the Scandinavian approaches to migration, feminist research has recently identified similar tensions in the different gender models between principles of gender equality and cultural diversity. The studies indicate that during the 1990s gendered conflicts between the cultural values and norms of the majority and ethnic minorities, including family norms, have contributed to constructing a barrier between 'them' and 'us' (Siim, 2003; Andreassen, 2005; Bredal, 2006, Langvasbråten, 2007).

Post-colonial feminists have criticised the notion of 'women-friendliness' (see Mulinari, Chapter 9 in this volume) because it hides the diversity between women of different races and ethnicities (de los Reyes et al, 2003). This approach has analysed how public policies and discourses contribute to separating 'them' from 'us' and raises critical questions about the potentials to include visible minorities in society as equal citizens (Andreassen, 2005). The dual breadwinner model and strong gender-equality norm can be both a potential for equal treatment of young migrant women (Mørck, 2001) and a barrier to respecting the diversity in family cultures, norms and values (Siim, 2003). The strong normative power of the official gender-equality discourse (Borchorst and Siim, 2002) tends to exclude, marginalise and assimilate minority perspectives on the family and gender equality (de los Reyes et al, 2003). The Nordic approach to gender equality may therefore have exacerbated the tensions between gender equality and respect for cultural diversity (Siim, 2007).

Migration, integration and gender – Danish exceptionalism?

This section explores the Danish approach to migration and integration, focusing explicitly on the tensions between gender equality and diversity. Migration issues include both asylum policies that regulate entry to the country and integration legislation, that is, the rights and obligations of those living legally in the country. Migration policies have an external and an internal dimension that express a tension between realpolitik and human rights (Brochmann and Dölvik, 2004).

Denmark has been described as an extreme case because the country moved from being one of the most liberal to being one of the most restrictive migration regimes between 1983 and 2002 (Fenger-Grøn et al, 2003). During the 1990s the political regulation of migration became gradually more restrictive and the formal naturalisation laws made access to the country for migrants more difficult. During the same period public policies intensified efforts to integrate those living legally in the country. Scholars agree that since 1998 integration has moved away from the pluralist pole, with an increasing emphasis on restricting access to the country as well as on assimilation of minorities to Danish values and the Danish way of life (Togeby, 2003; Hedetoft, 2006).

'Integration' is a fuzzy term, and scholars often differentiate between pluralist integration and assimilation. Integration is Janus faced and may often have the double effect of including and disciplining citizens (Lister et al, 2007). Danish integration policies include policies, norms and discourses that specify the rights and obligations of a good citizen and establish boundaries between 'them' and 'us', between 'citizens' and 'non-citizens'.

The first Danish integration law, introduced by the Social Democratic and Social Liberal coalition government and adopted by Parliament in 1998,[2] presented a relatively broad definition of integration which refers to the social, political, cultural and civil rights and obligations for those living legally in the country, including anti-discrimination legislation. It was based on conflicting principles that were used to legitimise both assimilation and discrimination (Ejrnæs, 2001, p 3). Ethnic discrimination has been illegal since 1971, but the first law against ethnic discrimination in the labour market was not adopted until 1996 (Hansen, 2003).[3]

The Danish approach to migration and integration thus combines a mix of restrictive migration policy with ambitious integration policy. Migration became politicised during the 1990s, and in the electoral campaign in 2001 the issue contributed to a change of government. The Social Democrats and the

Social Liberals, in power since 1993, were replaced by a Liberal–Conservative coalition supported by the anti-immigration Danish People's Party. In 2002 the government adopted one of the most restrictive Alien Acts, prolonging the residency requirement for nationality from seven to nine years. The package included the infamous '24-year provision', which severely restricts the rights to family unification with non-Nordic and non-EU citizens, requiring that both spouses must be 24 years old before a residence permit will be issued if one of the parties is a non-citizen (§9 in the 2002 Danish Alien Act).

The labour market is increasingly seen as the key to integration, and the high unemployment among migrants as compared with ethnic Danes has raised public concerns about the cost of integration to the universal welfare state. One example is the adoption of an 'introductory grant',[4] called the 'start aid', as a tool to integrate refugees into the labour market. The 'start aid' is highly contested, because the grant is lower than the amount given to people on social assistance [*kontanthjælp*], and refugees only gain the right to full and equal social benefits after seven years' residence. The official claim is that the grant is a positive incentive to integration into the labour market, but critics claim that the effect has been not to create jobs, but to increase poverty (Ejrnæs, 2003, p 233).

The issue of family unification is one of the most visible examples of the problems with navigating between realpolitik and humanitarian principles (Brochmann and Dölvik, 2004, p 8). The Danish case illustrates that the move from an open to a strict immigration regime has had dramatic effects on the discourse and regulation of 'family unification' (Grøndahl, 2003). Since the general migration stop in 1973, people have arrived in Denmark either as refugees or as family members of migrants, and during the 1990s governments turned to immigration laws and used the issue of forced marriage to legitimise a stricter immigration control in relation to family members by means of the 24-year provision.[5]

Debates about the family, religion and gender issues

Civil and cultural rights may refer both to the right to be equal and to respect for cultural diversity, including the right to practise your own language, religion, dress and behaviour (Lister et al, 2007). During the 1990s the relationship between the public and the private arena became repoliticised, and migrant families increasingly became the target of political regulation. The debate was highly gendered, often differentiating between 'oppressed migrant women' and 'criminal migrant men' (Andreassen, 2005).

The issues of forced and arranged marriages, domestic violence, and the right to wear a headscarf to work have sparked highly gendered debates (Siim, 2007). In Denmark, Norway and Sweden in the 1990s, forced marriages and 'honour-related violence' became subjects of public concern expressed through gender equality, women's rights and the oppression of girls in patriarchal families (Bredal, 2005). Denmark's approach is unique because the official discourse does not differentiate between forced and arranged marriages, while Norway's action plan is directed solely at forced marriages. The Swedish action plans are directed against the *general* oppression of girls in patriarchal families and do not target specific groups.

From 2001 to 2007 the Danish approach to migration has predominantly focused on restrictive policies and negative discourses rather than on preventive measures and dialogue. The public debate[6] about how to prevent forced marriage is part of the 'immigrant debate' and was therefore polarised from the start (Grøndal, 2003). According to the official Danish discourse, gender equality has already been achieved and patriarchal oppression is primarily a problem for minority women. The government's 'Action Plan for 2003–2005 on Forced, Quasi-forced and Arranged Marriages' of August 2003 illustrates this point. The objective is to support young people exposed to force in relation to marriage and to reinforce preventive initiatives by the authorities (*The Government's Action Plan*, 2003, pp 5–10) through projects financed by special allocation funds. This includes funds to Landsorganisationen for Kvinde- og Krisecentre, LOKK (the National Organisation of Shelters for Battered Women and Children) to start a nationwide team of professional counsellors to offer free advice to local authorities in cases of forced marriage or marriages where coercion seems to have been a factor.

The Action Plan does not differentiate between marriages based on force and those based on consent, arguing that both lead to oppression and lack of self-determination. It thus identifies the main problem as a conflict between the Danish majority norms about gender equality and 'normal' families on the one hand and the cultural tradition of forced and arranged marriages on the other. The discourse is constructed by ignoring the difference between forced and arranged marriages, both of which are regarded as major problems in need of political regulation. The rhetoric is constructed by means of arguments that stress that the two have the same negative effects in relation to self-determination, cultural conflicts, force and lack of integration. The references in the Danish law against forced marriage to the Norwegian and British Action Plans against Forced Marriages and to the European Human Rights Convention further blur the difference between forced and arranged marriages.

The issue of forced and arranged marriages thus illustrates the tension between the dominant individualist political culture and the cultural diversity in family forms. It indicates that the strong normative pressure towards cultural assimilation tends to exacerbate gendered conflicts between minority and majority groups about gendered rights. The lack of differentiation between forced and arranged marriage in the official Danish discourse is problematic because it does not acknowledge the interrelation of generational and gender problems in migrant families. This approach to integration denies migrant women autonomy and agency because they are perceived as potential victims of their own culture and religion (Andreassen, 2005; Siim, 2007). In this way the political discourse, and also the media, use the Danish gender model to legitimise political regulation of migrant families. The Danish approach to integration has arguably exacerbated the gendered conflicts between the majority and the minority. The Norwegian and Swedish approaches to preventing forced marriage are somewhat different because the action plans differentiate between forced and arranged marriages and give higher priority to preventative strategies and dialogues with minority families on the level of social practice (Bredal, 2005).

Lived citizenship – tensions between gender equality and cultural diversity

This section addresses the multicultural challenge in more detail, focusing on the voices, identities and practice of migrant women from the perspective of politically active migrant women. One of the key questions is how the Danish gender model deals with cultural diversities among women on the level of 'lived citizenship', including tensions between the public and private arenas.

Sociological research has explored the tensions between the patriarchal control of migrant women and the Nordic gender-equality model on the level of everyday life (Mørck, 2001; Prieur, 2002; Bredal, 2006). Yvonne Mørck's dissertation (1998) was one of the first Danish studies of young ethnic minorities from a generational perspective. The study explored the double or 'hyphenated' identities of young second-generation minorities from an anthropological approach. Mørck (2001) finds that young minority women living in Denmark have the potential to gain from the Danish citizenship model and gender-equality norm in their everyday life as well as in their political participation/voice.

Annick Prieur[7] has also addressed the conflicts between the Nordic equality ideals and patriarchal family forms in ethnic minority cultures. She emphasises that conflicts about gender equality are generational and dynamic and that domination is often a question of consent based on emotions, not on force. The study illustrates that changes are contradictory, in the sense that many young migrants apparently accept living up to their parents' expectations of traditional gender roles, but at the same time they share Nordic ideals about gender equality. Prieur concludes that migrant families experience and practise dramatic generational changes, which are often invisible from the perspective of the majority, especially changes that expand the freedom of women and children (Prieur, 2002, pp 163–5).

These studies raise important questions about the interaction of dominant institutions, discourses and everyday life. Some of these issues were addressed in a research project carried out for the Danish Democracy and Power Study. The study of political mobilisation of ethnic minority women explored the implications of the Danish approach to integration by looking at 'lived citizenship', that is, citizens' values, norms and practices related to gender equality, family and marriage in everyday life (Siim, 2003). The following section briefly summarises some of the findings of the study.

Lived citizenship: the voices, norms and values of political activists

The explorative study of the political empowerment of ethnic minority women focused on conflicts and tensions between women's public and private lives. How does the majority perceive and interact with minority groups and how do minorities experience the majority? How do ethnic minorities negotiate the tensions between the private and public arenas and between the dominant gender-equality and family norms in everyday life?

The informants[8] were political activists selected as leaders and founders of voluntary associations directed towards migrant women.[9]

The investigation explored five main themes: (1) individual and collective identity; (2) family and religion; (3) gender equality and feminism; (4) political confidence and empowerment; (5) equality, recognition and political influence (Siim, 2003, p 69). Identity was defined as social identity,[10] which may express belonging to a specific nationality, a social and cultural group or an individual person/self (Jenkins, 1997, pp 13–14).

The study illustrates that identity is dynamic and influenced by the interactions between the majority and the minority groups. The informants were relatively reflective of the perceived conflicts and tensions between the dominant family norms and gender values and the practice and norms in minority cultures. Many expressed a 'double' identity, for example as 'Danish–Turkish' or 'Danish Muslim' (Siim, 2003, p 71), which was not always perceived as a problem. The narratives illuminated how many of the informants negotiated the cultural conflicts between majority norms and their own family culture in their private and public lives.

Some of the younger informants who, like Sevil and Rubina, grew up in Denmark, feel 'mostly Danish' but also have a strong attachment to their country of origin. Sevil, who wears a headscarf, states that she would like to say that she is Danish, but is not sure that she will be accepted as 'Danish'. She feels forced to adopt an identity as a 'Muslim' or 'Danish Muslim'. In the focus-group interview the young Muslim women[11] say that they have formed an identity as 'Danish Muslims', because nobody can take that away from them. They are afraid that ethnic Danes will not accept them as 'Danish' because they look too different with their scarves, black hair or olive skin (Focus-group interview, 7 December 2001). Rubina also feels 'mostly Danish', but she expresses a stronger religious identity and ends by saying that 'I am first a Muslim' (Siim, 2003, p 71).

The narratives illustrate that many informants have strong family feelings and attachment to their own culture. They know that many migrant families are oppressive, but they perceive their own large families as a potential resource that they can turn to for support in their work, family and political life. Both Sevil and Rubina express a double perspective on the family. They are aware of the oppressive aspects of 'traditional' family norms and speak out against forced marriages, but they tend to accept arranged marriages if both partners agree.

What I love about my parents' culture is the family feeling. The family attachment is enormous. The negative side is of course the social control because everybody knows everybody, but I find that very good. If somebody has a problem it is quickly discovered, so you can prevent that the problem develops.... I cannot live without my parents. They also live here ... and I will never move away from here. If you need your family, then they are here for you. For example, I can always send my daughter to my parents' house – every day if necessary, without feeling sorry for them. (Sevil, in Siim, 2003, p 77)

Sevil was married to her cousin from Turkey when she was 19. She does not see it as an arranged marriage, because she herself chose him after falling in love during a vacation in Turkey. She is ambivalent about traditional family norms: she is positive towards individualisation and would like to 'arrange' to postpone her daughter's marriage till she is over 30, but at the same time she is afraid that modernisation and individualisation will destroy the family attachment and fears that people will be lonely (Interview, 31 January 2002).

The study illustrates that the young women are often confronted with a dilemma between the freedom to choose their own partner and the wish to marry someone from their own culture and religion. They like the large families, which support them in their daily life and protect them from loneliness, but they are also critical of the social control that is often connected with close family relations. They try to overcome the dilemma by presenting an ideal about strong families that are not oppressive but are able to combine the strength of a community with the promise of self-determination and equal rights for women and men (Siim, 2003).

The narratives illustrate that the informants often experience conflict between the demand for equal rights in relation to education and work and their acceptance of gendered family values. Most informants express a positive attitude towards feminism and full support for demands for gender equality in society, but some find that Danish women focus too much on sexual freedom, the body, and equality in the family.

One example is Sevil, whose gender profile is formed by the shifting roles of housewife in the kitchen and independent woman in public life and at work, which are constantly negotiated and renegotiated.

She tells with a grin how she often plays with shifting identities and roles at home and at work. When she is at home with her parents/family/guests she is Pakistani and plays the role of housewife. When she is outside the home, for example in school or at work, she is 100% Danish and plays by the Danish rules (Siim, 2003, p 83).

Another example is Rubina, a university student, who tells how she combines gender-specific roles at home with equal rights outside the home. She is positive towards women's rights to education and divorce but critical of the Danish equality debate's focus on 'who should do the dishes', because it breaks 'the peace in the home'. She has her own vision about gender equality, saying that housework should be fairly divided between both parties: 'There should be equality in both spheres but equality in the family is for the parties to decide, dependent on what kind of person you are' (Siim, 2003, p 84). She is aware of the potential conflict between the visions of 'peace in the family', motivated by her religious faith, and equality 'everywhere'. She expects both spouses to make sacrifices for the family, although she knows from experience that this is a difficult ideal and expects that her marriage may end in divorce.

What makes the group of political activists different from other migrant women is their political activism and leadership of voluntary organisations as well as their ambitions to influence political institutions. In Denmark migrants gained the right to vote in local elections in 1983, and, while they are relatively well represented in local municipalities (Togeby, 2003), research indicates that especially migrant women are under-represented in voluntary organisations, public debates and political institutions.[12] The informants address some of the tensions in the Danish political culture between inclusion and exclusion in politics

They generally experience the local political arena as an inclusive and open opportunity structure for the self-organisation of minority women. One example is that they have found it relatively easy to get public funding to establish voluntary associations for minority women. At the same time many of them find the political system as a whole and the media oppressive, and they note that the small associations lack the power to make a difference in political life. And some would like to join political parties to make an impact (Siim, 2003, p 91):

The study illustrates that many activists experience a feeling of powerlessness, because they do not have a voice in the public debate. Some informants talk about the multiple difficulties they encounter when they enter the public sphere both as individual women in relation to minority cultures and as minority women in relation to the majority culture. The narratives illuminate that the difficulties are not only connected to the oppressive political system and negative political discourse, but are also rooted in the norms and practice of minority cultures.

> It is difficult for a woman to go to a group of men and argue for her views without it being misunderstood. It is difficult for Turkish women to enter politics, especially because of the media's role in politics. The media wants to find something interesting or controversial. It is the same with Turkish people; they also need to have something on a person ... If you enter politics you really need basic skills. You need to be very convincing on the basis of your education and show that you are something, independent of other people. You have to be strong enough to stand alone, and that is what I think many Turkish people do not feel they are. You need to be able to stand up for yourself towards the critical Danes, but also to defend yourself vis-à-vis your own culture. This is a difficult balance and I think that this frightens many Turkish women from entering politics. (Rubina, in Siim, 2003, p 95)

The above quote illustrates that many politically active minority women experience a double or even triple barrier when they enter the public arena. They are looked upon with suspicion by the Danish media, by their own culture and country of origin – and sometimes even by Danish majority women. Some tell that they must pass a double loyalty test to prove that they embody both 'Danish' political norms and minority norms, with conflicting values about femininity.

The study illuminates that many informants experience strong feelings of discrimination and marginalisation in the public arena as 'the other'. Some, like Serena, tell stories about ethnification and stigmatisation of them as minorities in the public debate and about pressure to conform to the Danish majority norms (Siim, 2003, p 90). This is perceived as a barrier to attempts to influence the public debate and have their interests represented in politics. Others, like Rubina, stress that both majority institutions and minority organisations can become barriers in women's struggle to gain a voice in the public debate and be represented in politics. Many express a strong wish to strengthen the dialogue and cooperation between minority women's and Danish majority women's organisations.

In terms of democracy, the overall message of the study is twofold: the narratives illuminate the empowerment of a diverse group of political activists who have successfully founded organisations able to mobilise migrant women. At the same time they also indicate that discrimination and stigmatisation have created disempowerment, distrust in the political system and lack of belief in their ability to influence both political institutions and minority organisations.

What can we learn from the study of the meaning of citizenship for this exceptional elite group that has succeeded in breaking barriers to education and work, with the active support of their families? The study illustrates that the political activists have developed personal strategies in order to combine individual self-determination with respect for a collectivist, family-oriented culture and practice, and actively negotiate between different equality norms in their private and public lives at the level of lived citizenship.

What distinguishes this group of informants from Danish majority women with a similar background, as well as from the majority of ethnic minority women, is their political activism and strong wish to make a difference in politics. This has arguably enabled them to successfully bridge the tensions in their daily lives and to negotiate actively between two cultures – an individualist majority culture and a more collectivist family-oriented minority culture. Their collectivist family norms and strong family attachment set them apart from similar majority women, but they constitute a close connection with many groups of minority women.

To sum up: the qualitative studies of different groups of minority men and women have illuminated the gendered aspects of *the multicultural challenge*. They illustrate that at the level of lived citizenship there are tensions in the public and private lives of minority women (and men) connected with gender-equality norms and family values. The citizenship study further illuminates how a group of political activists, through personal strategies, has been able to bridge some of these tensions and conflicts and negotiate effectively between their own family cultures and values and the dominant gender-equality norms of the Danish majority.

Reflections on the intersection of gender and ethnicity from the Nordic contexts

In spite of different approaches to integration, the Nordic welfare states have similar problems with the marginalisation of ethnic minorities in the labour market and in society. Feminist scholarship has recently identified similar tensions and conflicts in the Nordic welfare, citizenship and gender regimes around gender equality and the cultural diversity of women. These studies raise critical questions about the intersections of welfare and migration and illustrate that the women-friendly social policies do not include all women.

Despite the Danish exceptionalism on migration and family unification, recent studies have identified similar problems in the relationship between the dominant gender-equality norm, family values and multiculturalism. The studies emphasise that we need more comparative Nordic research of the interactions of family, welfare and nation and of the interaction of public policies, discourses and lived citizenship. How do people experience the intersection of inequalities attached to gender, class and ethnicity in everyday life? What potential and barriers does the Nordic citizenship and gender-equality model hold for the inclusion of migrant women as equal citizens? What are the potentials and barriers of the Nordic gender-equality model for recognising cultural diversity, including the diversity of family forms and gender-equality norms?

The studies of lived citizenship raise important questions about the interconnection between the welfare institutions and gender-equality norms and values from the perspective of migrant women. They illustrate that we need institutional research sensitive to gender issues, focusing on the gendered conflicts around majority and minority cultures, norms and values. We also need more research focusing on the political strategies and voices of ethnic minority women's organisations. Finally, we need research that is sensitive to how the conflict between gender equality and cultural diversity is constructed and negotiated in daily life by the interactions between the majority and the minorities.

The arguments in this chapter are, first, that it is a democratic challenge for the political system to give minority women equal citizenship rights, recognition and influence in their daily life and in politics. Second, it is a gender-political challenge to respect the equal values and cultural norms of minority women and their search for their own ways to emancipation and to support them in developing strategies able to bridge between majority norms and the values of minorities concerning family norms and gender equality.

Nordic feminist research needs to analyse to what extent the official gender-equality discourses and policies, including the dominant approach to gender research, tend to marginalise and assimilate minority perspectives on gender equality. Arguably, it is a challenge to develop feminist strategies that respect the right to diversity of religion, culture and family forms without accepting patriarchal oppression and unequal treatment of migrant women.

Notes

[1] The notion of 'lived' citizenship is a way to address citizenship 'from below'. It has been defined as 'the meanings that citizenship actually has in people's lives and the way in which people's social and cultural backgrounds and material circumstances affect their lives as citizens' (Lister, 2003, p 3).

[2] According to the integration law, integration is a municipal responsibility. The law was revised by the Liberal–Conservative government in 2003. Since then, all refugees have to sign an individual contract with the Danish authorities, and all refugees must participate in a three-year introductory course where they acquire basic knowledge about Danish language, society and culture if they receive an introductory grant. The grant may be reduced if they do not honour the contract. From 1 January 2004 the full integration programme is about 37 hours per week (Tænketanken, 2004, Ch. 2, p 31).

[3] The Board for Ethnic Equality was established in 1993 but dissolved in 2002, and the tasks were transferred to the Institute for Human Rights. There is growing international criticism of Danish discrimination and intolerance, for example from the European Commission against Racism and Intolerance (ECRI), the United Nations Committee against Race Discrimination (CERD), and UN's Women's Committee (CEDAW) (Justesen, 2003, p 70).

[4] The low grant to refugees was introduced by the previous government headed by the Social Democratic Party in 1999, but lasted only 13 months because it was criticised and did not have the intended effect in terms of integrating refugees into the labour market (Ejrnæs, 2003, pp 224–5).

[5] The '24 year provision' in the Danish Alien Act has been widely criticised, but there have been similar proposals and debates in Norway (Bredal, 2005). In Norway the government initially had another strategy based on the National Plan of Action on Forced Marriages of 1998 that focused on both prevention and remedy (Bredal, 2005), but both strategies were motivated by women's rights.

[6] The government referred to a growing number of cases of forced and arranged marriages, arguing that the known cases were only the tip of the iceberg, but critics of strict regulation claimed that there were only a few reported incidents of forced marriage and complained about media generalisations stigmatising minority groups (Grøndal, 2003).

[7] Prieur's study was based on 52 interviews with young men and women from ethnic minorities in Norway.

[8] The interviews with 14 women from five different organisations were carried out between December 2001 and January 2002. The informants were perceived both as representatives of their organisations and as individuals. Two of them, Sevil and Rubina, were selected for in-depth interviews on the basis of their gender-political profiles. Most interviews were individual, two were group interviews with refugee women from Iraq and Afghanistan and one was a focus-group interview with the leadership of Dialog 2. The informants were diverse in terms of religion, age, education and family situation. Most were second-generation migrants, one was first-generation and the rest were refugees. Some were Danish citizens, others were not. Some were born in Denmark, some came to Denmark as children and the rest arrived as adults. Most were Muslims, one was Catholic and the two majority Danes were not religious. Four declared that they were reformed Muslims, seven were practising Muslims, three of whom wore headscarves.

[9] The organisations included: INDSAM, an umbrella organisation for ethnic associations, Dialog 2 and VISION, two small associations headed by young minority women as well as Kvinderådet (The Women's Council), and two Danish majority organisations, Kvinderådet and Evas Ark, which both aim to create dialogue with minority women.

[10] The understanding of identity as social identity formed in the meeting between minority and majority is inspired by Richard Jenkins. He finds that identity expresses a dialectic relation between equality and diversity (Jenkins, 1997, pp 13–14).

[11] In the focus-group interview with five young women who all were practising Muslims, three of them wore a headscarf and two did not.

[12] Democratic politics includes voting and representation in local and national elections, participation in voluntary associations and having a voice in public debates. Research indicates that there is a political marginalisation of minority women, who are generally under-represented in minority organisations, in public debates and in the political institutions. The only exception is the voter turnout among young ethnic minorities between 28 and 36: in this age group ethnic minority women vote as much as young men (Togeby, 2003, p 91).

Bibliography

Andreassen, R. (2005) 'The Mass Media's Construction of Gender, Race, Sexuality and Nationality. An analysis of the danish news media's communication about visible minorities 1971–2004', PhD dissertation, Toronto: Department of History, the University of Toronto.

Benhabib, S. (2002) *The Claims of Culture. Equality and diversity in the global era*, Princeton, NJ: Princeton University Press.

Bergqvist, C., Borchorst, A., Christensen, A.-D., Ramstedt-Silén, V., Raaum, N.C. and Styrkárdóttir, A. (eds) (1999) *Equal Democracies? Gender and politics in the Nordic countries*, Oslo: Scandinavian University Press, Nordic Council of Ministers.

Borchorst, A. and Siim, B. (2002) 'The women-friendly welfare state revisited', *NORA, Nordic Journal of Women's Studies*, vol 10, no 2, pp 90–8.

Bredal, A. (2005) 'Tackling Forced Marriages in the Nordic Countries: Between women's rights and immigration control', in L. Welchman and S. Hossain (eds) *Honour Crimes. Paradigms and violence against women*, London: Zed Books, pp 482-509.

Bredal, A. (2006) 'Vi er jo en familie'. Arrangerte ekteskap, autonomi og fellesskap blandt unge norsk-asiater', thesis, Oslo: Institutt for Samfunnsforskning.

Brochmann, G. and Dölvik, J.E. (eds) (2004) 'Is Immigration an Enemy of the Welfare State? Between human rights and realpolitik in European immigration policies', in *Managing Migration. A policy agenda for economic progress and social cohesion*, Washington, DC: Migration Institute, pp 155-79.

Brochmann, G. and Hagelund, A. (2005) *Innvandringens velferdspolitiske konsekvenser. Nordisk kunnskapsstatus*, Copenhagen: Nordic Council of Ministers.

de los Reyes, P., Molina, I. and Mulinari, D. (2003) *Maktens olika förklädnadar. Kønn, klasse og etnicitet i det post-koloniale Sverige*, Stockholm: Atlas.

Ejrnæs, M. (2001) 'Integrationsloven – en case, der illustrerer minoriteters usikre medborgerstatus', *AMID Working Paper Series 1/2001*.

Ejrnæs, M. (2003) 'Andenrangsborgere fra begyndelsen', in C. Fenger-Grøn, K. Qureshi and T. Seidenfaden (eds) *Når du strammer garnet – et opgør med mobning af mindretal og ansvarsløs asylpolitik*, Aarhus: Aarhus University Press, pp 212–34.

Fenger-Grøn, C., Qureshi, K. and Seidenfaden, T. (eds) (2003) *Når du strammer garnet – et opgør med mobning af mindretal og ansvarsløs asylpolitik*, Aarhus: Aarhus University Press.

The Government's Action Plan for 2003–2004 on Forced, Quasi-forced and Arranged Marriages, 15 August 2003.

Grøndahl, M. (2003) 'Familiesammenføring – fra verdensrekord til verdensrekord', in C. Fenger-Grøn, K. Qureshi and T. Seidenfaden (eds) *Når du strammer garnet – et opgør med mobning af mindretal og ansvarsløs asylpolitik*, Aarhus: Aarhus University Press, pp 184–211.

Hansen, N.E. (2003) 'Diskrimination på arbejdsmarkedet', in C. Fenger-Grøn, K. Qureshi and T. Seidenfaden (eds) *Når du strammer garnet – et opgør med mobning af mindretal og ansvarsløs asylpolitik*, Aarhus: Aarhus University Press, pp 235–53.

Hedetoft, U. (2006) 'More than Kin and Less than Kind: the Danish politics of ethnic consensus and the pluricultural challenge', in J.L. Campbell, J.A. Hall and O.K. Pedersen (eds) *National Identity and the Varieties of Capitalism: The Danish Experience*, Montreal: McGill-Queens University Press, pp 398–480.

Hedetoft, U., Petersson, B. and Sturfelt, L. (eds) (2006) *Invandrare och integration i Danmark och Sverige*, Göteborg-Stockholm: Makadam.

Hernes, H.M. (1987) *Welfare State and Women Power. Essays in state feminism*, Oslo: Norwegian University Press.

Jenkins, R. (1997) *Rethinking Ethnicity, Arguments and Explorations*, London: Sage.

Justesen, P. (2003) 'International kritik – den nationale arrogance', in C. Fenger-Grøn, K. Qureshi and T. Seidenfaden (eds) *Når du strammer garnet – et opgør med mobning af mindretal og ansvarsløs asylpolitik*, Aarhus: Aarhus University Press, pp 69–86.

Koopmans, R. and Statham, P. (eds) (2000) *Challenging Immigration and Ethnic Relations Politics. Comparative European perspectives*, Oxford: Oxford University Press.

Koopmans, R., Statham, P., Giugni, M. and Passy, I. (2005) *Contested Citizenship. Immigration and cultural diversity in Europe*, Minneapolis/London: University of Minnesota Press.

Kymlicka, W. (1999) 'Liberal complacencies', in S.M. Okin with Respondents, *Is Multiculturalism Bad for Women?* Princeton, NJ: Princeton University Press, pp 31–4.

Langvasbråten, Trude (2007) 'A Scandinavian model? – Gender equality policy and multiculturalism in Sweden, Denmark and Norway 2000–2005', *Social Politics* (forthcoming).

Lister, R. (2003) *Citizenship. Feminist perspectives*, 2nd edn, London: Macmillan.

Lister, R. et al (2007) *Gendering Citizenship in Western Europe. New challenges for citizenship research in a cross-national context*, Bristol: The Policy Press.

Lov om integration af udlændinge i Danmark (integrationsloven). *Lovbekendtgørelse nr. 1035, den 23. november, 2003.*

Marshall, T.H. (1949) 'Citizenship and social class', The Marshall Lectures, in T.H. Marshall and T. Bottomore, *Citizenship and Social Class*, London: Pluto Press, pp 1-51.

Mørck, Y. (1998) *Bindestregsdanskere. Fortællinger om køn, generation og etnicitet*, Frederiksberg: Forlaget Sociologi.

Mørck, Y. (2001) 'Etniske minoritetsunge og demokratisk medborgerskab', in A.-D. Christensen and B. Siim (eds) *Køn, demokrati og modernitet*, Copenhagen: Hans Reitzel Publishers, pp 223–37.

Mørck, Y. (2002) 'Multikulturalismens kønsblinde øje. Mangfoldighedsudfordringer og kønsligestilling', *Dansk Sociologi*, vol 13, no 3, pp 7–25.

Mørck, Y. (2005) 'Multiculturalism and Feminism: No simple questions, no simple answers', in A. Eisenberg and J. Spinner-Halev (eds) *Minorities within Minorities. Equality, rights and diversity*, Cambridge: Cambridge University Press.

Okin, S.M. with Respondents, edited by J. Cohen, M. Howard and M. Nussbaum (1999) *Is Multiculturalism Bad for Women?*, Princeton, NJ: Princeton University Press.

Parekh, B. (1999) 'A Varied Moral World', in S.M. Okin with Respondents, *Is Multiculturalism Bad for Women?*, Princeton, NJ: Princeton University Press, pp 69–76.

Phillips, A. (2005) 'Dilemmas of Gender and Culture: The judge, the democrat and the political activist', in A. Eisenberg and J. Spinner-Halev (eds) *Minorities within Minorities. Equality, rights and diversity*, Cambridge: Cambridge University Press, pp 113–34.

Prieur, A. (2002) 'Magt over eget liv: om unge indvandrere, patriarkalske familieformer og nordiske ligestillingsidealer', in A. Borchorst (ed) *Kønsmagt under forandring*, Copenhagen: Hans Reitzel Publishers, pp 149–67.

Siim, B. (2000) *Gender and Citizenship. Politics and agency in France, Britain and Denmark*, Singapore: Cambridge University Press.

Siim, B. (2003) *Medborgerskabets udfordringer – belyst ved politisk myndiggørelse af etniske minoritetskvinder*, Aarhus: Magtudredningen/Aarhus University Press.

Siim, B.J (2007) 'The Challenge of Recognising Diversity from the Perspective of Gender Equality', *Critical Review of International Social and Political Philosophy (CRISPP)*, Special Issue, vol 10, no 4, pp 491-511.

Tænketanken om udfordringer for integrationsindsatsen i Danmark i samarbejde med Socialforskningsinstituttet (2004) *Udlændinge og integrationspolitikken i Danmark og udvalgte lande – en Baggrundsrapport*, Ministry for Refugee, Immigrant and Integration Affairs.

Togeby, L. (2003) *Fra fremmedarbejdere til etniske minoriteter*, Aarhus: Aarhus University Press.

NINE

Women friendly? Understanding gendered racism in Sweden

Diana Mulinari

Introduction

This chapter offers a re-reading of the Swedish welfare state based on everyday experiences of women from the Latin American diaspora (Sawyer, 2000; Alinia, 2004) living in Sweden. Central to the chapter is to explore the specific experience of a group of migrant women at the crossroads between their transnational communities and the public policies of the Swedish welfare state.

Hegemonic trends in Swedish gender studies primarily focus on the conditions of women conceptualised as belonging to the nation. An under-theorisation of gendered racism(s) is common in these studies (Mulinari, 2001). The expansion and academic institutionalisation of queer and post-colonial feminism in the late 1980s changed the landscape of Swedish feminism. Studies inspired by intersectional analysis are today at the core of developments in the field.

While few feminist post-colonial studies have been carried out in Sweden, the dominant strands of research continue to represent migrant women as 'different', 'passive', 'traditional', lacking democratic traditions and with backgrounds in 'patriarchal' cultures. The chapter takes its theoretical point of departure from both international and Swedish debates on intersectionality (Collins, 1998; de los Reyes and Mulinari, 2004) and aims to grasp the diversity of migrant women's experience of the Swedish welfare state.

Theoretical starting points

Recognition of the narrow and problematic understanding of the world that is embodied in the word 'immigrant' has evolved over the last few years (Brah, 1996; Räthzel, 1997). Recent studies in the field of social policy have highlighted the significance of 'race'/ethnicity, especially the central role that the welfare state and its institutions play in creating and reproducing specific categories of people (Clark, 2004).

Sweden is today the EU country with the highest proportion of migrants in relation to total population (16% of 9 million when citizens with 'migrant background' born in Sweden are included). Castles and Miller (1993) classify Sweden in their analysis of migration regimes together with Australia and Canada with a migration system of permanent settlement, where immigrants are formally granted access to social rights. The concept of subordinated inclusion grasps the specificities of this regime, grounded in the establishment and development of a racialised and gendered working class, where racialised groups are included, but placed in subordinated positions in all spheres of life (Ålund and Schierup, 1991; Mulinari and Neergaard, 2004).

Some researchers argue that Sweden, along with Britain, constitutes one of the most clear-cut cases of regime change (Pontusson, 1992). In the 1980s and 1990s conflict over the meaning of culture increased and discourses of national belonging became more racialised, with larger groups of racialised citizens outside the labour market, in the context of cutbacks in the social security systems and (more) restrictive refugee policies.

Since the Second World War, Sweden has constructed a national identity based on a self-image as tolerant towards multiple forms of cultural and ethnic difference. The tensions between rhetoric and practices can be grasped today in the manifest intentions favourable for the development of an anti-racist agenda embedded in a broad political consensus on the one hand, and in the systematic forms through which division of labour is racialised and urban segregation increases along racialised class lines on the other (SOU 2005:56; SOU 2005:69).

A women-friendly welfare state?

While many feminist studies examine the specificities of the Swedish welfare state, the means through which the state is racialised and how this affects the construction of specific types of racialised femininities and masculinities remain highly authorised and poorly empirically researched.

Central to my understanding of the Swedish welfare state and its role in the creation and regulation of gender relations is the critical challenge posed by several feminist researchers to the ideology of gender equality (Rönnblom et al, 1998; Eriksson, 2003; Dahl, 2005). These researchers have identified the gap between gender-equality ideologies and the lives of women (and men) as well as the ways discourses of gender equality emphasise consent and collaboration between the category 'women' and the category 'men', but also assume heterosexuality as the norm by which society is organised.

Social anthropologist Annika Rabo suggests that policies of equality between women and men have become one of the most important goals of public life. She further argues that there are important connections between the welfare model and nationhood, and even those citizens who opposed the dominant social-democratic rule agree that Sweden has a unique position as the nation that pioneered and provided inspiration for the Nordic welfare model. Most official documents insist that gender equality is not a matter of opinion, but a matter of lack of knowledge and that it is almost impossible to voice an opinion against gender equality and to be inside the moral universe of Swedish-ness. In her own words: 'Hence Swedes, in general are convinced that immigrants especially from outside Europe need to be educated into the Swedish ideals of gender equality' (1997, p 109).

Post-colonial Swedish feminists have suggested that notions of gender equality are being used as a central feature in defining boundaries between those who belong to the nation and those who do not (Bredström, 2002; de los Reyes and Molina, 2002). At the core of these discourses lies a projection of 'bad patriarchies' to distant places and onto racialised bodies.

In the 1990s several policies based on the notion of 'risk groups' were developed that specifically targeted racialised women through assumed cultural differences (Essed, 1991; Lewis, 2000). The culturalist discourse constructs 'migrants' as an undifferentiated whole in terms of assumed uniform 'cultural' traits that distinguish the 'west' from the 'rest' and 'them' from 'us'. These policies not only increase the criminalisation of racialised men, but silence issues of poverty, institutional racism and exclusion.

Methodological contentions: the construction of a community

I have used a patchwork method in an attempt to grasp the experiences of Latin American women in Sweden through different interventions and voices. The material presented in this chapter evolves from 20 in-depth interviews with women who, I believe, to some extent cover the heterogeneity of the group in terms of class, sexuality, religion, ethnicity, family status and length of residence in Sweden. Many of the women I interviewed are divorced, most of them are mothers, two of them declare themselves lesbians, some returned to their country of origin but are now living in Sweden, most of them are employed. I believe that my findings are analytically generalisable and can relate back to broader theoretical insights on the modes of gendered racism in European welfare states.

My informants often use the term *la comunidad* to refer to the Latin American transnational space(s) of belonging in Sweden; my use of the concept of community is influenced by both sociological and feminist debates (Cohen, 1985; Anthias and Yuval Davis, 1992).

Follow me today, a Saturday morning, and meet 'my' community. Let us go to the city plaza. Are you hungry? Then maybe you can taste a chorizo that the Victor Jara, a Chilean solidarity organisation, sells while it collects signatures for Pinochet's trial. If you are not hungry, you can watch and even participate in a performance organised by another Latin American group (this time a 'cultural' one) for children. You may meet somebody who invites you to a salsa party next week or has information about the Latin American film festival taking place in a nearby city next month. And did you miss the last tango performance? Well, shame on you ... there are five different tango courses you can choose. Or would you like to stop with a group that sells books and crafts from El Salvador around a little table? Even if you do not want to stay with them, you may sign a petition to the Swedish government about Peruvian political refugees who are not recognised as such. And if you fancy hip-hop, ask the teenagers – they may even have extra tickets for the Latin Kings who are playing tonight. Listen to their languages. Do they speak Spanish? Well, yes and no. They speak Latin American Spanish, and their languages vary enormously, because they are embodied in different regions, in different social classes, ethnicities and generations. They speak Latin American Swedish because their language mirrors not who they are, but what they have become, through the use of thousands of Swedish words that (with the profound criticism of mother-tongue teachers) Latin Americans refuse to translate. Or they may speak a Latin American Swedish dialect where words and meanings are specifically constructed to embody and mirror their transnational experience. But if you ask them, all these very, very, very different people will call themselves *Latinos in Sweden*.

A risk associated with this ethnographic narrative is the reinforcement of neocolonial representations of Latin Americans in Sweden as ontologically left political activists, salsa and tango dancers who know each other. My aim with the narrative is to illuminate diversity in a public space. Insiders in the community are capable of reading class background, ways of doing gender (feminism, lesbian, single women, married to a Latin American, married to a 'Swede' and so on) and the different positions and locations of different groups. The community is also geographically dispersed, and interaction for most informants is narrowed to ritual gatherings (birthday parties, Christmas and so on), public events, close friendships and extended families.

While it is often argued that the Latin Americans in Sweden represent a political migration (Chile, Argentina, Uruguay, El Salvador), the Latin American community has undergone significant changes over these 30 years. The community has also come to include other regions that have suffered from political instability and human rights violations, for instance Guatemala, Venezuela, Colombia, Peru and Cuba (the latter often due to state policy on homosexuality) and has received new groups that migrate in response to the collapse of Latin American economies and the politics of 'structural adjustment' (Lundberg, 1989; Lindqvist, 1991; Leiva, 1996; Olsson, 1997).

Racism(s) constitutes one important level on which to analyse the identity of Latin Americans in Sweden today. If the notion of 'Latin American' or 'Latino' describes belonging to the community, the notion of *cabeza negra* (in Swedish: *svartskalle/blatte* = black skull), a derogatory word that has been transformed into a positive identification, describes belonging to the 'nation', showing the identification the group has developed through the experience of racialisation towards Swedish pan-ethnic collectivity.

Central to my research is the historical context. Most research on Latin Americans in Sweden was done *during the time they loved us*, to rephrase the ironic description of one of my informants: 'It was the time when they thought we were going back'. I am doing research in the context of increasing visibility of xenophobic political parties and of a stable community where most people acknowledge that they (and especially their children) are here to stay. There are generational changes too. The 'second generation', which, according to my material, has been taught that misbehaving creates trouble for all Latin Americans and migrants, struggles against racism(s) from within. In Andrea's words: 'They do not go around, as we do, asking for permission, being grateful.'

Ethnocentric policies/migration narratives

The group of Latin Americans that arrived in Sweden in the late 1970s had not only a model for how to change the world, but also a model of gender relations. Many women (and men) had experienced and fought for changes in gender relations before they confronted migration and exile:

> It was not easy to be in charge of groups with only men, but after a while they learned to respect me … I moved through the whole country [laughs] and I know what you are thinking … Yes, it was not so easy to do all that and then come back home and try to be a good wife … because in a sense that was also expected from you … And that is where I learned that my vocation as a wife was limited [laughs]. (Cecilia from Colombia)

Needless to say this (political) culture that defines courage as a masculine quality located in the male's testicles had a very ambivalent relation to women. Political status was within this culture established through a clear division of labour, where women were equal to men after they accomplished their female reproductive tasks, which were difficult and dangerous when struggling against military dictatorships. The specific violent repression of women prisoners and the centrality of discourses about 'the family' among the authoritarian regimes of the 1980s show that patriarchal order had, in serious ways. been challenged by women's practice in the resistance movements.

Research on gender and migration within the acculturation paradigm often focuses on the changes in gender relations *after* migration. This focus that constructs racialised subjects as social groups without history often marginalises and silences processes of gender struggle and gender confrontation that many migrant communities experience before migration (Westwood and Radicliffe, 1993). Especially for female political refugees, forced migration and exile is itself a product of their active participation in forms of action that challenged patriarchal norms. Nationalist ideologies (Billig, 1995) that understand gender equality as a Swedish cultural product are based not only on the closure to other ways of thinking about gender equality, but on the systematic resistance to learning from others, especially if those others are migrant women.

Migrant women at 'risk'

Mainstream discourses on political refugees and exile begin by recognising and underlining the traumatic experience of being forced to leave your 'own country' and confronted with a new and, as it is often mentioned, different 'culture'. Cultural theorist Paul Gilroy (1987) has suggested that there are strong links between popular notions of individuals' and groups' needs for roots and the ways through which the links between belonging and place have been understood in sociology. Social anthropologist Marita Eastmond (1998) comes to a similar conclusion based on her study of Bosnian refugees in Sweden. The author argues that research models and state policies of receiving societies often reflect essentialised notions of identity and cultural belonging that are very similar to nationalist discourses that claim a 'natural' relation between a people, a place and a culture.

The scientific representation of migrant women as different and in need of institutional support continues to guide state intervention in migrants' family lives through social workers, teachers and the health profession in Sweden. Central to these policies is the construction of 'other' cultures as patriarchal and in opposition to Swedish cultural values on gender.

Mainstream literature often portrays political refugees as males, and it is often assumed that women 'follow' their husbands or fathers into exile (Mousa, 1983; Knocke, 1995). Despite the growing literature that illuminates the central role Latin American women played in guerrilla movements and movements of social protest, discourses in the receiving countries create men as 'political' and redefine women as 'lacking' political identities. In her book *Socialarbetare och invandrare* (*Social workers and migrants*) (1984) Barbro Holmberg focuses specifically on the 'problem' of migration and exile. The author suggests that family crises may in part be explained by the differences between family forms in Sweden and in Latin America. Exile confronts men with terrible losses. They lose their roles as providers as well as their political identities. The representation of migrant women as 'only' mothers, economically dependent, politically passive, living in a 'traditional patriarchal culture', is at the core of these analyses grounded in ethnocentric assumptions about 'Third World Women'. An interesting paradox evolves between these hegemonic representations of migrant women as 'dependent' and migrant women's employment rates in Sweden. Not only was their participation in the labour market – up until the economic crisis of the 1990s – very high compared with 'Swedish' women, they also worked in male-dominated workplaces.

The same kind of argument, but moving from social work to psychology, is found in another book, *Att möta flyktningbarn och deras familjer* (*Meeting refugee children and their families*) (Angel and Hjern, 1992). Here, the refugee experience is described by the title 'Exile – the Never Ending Pain' and understood through the concept of post-traumatic stress syndrome. Needless to say, the recognition of trauma as a consequence of violent repression is central to the notion of an inclusive healthcare system. My argument aims at challenging psychological models that underestimate the role of sexism, homophobia and racism in an analysis of the mental health of political refugees and create practices that reinforce their pathologisation (Hollander, 1996).

In addition to these (hetero)sexual and normative notions of psychological health that create women as victims, the conceptualisation of divorce as a sign of crisis in migrant families, silencing women's gender struggles, developed in the mid-1980s. An illustration of this trend is the creation of several 'community projects' inspired by social-welfare bureaucrats and supported by psychological studies targeting 'families in crisis'.

For the Latin American community the high divorce rate has been often interpreted in terms of 'unstable family relations' and spoken of in terms of family breakdown. Family pedagogy was one of the multiple measures created by the authorities and upheld by the healthcare professions to support Latin Americans whose symptoms of the 'family crisis', according to the authorities, were illustrated not only by the divorce rates, but also by the 'sexual promiscuity' of many women and their tendency to practise masturbation. The family pedagogy project is alive in the collective memory in the south of Sweden as one of the first struggles that divided the community between those who upheld and even worked in the project and those who resisted it.

> The worst thing was that it was our people, our own people you know …
> I meet these idiots today… they were only jealous … we were young and
> even if we had children we allowed ourselves to search for new things …
> and now that most of us live in stable relationships they begin to divorce.
>
> – Do you remember what the project was about?
>
> – [Laughs] Actually no … offering therapy. I actually I do not know …
> but I do remember that we had a lot of fun organising against the project
> … we had a lot of meetings, we had a lot of free time those days; most of
> us were students. The project was about offering support because of what
> they thought the family breakdown was about … Thinking about it now,
> it was also strongly anti-women, describing women as promiscuous and so
> on … One must be stupid – first they gave us all the material possibilities
> of managing alone with your children and then when we … when many
> women chose this option, then they put money into preventing divorces
> … (Norma from Uruguay).

Discussing the family pedagogy project, another informant suggests that, despite gendered forms of racism, the inclusive policies of the Swedish women-friendly welfare state provided an arena for empowerment. Her reflection is interesting because she names some of the changes in public policy that have taken place over the past 10 years:

> It was different before, and it was good. Speaking about family pedagogy ... When I divorced, I went to the housing office and I got a new apartment after two months ... today your husband can beat you to death ... there is not even a list to put your name on if you want to apply for an apartment. (Maria from Chile)

While divorce in Swedish hegemonic social research literature is understood as a product of migrant women facing and 'discovering' modernity, it is important to underline that, due to armed conflict, internal migration and matrilineal households for a vast proportion of the population has been one way to organise and negotiate gender relations in Latin America's multiple modernities. Moreover, divorce patterns, especially in the vast majority of middle-class backgrounds, should also be understood in terms of the development of new family forms evolving in the context of late modernity.

Through all these texts and policies there is not one reference to the increasing visibility of political articulation of racism in the country, nor any reflections on the health profession as a vehicle of white ethnicity; nor any discussion of the conditions of segregation, unemployment and racist violence that these groups suffer. The projection (in psychoanalytical terms) of evil onto other places and other times is a central self-defence mechanism from within the healthcare system when it encounters racialised patients who suffer from mental disorders.

At the same time as women's sexuality was targeted, policies prioritising migrant men were introduced: 'You will not find one Latin American woman working in radio, or magazines or in an organisation, not one Latin American woman who makes a living through this immigrant thing' (Maria from Chile).

Through resource allocation, the Swedish welfare state has contributed to reinforcing patriarchal relations in migrant communities by emphasising men's roles as spokespersons for the community and by imbuing men with 'ethnic' authoritative knowledge. These policies towards creating migrant men as the main interlocutors with the welfare state have not only marginalised women from resources, it is one arena where the patriarchal racialised welfare state reinforces and even introduces (new forms of) male dominance in transnational communities.

Unpacking gendered racialised responses to the welfare state

An intersectional perspective not only grasps the diversity of women's relationship to the state in terms of differences between majority and minority populations, but also explores the differences between and within transnational diasporas in the same nation-state. It could be argued that migrant women's relationship to the welfare state differs from that of (migrant) men (Jones-Correa, 1998) and that, due to policy changes, newly arrived migrants' experiences differ from the experiences of those who arrived in the country earlier. It could also be argued that class, ethnicity, sexuality and generation are central clues to understanding the diversity of experiences vis-à-vis welfare-state policies.

Listen to this conversation:

– I tell you something, Diana. I stay here because I like it [laughs]

– Me too.

Why are both informant and researcher laughing like two teenagers coming home late? Because they are breaking a rule that demands that arguments about living outside one's nation must be constructed in ways that represent individuals as forced to live away from 'home' for structural reasons outside individual control, such as children who want to stay or an economic crisis and unemployment in the country of origin making a return impossible. This is not only a rule within community boundaries; it is also central to national Swedish discourses that demand representations of refugees as victims.

Two of my informants, Angelica, who defines herself as a black woman and comes from Uruguay, and Anastasia, with an indigenous background from Guatemala, belong to groups that have been targets of racism in Latin America. Ana defines herself as a lesbian.

They speak about how terrible things are … how they miss home … how racist the Swedish are. Well I am a Maya woman. These people had to come to Europe to discover racism (Anastasia from Guatemala).

I am a black woman. I was a black woman before migration. I know how things are. But most of the Latin Americans that came here are white: they did take time to understand that social workers did not see them as they saw themselves, that here in Sweden we are all the same: a problem, a migrant, a black skull (Angelica from Uruguay).

And I told him [her brother in Chile], if you think Sweden is a sick country because homosexuals can marry, well I am also sick, I am a lesbian and that country that you think is sick is where I live (Ana from Chile).

Maria Graciela, a 63-year-old working class-woman from Chile, illuminates the excluding narratives of nation and culture:

Sweden is home for the children, exile is a curse … to return is to give this curse to the children … And then you have all the others … those who did not like Sweden because they could not get a bloody private doctor, because they want to be called Señor again and not *jävla blatte* [derogatory 'black skull'].

A pattern emerging from my research is that most informants embodying unprivileged positions before migration interact with the Swedish welfare state very differently from those groups (of class-privileged 'white' heterosexual men) whose class positions have weakened through the racialisation process (George, 1997). The experience of migration and exile is an experience of loss, but the ways these losses are named, acted upon and (if possible) healed varied from different locations.

Motherwork: resisting victimisation

Not to be constructed as a victim in need of psychological help was a central survival strategy to protect families and children from the goodwill of the helping professions. The gossip that Swedish authorities took children away from parents was undoubtedly a central point of departure for resisting any acknowledgement of the need for help. Amalia is now in her late 40s, working as a nurse. She has three – as she calls them – nearly grown-up children. The biological father lives in another city, and Amalia has raised her children alone, even if she dislikes (even disapproves of) the term 'alone' because there are always people in her home.

– You know how they are … if they get in, you never get them out. Especially then when we were so … well, we did not know the language, no jobs … and they always smile and smile while they check if your damn toilet is clean. No, no and no. They offered me help when I divorced (we had been here for I believe eight months). But I said to my children, here at home we can scream, fight, whatever, but for them, we are OK … you have problems; you come to me, never to them. Time showed that I was right. Those who asked for help were not helped …

– What about your husband, the father of the children?

– Well, as most Latin American men … In Chile I thought that I had to take the children to meetings and so on because his meetings were more important than mine … Here in Sweden he continued to go to meetings … and well. As my mother says, thank God that I was here so I could leave him.

For the Latin American women I interviewed, protecting the children was considered a vital arena of political resistance. Amalia links good mothering to silence, almost to the point of no form of cooperation with the Swedish welfare state. She also illuminates these issues as a point of conflict within the community, and more particularly among women who are often divided in terms of what strategies are successful. Amalia's silence and the silence of many Latin American women must be understood as a strategy to resist pathologisation as traumatised mothers. Listen to Beatriz reflecting on her situation with a husband who was imprisoned in Uruguay during the first 10 years of her settlement in Sweden:

> They never understood. The first thing a social worker said to me was that I had to get on with my life. She said: 'For your son's sake. You have to learn to live a normal life. Go on. You cannot wait for him. It is not natural ... you need, here in Sweden we believe that you have the right to your own sexuality.' You know what they think about us. With the Virgin Mary on one side and the children on the other ... After all I had been through. It did not help to argue that it was a good time for me. To be alone for myself. I did a lot of things. Studied, took care of my son ... I could never have done those kinds of things if I stayed in Latin America: the day-care centre and the support to study. I did not wait for him like Penelope. I know what they think, that I am dependent ... but who says that sex is that important? ... After this first encounter I developed a stone face as a strategy ... Well, then I became a cleaner in a day-care centre and that was like being ... do you remember that film, *The invisible man*? (Beatriz from Uruguay)

Beatriz makes a connection between her silence as a migrant woman/mother and how she is silenced/made invisible as a migrant women/worker. There is a different dimension between the two events. In the first she is in her capacity as mother, an object of education for the social worker; she is too visible, too present as an object of institutional intervention. In the second event, in her capacity as cleaner, she experiences herself as totally unseen, a non-person. Women have also been constructed as having too many children and, as a result, a 'drain' on welfare provision:

> I have six children, but I always worked, I worked in Santiago before we left and continue to work here. I got a cleaning job in a day-care centre after three weeks. I worked shifts so that I could be with the children. So well, I have not been a burden to them. I wish you would write that. (Marta from Colombia).

> And then a nurse comes and asks me if I am religious [after her fourth pregnancy]. I did not understand at first, it was so bizarre ... and then she continued with a lecture about own decisions on body and sexuality ...

> I am sure she had been to some of these multi-culti courses and learned
> that Latin Americans are Catholics ... I got the lecture because I am a
> svartskalle.... (Betty from Argentina)

Very few racialised female subjects are employed in schools and day- and healthcare
centres in positions of authority. Latin American women often confront racialised
representations that neglect the strengths and resources of most migrant families.
The women in the narratives report confronting racist prejudices in the ascribed
identities given to their children by well-meaning social workers, teachers, nurses
and day-care workers, most of them women who are conceptualised as belonging
to the nation. How to mother in these conditions is one of the recurrent themes
in the narratives.

> I fetched her in the school; I took her by her hair ... she did not listen
> whatsoever. I told her that if she took drugs again I would kill her ... Those
> who did as the Swedish authorities said, their children went to hell. It is true
> that I screamed ... I was terrible with her, but she managed. I was able to
> support the two of them; I got help from the employment office and got a
> job. She is 26 now. (Alicia from Chile)

Alicia's story illustrates the contradictory ways in which the welfare state may be
experienced. While the interventions of social workers are resisted, the informant
is grateful for the 'help' (informant's word) provided by the employment office.
But my informant is not only saying that what she did was right, but that what
others (co-opted by what she considers the ways of the Swedish authorities) did
was wrong. While another informant of middle-class background can sound very
different, the two women draw the same conclusions:

> Children need a lot of support. You have to be there for them if you want
> them to manage with all this racism around. If you believe that the Swedish
> authorities are going to educate the children ... well the consequences are
> clear. Those who accepted what social workers and teachers said did not
> help their children ... Besides in Sweden it is not like in Latin America,
> like my sister who needs three jobs to manage ... here you have more time
> for the children. (Andrea from Chile)

In some of the narratives, women's resistance to being turned into objects, victims
or cases by others who define their needs is developed through a withdrawal
from the welfare-state services. The strong ambivalence many women feel towards
the Swedish authorities may make them withdraw from demanding services and
rights to which they are entitled:

> Well and then I thought I have to tell my story from prison to divorce to get some money, and then he is Swedish you know ... they like him more than they like me. I cannot handle that. No, I borrowed the money from a friend and ate canned soup all summer ... then somebody told me that it was my right to get the money. That I did not need to humiliate myself ... (Virginia from Ecuador)

In this narrative the informant experiences the social services not only as threatening, but also as supporting her ex-husband. She also relates how mortifying interactions with the Swedish authorities are. Most of the illustrations provided by my informants describe resistance as withdrawal. However, I have collected many narratives that emphasise a confrontational strategy. In the context of increasing racism there are no more 'innocent' questions about origins.

> I hated when my son's schoolteacher smiled and asked me 'where do you come from?' I usually answered from my mother's belly. Well you know they ask to make you feel like a stranger here. Otherwise you can pose the question back to them: Where do they come from? They always get embarrassed. (Andrea from Chile)

> And then the teacher who tells her that she is as good as the Swedish pupils in the Swedish language ... I got so angry ... it was so embarrassing for her. You know that the children do not want us to make trouble, but I was forced to tell her that she was a racist. My daughter is born in Sweden and goes to school in this country. I hate their paternalism. And I told her. (Norma from El Salvador)

Feminist sociologist Patricia Hill Collins (1998) provides an understanding of maternal work, underlining that migrant women, unlike white middle-class mothers, cannot take the survival of their children for granted. The author illuminates women's activity of helping children to develop a sense of self in a society whose dominant culture provides a negative representation of his/her group. My research unveils the ways in which migrant women experience gendered racism through their interaction with the welfare state in their capacity as mothers and uncovers the tension between being conceptualised as both a citizen and an essentialised other.

Reflections

With women's narratives as my point of departure, I have tried to grasp the specificities of the Swedish race formation where a regime of welfare nationalism produces discourses of belonging and boundaries against the other through a narrative where national pride is symbolised in the welfare system. Over the last

10 years and in the context of visible racist articulation and increasing mobilisation of racialised citizens, as well as serious cuts in the welfare system, 'gender equality' has developed as the central ethnic signifier of national belonging and the most important boundary between 'us' and 'them'.

Women's narratives illuminate the centrality of gender analysis in exploring the differences between migrant men and women in relation to the Swedish welfare state. The material emerging from my study grasps a strong ambivalence in the women's relationship with the Swedish welfare state. While they had to confront on a daily basis the discriminatory practices at the core of the Swedish ethnic and gender regimes, they also enjoyed many of the inclusive 'women-friendly' policies. In my view, these policies have been central in transforming gender relations in ways that, to a certain extent, empower women in the Latin American diaspora in Sweden.

Contrary to what is commonly believed, the women I interviewed did not emphasise the cultural differences between Latin America and Sweden in their narratives. They often focused on the gendered racism of the Swedish welfare state and the forms of everyday racism they experienced. Central to the narratives is a resistance to being conceptualised as others, expressed for these women in discourses of victimisation and incommensurable cultural differences. Contrary to what is commonly believed, the struggle against gender hierarchies was central to the women's lives before migration, and these struggles are important clues to understanding both their migration patterns and settlement in Sweden. Women's narratives illuminate their resistance towards discourses that define the experience of living outside the country of origin as only fracturing and traumatic, and their highly ambivalent relationship to discourses of national belonging and essentialised forms of ethnicity.

Bibliography

Alinia, M. (2004) *Spaces of Diasporas: Kurdish identities, experiences of otherness and politics of belonging*, Gothenburg: Department of Sociology, Gothenburg University.

Ålund, A. and Schierup, C.-U. (1991) *Paradoxes of Multiculturalism*, Addershot: Avebury.

Angel, B. and Hjern, A.(1993) *Att möta flyktingbarn och deras familjer*, Lund: Studentlitteratur.

Anthias, F. and Yuval Davis, N. (1992) *Racialised Boundaries*, London: Routledge.

Billig, M. (1995) *Banal Nationalism*, London: Sage.

Brah, A. (1996) *Cartographies of Diaspora. Contesting identities*, London: Routledge.

Bredström, A. (2002) 'Maskulinitet och kamp om nationella arena', in P. de los Reyes, J. Molina and D. Mulinari (eds) *Maktens (o)lika förklädnader*, Stockholm: Atlas, pp 182-207.

Castles, S. and Miller, M. (1993) *The Age of Migration*, London: Macmillan.

Clark, J. (2004) *Changing Welfare, Changing States. New directions in social policy*, London: Sage Publications.

Cohen, A. (1985) *The Symbolic Construction of a Community*, London: Routledge.

Collins, P.H. (1998) 'It's all in the family: Intersections of gender, race and nation', *Hypatia*, vol 13, no 1, 62–82.

Dahl, U. (2005) 'Scener ur ett äktenskap: jämställdhet och heteronormativitet', in D. Kulick (ed) *Queersverige*, Stockholm: Natur och Kultur, pp 48–71.

de los Reyes, P. and Molina, I. (2002) 'Kalla mörkret natt. Kön, klass och etnicitet i det postkoloniala Sverige', in P. de los Reyes, I. Molina and D. Mulinari (eds), *Maktens (o)lika förklädnader*, Stockholm: Atlas, 2002, pp 295–317.

de los Reyes, P. and Mulinari, D. (2004) *Intersektionalitet, kritiska reflektioner över (o)jämlikhetens landskap*, Malmö: Liber.

Eastmond, M. (1998) 'Nationalist Discourses and the Construction of Difference. Bosnian Muslim refugees in Sweden', *Journal of Refugee Studies*, vol 11, no 2, pp 160–81.

Eriksson, M. (2003) *I skuggan av Pappa: familjerätten och hantering av fäders våld*, Polen: Stehag Gondolin.

Essed, P. (1991) *Understanding Everyday Racism,* Series on Race and Ethnic Relations, vol 2, London: Sage.

George, R. (1997) 'From Expatriate Aristocrat till Immigrant Nobody. South Asian racial strategies in the southern California context', *Diaspora*, vol 6, pp 283–303.

Gilroy, P. (1987) *There ain't no black in the Union Jack*, London: Hutchinson.

Hollander, N. (1996) 'The Gendering of Human Rights. Women and the Latin American terrorist state', *Feminist Studies*, vol 22, pp 41–80.

Holmberg, B. (1984) *Social Arbetare och Invandrare*, Stockholm: Liber.

Jones-Correa, M. (1998) 'Different Paths: Gender, migration and political participation', *International Migration Review*, vol 32, no 2, pp 327–49.

Knocke, W. (1995) 'Migrant and Ethnic Minority Women. The effects of gender-neutral legislation in the European community', *Social Politics*, vol 2, pp 225–38.

Leiva, M. (1996) *Latinoamericanos en Suecia*, Uppsala: Uppsala Multiethnic Press.

Lewis, G. (2000) *'Race', Gender, Social Welfare: Encounters in a postcolonial society*, Cambridge: Polity Press.

Lindqvist, B. (1991) *Drömmar och vardag i Exil. Om chilenska flyktingar kulturella strategier*, Stockholm: Carlsson.

Lundberg, S. (1989) *Flyktingskap. Latinamerikaner i Exil i Sverige och Västeuropa*, Lund: Arkiv.

Mousa, H. (1983) *Storm and Sanctuary. The journey of Ethiopian and Eritrean women refugees*, Ontario: Artemis Enterprise.

Mulinari, D. (2001) 'Race/Ethnicity in a Nordic Context: A Reflection from the Swedish Borderlands', in A. Johansson (ed) *Svensk genusforskning i världen: globala perspektiv i svensk genusforkning och svensk genusforskning i ett globalt perspektiv*, Örebro: Sekretariatet för Genusforskning, pp 6–24.

Mulinari, D. and Neergaard, A. (2004) *Den nya svenska arbetarklassen: rasifierade arbetares kamp inom facket*, Umeå: Borea.

Olsson, E. (1997) 'Att leva nära en flygplats. Chilenska migranter mellan hemland och värdland', *Socialvetenskapliga Tidskrift*, vol 4, no 1, pp 43–62.

Pontusson, J. (1992) *The Limits of Social Democracy, Investment Politics in Sweden*, Ithaca: Cornell University Press.

Rabo, A. (1997) 'Free to make the right choice? Gender equality policy in post-welfare Sweden', in C. Shore and S. Wright (eds) *Anthropology of Policy. Critical perspectives on governance and power*, London and New York: Routledge, pp 107–35.

Räthzel, N. (1997) 'Gender and Racism in Discourse', in R. Wodak (ed) *Gender and Discourse*, Sage: London, pp 57–80.

Rönnblom, M., Tollin, K. and Mattson, Å. (1998) *Jämställdhet retorik och praktik*, Umeå: Länstyrelsen.

Sawyer, L. (2000) *Black and Swedish: Racialisation and the cultural politics of belonging in Stockholm, Sweden*, Ann Arbor, MI: UMI.

SOU 2005:56. *Det blågula glashuset. Strukturell diskriminering i Sverige*.

SOU 2005:69. *Sverige inifrån. Röster om etnisk diskriminering*.

Westwood, S. and Radicliffe, R. (eds) (1993) *VIVA. Women and popular protest in Latin America*, London: Routledge.

TEN

Young women's attitudes towards feminism and gender equality

Ann-Dorte Christensen

Introduction

For young Scandinavian women, certain central elements in the Scandinavian welfare states have been part of their upbringing – for example, equal opportunity policy and the role of public provision in day-care institutions – and they therefore expect equal citizenship rights for men and women. Gender and equality have been hotly debated topics throughout the lifetime of young Scandinavian women.

Although the young generation did not live through the female political mobilisation that followed the second wave of feminism from the 1960s through the 1980s, feminism has had an effect on young women's gender-identity formation. Most of their mothers belong to the generation of women who were the driving force in the New Women's Movement, and although the mothers may not have participated actively in the movement, they were influenced by the increased female political radicalisation and mobilisation and by the equality debates and changes that followed in the wake of the movement. In Denmark, the label 'the daughters of the Redstocking Movement' symbolises the position young women are expected to have in relation to the new feminist movement (Sværke, 2005). Obviously, not all mothers are feminists, but it is still a fair assumption that parents as well as young people have felt the impact of the radical changes in gender relations brought about by the New Women's Movement and later institutionalised to varying degrees in the Scandinavian welfare states. These changes and influences constitute a dynamic interplay between general structural changes and new conditions and frameworks for individual subjectivity and (gender) identity work.

But what do contemporary young women think about feminism and equality? What are their dreams and visions for the future? How do they see themselves in relation to their future work life, perhaps combined with family and children? These are some of the questions that will be discussed in this chapter. The purpose is to identify young women's subject positions and their creation of gender identities by analysing (1) their attitudes towards feminism, and (2) their attitudes towards some key issues associated with gender equality in the Scandinavian welfare states. First of all, however, I want to introduce my approach, some key issues and the empirical data on which the analysis is based.

Approach, concepts and empirical data

The overall key concept is identity, specifically gender identity. My approach to the concept of identity is social constructivist and process oriented in the sense that I see identity not as something we 'have' or 'get', but as something we 'do'. We can work with identity at many levels. From a macro-oriented perspective we can narrow down different groups' relations with global, national or local communities; from a meso-oriented perspective we can analyse collective identity processes in an organisation or a social movement, or we can study identity formation in relation to significant processes at the subject level, and in relation to complexity and changes in lived experiences. Here the latter level is applied with the young women's subject positions and construction of gender identity as point of departure. I thus accept the structural framework and the specific Scandinavian context as discussed in other chapters in this book. My analysis concentrates on the meanings of gender in the young women's lived lives (1) in relation to contemporary feminist movements/debates, and (2) in relation to gender-equality policies in the Scandinavian welfare states.

The general approach is the basic conditions for identity formation as defined by modernity. I thus expect that everybody is (more or less) affected by detraditionalisation, by individualisation and by the demand for reflexivity in relation to our personal life biographies. According to Giddens (self-) identity in late modernity is a reflexive process that consists of maintaining a cohesive but constantly revised biographical self-narrative where we not only are able to make choices, we are forced to do so (Giddens, 1991).

Stuart Hall sees identities as more dislocated and fragmented than Giddens does. He deconstructs essentialist conceptions of identity (such as gender and race) and instead emphasises their dual dimension: an individual dimension that can be described as *a process of becoming*. In this dimension, identity is a construction of the individual subject, but each individual may have multiple identity positions, which may be both contradictory and overlapping. The collective dimension can be described as *a process of belonging*. This dimension emphasises belonging and the sense of belonging to/being associated with communities. Accordingly, the inclusion/exclusion issue also belongs in this dimension (Hall, 1991, 1996; Christensen, 2003).

As a principal element in subjectivity, gender is not static, and women and men are not a group with common interests and values. Rather, gender is constantly being created and maintained through processes where gender is communicated and 'done' in institutions, in social praxis and in the individual person's gender-identity work (West and Zimmerman, 1987; Butler, 1994). (Gender) identities can be seen as processes consisting of categorisations created at an individual and at a collective level through affiliations with groups. A part of individual identity work is to assert distance and dis-identification with other individuals, groups, movements, institutions and so on (Skeggs, 1997).

If we look at modernity's significance for identity construction among contemporary young people more specifically, Thomas Ziehe proposes a distinction between the different stages of modernity in relation to its impact on identity construction. He describes the young people of today as belonging to a second generation of culturally liberated, and thus highlights the generational difference in terms of individualisation and rebellion. Today, many young people have parents, teachers and so on who already *are* culturally liberated, for example because they have broken with traditional gender notions and practices. According to Ziehe, many of these parents have exploited the multitude of opportunities that opened up via detraditionalisation. A large part of this process was a rebellion against parents, so today's youth is facing a fundamentally different process. Ziehe also stresses that detraditionalisation for the parents was part of a rebellion, but for young people today it has become a standard of normalcy. In other words, 'rebelling' takes on a totally different meaning if it is expected of you (Ziehe, 1998a, 1998b, 2001).

The question is, however, whether the post-/late modern understandings overemphasise the disintegration of identities and underemphasise how slowly structures and identities change. Beverley Skeggs, for instance, has criticised Giddens' interpretation of the way individuals reflexively construct their identities. According to Skeggs, Giddens is departing from a class perspective, and she argues that what Giddens (together with Ulrich Beck) 'read as the decline of class culture and the rise of individualisation ... would be better understood as a shift from working-class to middle-class modes of individualisation, but classed, nonetheless' (Skeggs, 2004, p 52). I agree with Skeggs that class is absent in Giddens' perspective, and there is no doubt that the theories of modernity overlook the trends – unfolding alongside the disintegration – towards preservation of tradition and certain social representations and inequalities (Larsen, 2000; Prieur, 2002). Not only in relation to class, but more generally you can ask whether the disintegration of identity positions is really that pronounced; and whether the 'new' identity constructions really offer that many choices.

In my opinion, the actual impact of the struggle between tradition and renewal is an open and empirical question, which must be analysed in a dynamic perspective. The main question is how gender intersects with other differentiating categories such as class, ethnicity, generation, race and sexuality. The increasing focus on the concept of intersectionality in feminist research expresses the ambition to create such a dynamic and multiple approach. 'As opposed to examining gender, race, class, and nation, as separate systems of oppression, intersectionality explores how these systems mutually construct one another' (Collins, 1998, p 63). In this chapter, which focuses on young Danish women, not all categories of an intersectional analysis are considered. It is the intersection between gender and generation that is in focus but it is important to emphasise that it is seen from the perspective of the white middle class.[1]

The *empirical foundation* of this article consists of two qualitative interview studies of young Danish women aged 20–28.[2] One was carried out in 2002 as part of my project for the Danish Democracy and Power Study; the other is a pilot study from 2004 of political identities and gender identities in three generations, in which I cooperated with Mette Tobiasen. For the 2002 study 14 young women were interviewed, six of them politically active, eight not politically active (Christensen, 2003). The 2004 pilot study includes three focus-group interviews with three different generations: the crisis generation, the 1968 generation and the 1990s generation. Three women and three men participated in the latter group (Christensen and Tobiasen, 2007). In both studies the young people belong to the so-called 1990s generation, born between 1975 and 1983 and today aged 20–28. They both focus on resourceful young people enrolled in medium- or long-term higher education. The young people in the 2004 study are students at Aalborg University. In the 2002 study the participants who reside in Aalborg are students at either Aalborg Teacher Training College or Aalborg University. The other participants in the 2002 study live in the Nørrebro neighbourhood in Copenhagen and are all members of the left-wing movement. The analysis primarily concentrates on the young students from Aalborg, but the radical left-wing women's feminist positions are included in a comparison with other feminist positions. With 17 respondents the intention is not to make empirical generalisations about young Danish women's gendered identities but, through in-depth analysis, to grasp and illustrate some of the dilemmas and ambivalences in young women's constructions of gender identities.

Attitudes towards feminism and feminist movements

With public and often provocative actions, the New Women's Movement paved the way for a massive gender-political public awareness. In the Scandinavian countries, it was formed in the 1970s, but was replaced by a more subdued debate about gender equality in the 1980s. The new Scandinavian women's movements insisted – to varying degrees – on having influence on government gender-equality policies, and the movements did play a great role – directly or indirectly – in the subsequent institutionalisation of gender-equality legislation and agencies. It is also to their credit that gender equality became a major element in society's political value orientation (Dahlerup, 1998; Christensen and Siim, 2001).

Towards the end of the 1990s, New Feminism made its entry with new (young) actors and new topics. In a diachronic perspective, New Feminism has been designated as the third wave of feminism. This emphasises the relation to other key movements, namely the first wave of feminism around the end of the nineteenth century and the second wave of feminism from the 1960s to 1980s (Christensen et al, 2004; Sværke, 2004). Just as the New Women's Movement, New Feminism is primarily driven by intellectual women. But whereas the former emphasised public actions and, to some extent, alliances with working-class women, New Feminism remains an intellectual discourse, primarily based in metropolitan areas and a few large cities. Compared with the number of participants, the media impact has been enormous. However, it is debatable whether it is fair to call New Feminism a social movement – like the first and second waves of feminism – considering the relatively limited activity and collective organisation (Fiig, 2003, see also the next chapter in this volume).

Below I will discuss my respondents' attitudes towards feminist movements and to feminism as such. I will especially focus on the significance they attach to feminism, and equality in the construction of gender identities.

Although the Scandinavian countries have many things in common, in terms of feminist movements and the progress in gender-equality policies, they differ significantly in some areas. As the empirical basis of this chapter is young Danish women, I want to emphasise that several studies have shown that, since the mid-1980s, gender policies have been more anonymous and more antagonistic in the Danish public sphere than in the Norwegian and the Swedish (Bergqvist et al, 1999; Fiig, 2003). Likewise, the label 'feminism' is currently more negatively loaded in Denmark than in the other Scandinavian countries. For example, in a comparative study of equality concepts in Denmark and Sweden, Drude Dahlerup shows that although the legislation in the two countries is basically similar, the debates differ significantly. In Sweden the predominant attitude is that equality is far from achieved, and most political parties promote themselves as feminist. In Denmark the debate is much more ambiguous and ambivalent, and the Danish parties focus very little on equality and do not see themselves as feminist (Dahlerup, 2002). However, I agree with Harriet Bjerrum Nielsen that it makes sense to describe young women as 'made in Scandinavia', primarily because the detraditionalisation associated with gender in a comparative perspective has been relatively prevalent here (Nielsen, 2004).

Left-radical feminists

For *the young left-radical women*, who are declared feminists and a part of one of the feminist groups in the radical left-wing movement in Copenhagen, it is not a question of feminism or not, but rather of which segments of the feminist movements they identify with. They have extensive knowledge of feminist discourses, and they use both the New Women's Movement (also called the Danish Redstockings from the 1970s) and New Feminism (primarily related to a media debate among young middle-class feminists in the 1990s) as central identification markers – positive identification in relation to the Redstockings, dis-identification[3] in relation to the New Feminists.

The reason for the positive identification with the Redstockings is probably that the left-radical feminists' attitudes have many things in common with the feminism of the 1970s. They emphasise the link between left-wing attitudes and feminism, sisterhood and autonomous women's organisations (Dahlerup, 1998; Christensen, 2003).

Nina, one of the left-radical feminists, points out that she (unlike many other young women today, including New Feminists) does not feel a need to distance herself from the Redstockings. She finds that the New Feminists have helped construct so many myths about Redstockings and feminists, for example that they don't like sex, that they are ugly and wear ugly clothes. Nina uses her positive identification with the Redstockings as a provocation – as a kind of deviant position (in relation to other young women).

> We [the women in the radical left-wing movement] do not need to distance ourselves from the Redstockings. We need to say: We can use these experiences; these we can't use ... We started March 8 by saying: Yes, we are hopelessly old-fashioned and our tits are sagging, we're unshaved and don't wear make-up and all those things. Sure – we're all those things a big part of the way! We don't need to distance ourselves from it. But we can also be the opposite. (Nina)

The left-radical feminists also criticise the New Feminists for ignoring class. They find that this form of feminism represents well-off feminists who lack solidarity with other women and cultural representations far from 'normal women's' everyday lives.

Not feminists

In contrast to the left-radical feminists, the respondents who live in Aalborg and are not members of any feminist groups have extremely limited knowledge of New Feminism. It is surprising that the awareness of New Feminism is so limited among these young students, and it demonstrates how the phenomenon has been isolated to specific groups and urban areas, in a Danish context.

In comparison, most of the respondents have clear opinions about the Redstocking Movement, which they associate with feminism. The respondents in both 2002 and 2004 stress that the New Women's Movement may have been justified 'back then', but that it is 'totally absurd today'. The women clearly take a stand against a predefined discourse – both at a general level and as something that might be useful in their own gender identity work. For example, Line finds that the Redstocking Movement exaggerated and came across too much as a 'let's take off our bra movement. It gets more and more ridiculous when you think about the Redstockings because now it seems hysterical somehow. It didn't before, absolutely not, but when you think about it, and if it happened today, it would be totally absurd.'

In addition to using the terms 'ridiculous' and 'hysterical', they also describe Redstockings as angry women who hate men (2002, 2004). But dis-identification is not only associated with the women's movement. Studies show that the young women do not see themselves as feminists; rather, they see feminism as a contrast to the part of their gender-identity work that concerns the right to market femininity, have lovers and the right to be different.

In an analysis of young English working-class women, Beverley Skeggs shows how this group also has constructed a negative image of feminists as madwomen, angry, lesbian, bra-burning man haters. Here too, feminism is a negative identity marker that contrasts with modern femininity and the desire to build respectability (Skeggs, 1997, p 143). However, the negative image of feminists does *not* mean that the young women do not value gender equality. Skeggs sees this as an expression that feminism is not universal, but contextual; that it has been formulated from specific class positions, and that there has basically been a gap between the theory, which explains women's lives, and the experience of living women's lives. The young working-class women do not recognise themselves in the feminist discourse (in England), which has primarily been formulated by (white) intellectual women. However, they feel a strong identification with, for instance, the women's political work that was done in connection with a specific mining strike in their home-town (Skeggs, 1997).

Despite the large differences between young English working-class women and Danish students, Beverley Skeggs makes an important point in her distinction between attitudes towards feminism and attitudes towards gender equality. Along the same line, Pamela Aronson is critical towards uniform definitions of feminism that ignore generational differences. She explores young American women's attitudes towards feminism in relation to social background, and one of her findings is that, whether or not young women call themselves feminists, they support feminist goals (2003).

The findings in my investigations indicate the same tendencies. It seems that, to young women who do not subscribe to a specific feminist position, feminism is, in a broad sense, a mainly negative identification marker. It is primarily associated with the second wave of feminism; it represents a stereotypical perception of women that belongs to a specific era, which does not match the substance that body and femininity represent in modern women's identity. However, as in Aronson's American study, this negative perception of feminism is not associated with attitudes towards gender equality. Let us take a closer look at this.

Experiences and attitudes towards gender equality

Although the young Danish middle-class women do not think of themselves as feminists, they do see great inequality between women and men. They favour more equality and are very aware of unequal pay and a pronounced gender-based hierarchy in the labour market.

Experiences with gender inequality

The respondents have personally experienced gender inequality in childhood and adolescence, in the educational system and in social relations, where they have experienced gender as a barrier to personal autonomy and development. Likewise, the young women are certain that they will encounter inequality and unequal pay in a future labour market.

Most of the women come from families – mostly middle and/or working class – with limited detraditionalisation in terms of gender. A couple of the mothers stayed at home while the children were small and in most of the families the mothers were responsible for cooking and other chores. Although the traditional division of labour was under debate, none of the families are negotiation families where that topic was debated regularly. With few exceptions, the daughters think that their parents were happy with the gendered division of labour in the family, and they do not see the issue as problematic. Some of the young women talk about how they had to do more housework than their brothers, and at the same time the parents were more protective of their daughters than of their sons, which meant that the boys 'could do more' than the girls. The women who experienced gender differences in their upbringing felt that they were extremely unfair, and they have protested vigorously against them.

The young women generally feel that in order to change gender inequalities, you have to do something about it yourself. They do not assign much significance to collective strategies and policies for greater gender balance in the labour market or in politics. The reason they are critical of the collective idea is that they basically see inequality and oppression as personal, individual problems, and collective strategies counteract the individualisation they strive for.

The young women are thus aware of gender inequalities and strive for more gender equality. However, it is not, unlike in previous generations, linked to a collective project. Rather, it is integrated in the reflexive life planning as a central element in the individual woman's gender identity project. Some might say – seen from the dominant conception of equality – that there is an inherent contradiction between wanting more equality and insisting on free, individual and reflexive choices. If we look more closely at what the young women's notions of equality contain, it is clear that the ideals of gender equality are formulated in a different way and have another meaning than what we know from the general Scandinavian equality discourse. Below, I will describe these meanings in more detail with specific emphasis on the young women's notions of equality in terms of the work/family relation.

Equality paradoxes

In their Norwegian three-generation study, Harriet Bjerrum Nielsen and Monica Rudberg (2000, 2006) emphasise that although young Norwegian women do not think of themselves as feminists, the notion of equality has had a great impact. The level of involvement in equality policy differs, however, and the authors point out several differences in the young women's perception of equality.

Monica Rudberg defines three groups:

1. A group of young women who are strong advocates of equality, typically from a single-mum home or from middle-class homes where the parents were equal.
2. A group that also favours equality, but does not think it should be exaggerated because it hurts femininity and the 'natural' differences, which do 'after all' exist. This group is typically from middle-class homes with a traditional division of labour.
3. A group that strongly favours equality in the labour market, but not at home (for example, wanting a 'strong man' to handle things that women can't do). This schism between equality at work and at home is only found among young women from the lower middle class and working class, also if they grew up with equality at home (Rudberg, 2003, p 293).

Although the Danish material does not allow such a detailed categorisation or linking of political attitudes towards equality to the young women's class background, there are clear parallels. I have not identified the strong ideological relation to the equality project among the young female students in Aalborg, but there are clear similarities with the second and third position, which I will discuss below.

Basically, I find that the young women's expectations as to their future work and family life are driven by autonomy, individualisation and reflexivity. The young women express their quest for autonomy by emphasising that it is important to be independent of a male main provider and to make their own money. At the same time, however, they reject the pronounced focus on career, which they see represented by various well-educated women. It is clear that they want to combine family and work in a way that *differs* from the dominant equality political praxis. It is not a praxis they have encountered very much among their mothers, but rather a praxis they find rooted in a specific equality political discourse.

Christensen and Tobiasen (2007) compare the young women's attitudes towards work and family with those of the 1968 generation, and there is a remarkable difference in the way the two generations talk about gender relations in the family. Compared with the young women, more respondents from the 1968 generation have created negotiation families, where making agreements and hotly debating division of chores and childcare are important elements in family life. However, they also emphasised what the respondents describe as competent (and shared) parenthood.

When the young women from the 1990s generation talk about their future families, it is clear that the general tendencies towards increasing individualisation have also made their mark on their notions of family. Compared to the 1968 generation, it is much less a 'we project' and much more a 'me project'. The centre of gravity is the significance each woman expects the family to have in her own reflexive life planning. Expectations and thoughts about a future partner play a limited role, and there are no expectations regarding a future provider. Instead, the reflexive planning focuses on how the young women are personally responsible for combining family, children and career in a satisfactory everyday life. Anne says:

> It's not THAT important for me to find a super job. I don't want to work 60 hours a week. For me, some other things are more important, far more important ... I also want a family. And I don't think I could be a competent mother if I worked 60 hours a week. I just wouldn't do that to a child ... So it is a choice I've made (Interview with Anne, 2006, p 67)

Note that Anne does not talk about competent parenthood, but about being a competent mother. Like the other young respondents, her reflexive considerations about a future family are basically individual and formulated in opposition to the expectations about a career as the biggest driving force for well-educated young women. For example, several of the women point out that they 'are too lazy' for a top position; that they also want time to take care of their children and bake a cake; that they want to make their own money, but that they do not need a giant level of consumption. In those cases where a relationship with a partner is mentioned, it is emphasised that the time at home under no circumstances will be spent servicing him.

It is important to notice that the emphasis on individuality certainly appears stronger because the young women are taking about ideals and visions for the future. At the same time they are talking from the horizon of their present situation as students without children – none of them are married; some of them are living with a boyfriend.

The right to family focus

One of the main results from the 2002 study is that the respondents emphasise the right to put greater focus on the family than what they see among women in the types of jobs they are expected to take after their studies. The focus on family is not so much directed at house chores, but at childcare. Therefore it does not represent a traditional housewife role, but instead what the young women describe as the joy of being a woman, and revised to highlight femininity and gender differences. They insist that the family focus can be combined with a good job, but they also emphasise that breaking with oppressive gender praxis – in the family or at work – is something 'you have to do yourself' (Christensen, 2003, p 101). This position is practically identical to position (2) in the Norwegian material. Overall, the analysis shows that autonomy, self-determination and reflexivity play a great role in the young women's identity work. This is based on a high degree of individualisation where neither men, nor the state nor predefined equality policies decide how the women live their lives. If they feel like prioritising children higher than they assume that, for example, the Redstockings did in the 1970s, they insist on their right to do so. It is important for them that work/career is not everything, and they expect family, and especially children, to play a large role. However, it is unclear what role a partner will be assigned in their life planning.

The young women are aware of the general gender inequalities in society and of the injustices they encounter every day in the form of stereotyping and oppressive constructions of women and men. In that sense there may be an inherent contradiction between, on the one hand, the gender-based inequalities that are anchored in social structures and in subjective orientations, and on the other hand, the belief that equality is created through free choice. I presume that the distinction between gendered structures and free choices is quite easy to maintain in their present situation as students (without children), whereas it will be more difficult if they will have to create an everyday life based on both work/career and children/family. It is an open question how such changes will influence their strong endeavours for autonomy and the high degree of individualisation.

Anyhow, the equality paradoxes that are anchored in the young women's gender identities raise important questions regarding central elements of the equality political pillars in the Scandinavian welfare states. I will here discuss one of them, namely the relationship between the public and the private sphere.

Rethinking the public–private split?

One of the fundamental elements in the construction of the Scandinavian welfare and equality models is removing the gendered split between the private and the public (Siim, 1988; Borchorst and Siim, 2002). With their increasing focus on the family, the young women challenge this basic idea. For the young women, the family focus has positive connotations: a place where you can construct a competent motherhood; where femininity and gender differences can unfold; where you can be 'lazy' and creative. For previous generations of women, the responsibility for the family was a barrier between them and public life. For young women today, it is almost the opposite: career and work can become a barrier between them and family life. The family the young women imagine is primarily constructed with them as breadwinners and care providers. Thoughts about a partner do not take up much room, and it is obvious that the women do not expect to repeat their mothers' cook and maid services.

Nielsen and Rudberg found a similar trend in the Norwegian data. They highlight the change in the perception of the home, which for the young women who also expect to participate in public life has taken on a new meaning for them: 'Whereas the feminists of the mothers' generation claimed the private to be political, we see a tendency by the daughters to reinstall the border between private and public, but to dismiss the gendered structure. Also, women, as well as men, need rest and emotional support these days' (Nielsen, 2004, p 19; see also Rudberg, 2003).

Many feminists probably see this new focus on family and home as a backlash and a return to traditional gender divisions – and I agree that the risk is lurking right around the corner. However, I want to emphasise that the young women's visions of how to do family differ qualitatively from previous generations. Although they may be willing to reinstall the border between private and public, they have not reinstalled the border between a male main provider and a female care provider, which was the foundation of the gendered public–private split. Instead, the young women have reinvented the family as an element of their own endeavours for autonomy and individualisation – and here the men play a very limited role.

Conclusion

Gender researchers have always found the distinction between feminism and equality important – and the young women of today clearly confirm that this distinction is necessary. To young women who do not subscribe to, for instance, New Feminism or left-radical feminism, the concepts of 'feminism' and 'feminist' are highly negative identification markers. They are associated with a specific form of feminism from a specific period that is formulated in sharp contrast to the young women's self-image and the way gender, body and femininity are manifested in their identity construction. The analysis emphasises that feminism is not a universal, but rather a contextual concept and that certain feminist notions will be formulated from different social positions, typically (white) middle class or – as in this case – a certain generation, that is, the generation associated with the second wave of feminism.

Although the majority of the young women certainly are not feminists, they are fully aware of the lack of equality between women and men today. They have personally experienced gender differences in their upbringing, in the educational system, and they expect to encounter gender hierarchies and unequal pay in the labour market. In that way, their identification of inequality in the public space is very strong, and the areas that are highlighted in many ways belong to the common equality political areas that were formulated from the 1960s on in the Scandinavian countries. However, the young women have in no way taken over their 'mothers'' equality project – and there are several reasons for that.

First and foremost, the young women's approach to equality policy is characterised by individualisation and their own reflexive life planning. Specifically, this means that any changes must come from oneself. They do not see collective strategies as important; they do not see themselves in a collective context; and they have no affiliation with any of the collective movements with a historic or current focus on gender equality. Rather, they fear that collective decisions may limit their individual freedom.

In my analysis, I focus on the young women's expectations of the relationship between work and family, and the key words are here autonomy and individualisation. It is important for the women to be independent of a male breadwinner and make their own money, but they also stress that they do not want to just take over 'well-educated women's career-oriented praxis'. For them the focus on family is not just a necessary 'evil', but rather a 'haven' where you have the right to be feminine, lazy and creative. In these visions of a new balance between work and family, a partner/spouse only plays a small role – perhaps because binding love relations can be seen as a limitation to autonomy. In contrast, children play a large role and the expression 'competent motherhood' (not parenthood) is a concise symbol of the (individualised) meaning that is also assigned to parenthood in the young women's life planning.

Do young people question the public–private split, which was a key issue in the development in the woman-friendly Scandinavian welfare states? It is difficult to give an unequivocal answer, but it appears that they have a need to rethink the public–private split. They find it important to reinstall the border between private and public; they emphasise that exaggerated focus on career and work can become a barrier to family life, and finally they do not take the dual-provider model for granted, but emphasise women's autonomy and the opportunity to provide for oneself and one's children.

This chapter points out several paradoxes and contradictions in the young women's notions of equality, for instance between their strong awareness of gender inequalities and the emphasis on individual freedom. Their rethinking of work/family and public/private also harbours some warning signs in terms of equality. As I have emphasised, the results are based on investigations of young, white women who are students without children. And it is easy for 'the mothers from the Redstocking generation' to criticise, encourage caution and to say: 'Just wait, when they have children everything will be different, and they will realise how the conditions for women's lives are!'

But anyhow, if we want a dialogue between generations, we have to be more constructive in our attitude towards the visions of equality that are being formulated. I am thinking especially of the strong endeavours for autonomy and the high degree of individualisation, which means that neither men, the state nor predefined equality discourses will make decisions on their behalf. It is interesting that the focus on family is not associated with a male main provider. And it would therefore be wrong to interpret it exclusively as a retraditionalisation in the form of a return to earlier gender structures. Finally, it is noteworthy that the young women of today are so critical of the strong focus on work life, which they feel has been the foundation of the Scandinavian equality policy and of the lives of their mothers.

Notes

[1] For more information about the current debate on the concept of intersectionality in Scandinavia, see also Lykke (2003), Staunæs (2003), de los Reyes and Mulinari (2005), Mørck (2005).

[2] By 'young' I do not mean teenagers, but so-called 'young adults' over 20. I chose these rather 'old' youths, because they have more life experiences, for example with boyfriends/girlfriends; most live away from home; and they have a minimum of political experiences (for example, as voters). Another reason is the assumption that at this stage in life individualisation is at the forefront, since this is the time of life with most room for personal priorities (Frønes, 1997).

[3] The notion of dis-identification is developed by Beverley Skeggs in her analysis of young working-class women in Britain. She emphasises that it is important that theories of identification enable you to encapsulate not only the processes of identification but also dis-identification applied to class, femininity and feminism (Skeggs, 1997, p 13).

Bibliography

Aronson, P. (2003) 'Feminist or "Postfeminists"? Young women's attitudes toward feminism and gender relations', *Gender and Society*, vol 6, pp 903–22.

Bergqvist, C., Borchorst, A., Christensen, A.-D., Ramstedt-Silén, V., Raaum, N.C. and Styrkárdóttir, A. (eds) (1999) *Equal Democracies? Gender and politics in the Nordic countries*, Oslo: Scandinavian University Press, Nordic Council of Ministers

Borchorst, A. and Siim, B. (2002) 'The Women-Friendly Welfare States Revisited', *NORA. Nordic Journal of Women's Studies*, vol 10, no 2, pp 90–9.

Butler, J. (1994) 'Contingent Foundations: Feminism and the question of "postmodernism"', in S. Seidman (ed) *The Postmodern Turn: New perspectives on social theory*, Cambridge: Cambridge University Press.

Christensen, A.-D. (2003) *Fortællinger om identitet and magt. Unge kvinder i senmoderniteten*, Aarhus: Magtudredningen/Aarhus University Press, pp 153–70.

Christensen, A.-D. and Siim, B. (2001) *Køn, demokrati and modernitet. Mod nye politiske identiteter*, Copenhagen: Hans Reitzel Publishers.

Christensen, A.-D. and Tobiasen, M. (2007) *Politiske identiteter og kønsidentiteter i tre generationer. Pilotundersøgelse*, Aalborg: Aalborg University, forthcoming.

Christensen, H.R., Halsaa, B. and Saarinen, A. (eds) (2004) *Crossing Borders. Re-mapping women's movements at the turn of the 21st century*, Odense: University Press of Southern Denmark.

Collins, P.H. (1998) 'It's All in the Family: Intersections of gender, race and nation', *Hypatia*, vol 3, pp 62–82.

Dahlerup, D. (1998) *Rødstrømperne. Den danske Rødstrømpebevægelses udvikling, nytænkning and gennemslag, 1970–1985. Bd. 1–2*, Copenhagen: Gyldendal.

Dahlerup, D. (2002) 'Er ligestillingen opnået? Ligestillingsdebattens forskellighed i Danmark and Sverige', in A. Borchorst (ed) *Kønsmagt under forandring*, Copenhagen: Hans Reitzel Publishers, pp 226–47.

de los Reyes, P. and Mulinari, D. (2005) *Intersektionalitet. Kritiska refleksioner över (o)jämlikhetens landskap*, Lund: Liber AB.

Fiig, C. (2003) 'A Feminist Public Sphere. An analysis of the Habermasian public sphere in a Danish gender political context', PhD thesis, Aalborg: Aalborg University.

Frønes, I. (1997) 'The Transformation of Childhood: Children and families in postwar Norway', *Acta Sociologica*, vol 1, pp 17–30.

Giddens, A. (1991) *Modernity and Self-Identity. Self and society in the late modern age*, Cambridge: Polity Press.

Hall, S. (1991) 'Old and New Identities, Old and New Ethnicities', in A. King (ed) *Culture, Globalisation and the World-System. Contemporary conditions for the representation of identity*, New York: Macmillan, pp 41–68.

Hall, S. (1996) 'Introduction: Who needs "Identity"?', in S. Hall, and P. du Gay (eds) *Questions of Cultural Identity*, London: Sage Publications, pp 1–17.

Larsen, J.E. (2000) 'Klassebiografi and individuel biografi', *Social Kritik. Tidsskrift for Social analyse and debat*, vol 67, pp 58–78.

Lykke, N. (2003) 'Intersektionalitet – ett användbart begrepp för genusforskningen', *Kvinnovetenskaplig Tidsskrift*, vol 1, 47–55.

Mørck, Y. (2005) 'Intersektionalitetsanalyser and diversitetsudfordringer', in H. Bech and A.S. Sørensen (eds) *Kultur på kryds and tværs*, Aarhus: Forlaget Klim, pp 65–87.

Nielsen, H.B. (2004) 'Noisy Girls. New subjectivities and old gender discourses', *Young: Nordic Journal of Youth Research*, vol 1, pp 9–30.

Nielsen, H.B. and Rudberg, M. (2000) 'Gender, Love and Education in Three Generations: The way out and up', *The European Journal of Women's Studies*, vol 4, pp 423–55.

Nielsen, H.B. and Rudberg, M. (2006) *Moderne jenter. Tre generasjoner på vei*, Oslo: Universitetsforlaget.

Prieur, A. (2002) 'Frihet til at forme seg selv?', *Kontur*, vol 3, pp 4–13.

Rudberg, M. (2003) 'Våt såpe – Kjærlighet and likestilling i unge jenters fortellinger', in F. Engelstad and G. Ødegård (eds) *Ungdom, makt and mening*, Oslo: Gyldendal Akademisk, pp 284–303.

Siim, B. (1988) 'Towards a Feminist Rethinking of the Welfare State', in J. Kathleen and A. Jonasdottir (eds) *The Political Interest of Women. Developing theory and research with a feminist face*, London: Sage Publication, pp 160–87.

Skeggs, B. (1997) *Formations of Class and Gender. Becoming respectable*, London: Sage Publications.

Skeggs, B. (2004) *Class, Self, Culture*, London: Routledge.

Staunæs, D. (2003) 'Where have all the subjects gone? Bringing together the concepts of intersectionality and subjectification', *NORA. Nordic Journal of Women's Studies*, vol 11, no 2, pp 101–10.

Sværke, K. (2005) *Nyfeminisme and kønsidentiteter*, FREIA-skriftserie, nr. 59, Aalborg: Aalborg University.

West, C. and Zimmerman, D. (1987) 'Doing Gender', *Gender and Society*, vol 2, pp 125–51.

Ziehe, T. (1998a) 'God anderledeshed', in T. Størner and J.A. Hansen (eds) *Unge og ungdom i 1990erne*, conference report, Copenhagen: Danmarks Erhvervspædagogiske Læreruddannelse, pp 37–49.

Ziehe, T. (1998b) 'Adieu til halvfjerdserne', in J. Bjerg (ed) *Pædagogik – en grundbog til et fag*, Copenhagen: Hans Reitzel Publishers, pp 74–88.

Ziehe, T. (2001) 'Modernitets- og ressourceperspektivet. Læring i et hypermoderne samfund – mentalitetsforandring, læringskultur and fremmedfølelse', *Sociologiske Arbejdspapir nr. 8*, Aalborg: Sociologisk Laboratorium, Aalborg University.

ELEVEN

A Scandinavian feminist public sphere: discourses on feminism and gender equality

Christina Fiig

Introduction

A common thread in this volume is the recurring challenge to and questioning of the official Scandinavian gender-equality discourses, as expressed at state level. Other threads I discuss in this chapter are a generational perspective between two generations of feminists and whether feminism has maintained some type of 'intergenerational currency' (Budgeon, 2001).

One such challenge is a debate initiated in the late 1990s by young, predominantly white middle-class feminists who are, generally speaking, the 'daughters' of the feminists in the women's movement of the 1970s across the three countries. The 'daughters' have been brought up and socialised to believe that the Scandinavian welfare states have, to a large extent, realised an ideal of gender equality. However, the debate, which consists of personal narratives of everyday experiences, is inconsistent with the official state optimism and the ideals of their upbringing. These women have academic degrees, a media profile and more cultural and social capital than any generation of Scandinavian women before them (Nielsen, 2002). Paradoxically, they still identify aspects of gender (in)equality in their everyday life.

The phenomenon studied in this chapter was termed 'the new feminist debate', the term describing a specific Scandinavian media debate. Voices questioned the welfare states in relation to gender equality by examining types of discrimination and inequality. At the same time, these voices echoed a wish for agency and empowerment – that is 'the ability to act with others to do together what one could not have done alone' (Ferguson, 1987).

From an international perspective, the Scandinavian countries are often considered a type of gender-equal 'utopia' (Karvonen and Selle, 1995; Fiig, 2008). However, the new feminist debate, far from contributing to a 'discourse of utopia', challenged it by highlighting various examples of inequality.

The purpose of this chapter is to analyse the new feminist debate. I draw on the part of the debate published in Danish, enriched with materials from the debate in Norway and Sweden.[1] The chapter works as a reservoir of insights into Scandinavian discourses on feminism and gender equality. Two questions are addressed. First, what kind of feminist discourses become visible when the debate is observed from within a perspective of a public sphere? Second, in what ways does the debate challenge the Scandinavian state discourses on gender equality?

I embrace the public sphere as a central category of analysis. The debate is approached as a type of feminist public sphere drawing on a framework by German sociologist Jürgen Habermas. It captures the sense of the public sphere as an arena for identification of complex problems such as those related to the individual's private sphere and to public identification and recognition of societal problems. It is conceived as a common space in society divided into arenas, assemblies and other meeting places where citizens gather. It spreads out into a complex network of a multitude of overlapping global, national, regional, local and subcultural arenas and forms 'einen wilden Komplex' (Habermas, 1996, p 373).[2] American political philosopher Nancy Fraser (1992), in an influential formulation, suggests a range of alternative public spheres on different axes such as class, gender, power and profession, suggesting that the notion of the public sphere is de facto a multitude of different publics defined as parallel discursive arenas for formulating identities, interests and needs. She has termed these 'strong' publics and 'weak' publics. The strong publics are orientated towards decision making in the parliamentary system, whereas the weak publics are orientated towards opinion formation in a broader sense. Their deliberative practice consists exclusively of opinion formation. One type emphasises the place of rational argument and decision making within the parliamentary system, and the other hosts public communication in a wider sense, such as the mass media, public events and meetings reflecting discourses of hermeneutical self-understanding. These two types of publics are characterised by two types of logic: the logic of argument and impartial justification and the logic of discovery (Eriksen and Fossum, 2002).

The Scandinavian generation of feminists born after 1968 and the new feminist debate have been analysed within various frameworks: as a type of feminist, political identity (Christensen, 2003), as an example of a class and generational-specific type of feminism rooted in the Scandinavian 'creative class' (Bråten, 2002; Nielsen, 2002), and as a feminist public sphere (Fiig, 2003, 2006). The debate reflects another type of feminism and another type of public sphere than the one that has been characterised as a 'women's public' and linked to the external and internal debates of the women's movement during the 1970s and early 1980s (Richard, 1978).

I seek to analyse a weak public based on such types of communication as narrative, rhetoric and storytelling (Young, 2000) and on the logic of discovery. The analytical focus of Scandinavian gender research has covered parliamentary debates and issues on gender equality and feminism (Borchorst, 2003; Dahlerup, 2004), election campaigns in a gender perspective (Gomard and Krogstad, 2001), and various types of historical and arts publics focused on women's agency (Hagemann and Krogstad, 1994).

In order to analyse the new feminist debate, I have constructed a Scandinavian gender-political context of the 1990s. The design of the time period is due to the beginning of the new feminist debate that took off in 1999 with the publishing of the Swedish anthology *Fittstim* (*The Cunt Cascade*) (Skugge et al, 1999a). The underlying idea is that the context forms a background framework for the understanding of the new feminist debate. By this specific context, I mean some historical and institutional factors and the media debate in a given period. When it comes to a Scandinavian context, the three countries are considered homogeneous as regards broad socio-economic development and legislation (Bergqvist et al, 1999). The countries are considered heterogeneous when it comes to the gender debate. Parliamentary debates and the media debate on gender-related issues have been described as being less intense in the 1990s than in the previous two decades. This reduced intensity masks some intra-Scandinavian differences. A relatively vigorous debate took place in Sweden, whereas the Danish and the Norwegian debates were comparatively quieter (Nielsen, 2002; Dahlerup, 2004).[3]

An analytical perspective of a public sphere seems a particularly compatible arena for a Scandinavian gender-political context of the 1990s characterised by a demobilised women's movement and a demobilised generation of youth, as far as political institutions go. The public sphere becomes a central arena for articulating issues related to private experiences and to the private and intimate sphere. In relation to the debate on feminism, the context equally plays a role when it comes to generational differences. Another characteristic of the context is exactly the influence of second-wave feminism – that is, feminist currents based on the women's movement of the 1970s and early 1980s.

As Eriksen and Fossum (2002) show in an analysis of different types of publics in the EU, it is necessary to employ another term than the adjective 'weak' for a description of a type of public sphere whose arena and focus are outside the parliamentary complex. The same goes for a Scandinavian context and for the naming of a feminist public situated in civil society and based on a logic of discovery. The argument is – along the thesis of the context – that political culture and the significance of extra-parliamentary activities from 'below' play a significant role in Scandinavia. Eriksen and Fossum employ the term 'general publics' about an object that covers Fraser's term 'weak public'. I employ the term 'general public' in the following.

Feminist voices in the Scandinavian new feminist debate 1999–2004

The new feminist debate voiced new discourses across Scandinavia. The first books initiated a media debate in Sweden, which subsequently spread to Norway and Denmark. After a decade distinguished by its marked quietness on gender, especially in the Danish debate, the critical voices revitalised the conversation on gender and feminism. Despite this, the debate never had a popular breakthrough, as was the case with the women's movement and its related publics during the 1970s and early 1980s (Dahlerup, 1998; Christensen, 2003).

This section will briefly describe what I call the 'key actors' in the debate, that is, the young women who took part in the debate and whose experiences, narratives and life stories form its basis.[4] The empirical material consists of a series of debate books published in Danish, Norwegian and Swedish from 1999 to 2004 and some newspaper debates during the same period. The concept of a public sphere is applied to a range of book publications and newspaper articles, such as book reviews, features and letters to the editor.

The issues of the debate were multifaceted, with an emphasis on narratives on feminism, on bodily integrity[5] and personal autonomy, and on experiences with different types of discrimination and violence in everyday family life, among friends and in the educational system. The debate dealt less with policy initiatives on a state level and emphasised issues related to recognition of personal autonomy and discrimination.

The key actors were characterised by a range of identity markers such as class, ethnicity, gender, generation and race. Predominantly, they were white, ethnic Scandinavians with parents born in Scandinavia. They represented a new group of feminists born between 1965 and 1975, many of them 'daughters' of the active feminists of the 1970s. They grew up in a context marked by demobilisation of the women's movement and by second-wave feminist influence. However, only the intersection between *class, generation* and *gender* is considered in the following. By 'class' I mean the educational dimension. The key actors possessed a great amount of educational and social capital and reflected the profile of the women of the women's movements in the western countries in the late 1960s and during the 1970s (Hagemann, 2004). It is therefore a range of privileged stories these women tell (Nielsen, 2002). The intersection between class/education, generation and gender manifests itself in several ways: one is the use of interpersonal networks as a recruitment platform for the debate, another is the way the actors connect feminism with a type of discursive practice and a third is the type of personal narratives on bodily matters, education and work articulated in the debate.

Many of the key actors held an academic degree and a media profile, which were used as a platform to raise the profile of the debate (Bråten, 2002). Social networks and interpersonal links among individuals that existed prior to the phase of some type of collective mobilisation are crucial in this process (Bergman, 2002, p 255). Access to the media leads to agenda setting and to discursive power making, by which I mean production of identities and capacities for action. The actors chose the media and new technologies such as the Norwegian network *Female Bonding* and the Danish *Fem@il* and *Feminist Forum* for internal debates on feminism instead of an organisational form such as the basis group. These types of networks illustrate that it is possible to construct a sense of community and confidence across time and space. The networks are independent of large geographical distances. They function as a type of 'Polis on the internet', providing dialogue, knowledge and contacts (Bråten, 2002).

The feminist discourses articulated in the debate were associated with a discursive practice, that is, publication of articles, books and letters to newspapers, and linked to writing and speaking. It was an intellectual type of discourses: 'That is why feminism is very much about writing and speaking, and that is why I have chosen to assemble women for a book and not for a demonstration. Action is important. Of course. But without words, we cannot act. Without words, we can't do anything at all'(Skov, 2002, p 30).[6]

The intersection of class/education, gender and generation also manifests itself in the narratives concerning the complex of problems young intellectual women face in the educational system, in the labour market and in social relations with both women and men. The class position is also manifest in the way other young women related to the debate. For instance, other groups of young Danish women distanced themselves from the intersection of these identity markers in relation to feminism. These were women who did not identify themselves as feminists and also women participating in radical, left-wing feminist movements (Skeggs, 1997; Christensen, 2003).

Age as a source of difference[7]

The actors can be framed in a generational perspective when understood as a common framework of historical, social and cultural experiences that characterise a generation. The idea is that societal events can be linked to the development of youth culture and that there is a time-specific framework for each generation.[8] I will examine two narratives on the key actors' construction of the relationship to their feminist mothers and to the women's movement the mother belonged to. The intergenerational relationship will be analysed based on the voices of the young generation and will not include the second-wavers – that is, the feminists of the 1970s and early 1980s. The relationship is ambiguous: on the one hand, the feminist mum has become a role model, and on the other hand the daughters are in opposition to the idea of the specific women's movement of the period. The ideological feminist mum of the 1970s brought up her daughters with a strong sense of self-worth and with rights and opportunities. The daughters related to their mothers as feminists but not to the women's movement they belonged to, as, for example, the way of organising, dressing and other types of symbolic habita. 'The feminist mum' has become a feminist heroine and a role model. The second-wavers rebelled against the narrow gender roles their mothers' generation had been brought up with as a specific concept of womanhood, motherhood and housewifehood (Ravn, 1989).

> Danish women have achieved economic independence, independence and the vote – we are entitled to education, abortion and divorce. And thank you for that! Never have women lived as we do and had as many possibilities. Just 50 years ago, it would have been unthinkable to have a female chairman of the national bank or a female minister of economy. We are brought up to believe that women can do anything and we would like to believe that. If we point at the inequalities, it is often perceived that we claim victim status. This is why it has been so difficult to talk about gender equality. We have to stop thinking like that. (Goth et al, 2000, pp 10–11)

The discourse of 'the feminist mum' is explicitly formulated as an abstract thankfulness towards the achievement of earlier generations' women's movements, which have assisted in producing opportunities for the young generation of women. The feminist mothers are seen as having paved the way for women born in the 1970s to enter to the labour market, academia and politics.

At the same time, the discourses reflect a radical distance from the women's movement of the 1970s and early 1980s. Along the lines of earlier generations of feminists, the actors define themselves in opposition to the previous generation. Historically, the women's movement has experienced a greater degree of discontinuity compared to other social movements concerning collective processes of learning from one generation to the next (Streijffert, 1983; Dahlerup, 1998; Fiig, 2006).

> It is light years ago that a group of Redstocking feminists went down Stroeget [the main pedestrian street in Copenhagen] and stopped at the Town Hall Square, where they took off among other things wigs, artificial eyelashes, big bras and threw them into a sack labelled: 'Keep Denmark clean'. In the push-up-wearing young's eyes they look like a group of loonies. A group of old loonies. (Bom and Bjerke, 2002, p 35)

The feminist identities articulated in the debate are related to a generational distance to the feminists of the women's movement of the 1970s and early 1980s. The way the key actors in the debate construct these is mirrored in Budgeon's analysis of young British women. They display 'resistance to adopting an identification with a form of feminism they feel has no relevance to their daily lives' (Budgeon, 2001, p 11). The same kind of resistance can be identified in the new feminist debate, in which discourses on the young feminists are constructed such as:

> They do not sit around in a circle their toes entwined discussing a one-eyed view on the world, but are individualistic and hold different definitions of feminism from courage to rock 'n' roll. They look like true, smart women and not like men with lipstick. They are young, mid-20s. They do not hate men. They do not carry luggage full of hurt pride and ridicule which makes

their voices shrill and their eyes dark with bitterness. They do not fire live cartridges from a trench but expose their inner thoughts and feelings. (Skugge et al, 1999b, p 5)

Three discourses on feminism and gender equality

I suggest three discourses on feminism and gender equality on the basis of the new feminist debate. I will examine the discourse of rehabilitation, the discourse of public recognition and the discourse of consciousness raising in the following subsections and finally discuss the findings of the analysis.

Discourse of rehabilitation

One discourse concerns different ways of characterising feminism and it holds three elements: an individual understanding of feminism, the discursive practice and feminism as a common project for women and men.

One illustration of the individual definitions of feminism is the way each key actor presents her personal definition in the debate books. Feminism is talked about as an umbrella term and definitely is 'many, not one' (Tong, 1998). Besides, it is not linked to a specific political ideology or to the ideology of the women's movement (see Dahlerup, 1998). In the first publication, *The Cunt Cascade*, each contributor presents a short definition of feminism. The editors state that the only common denominator for all feminists is that they want men and women to be treated as equals with equal rights (p 8). Feminism becomes synonymous with a variety of things: not believing what they say (p 156), the whole wage and half the power (p 150), an instinct of self-preservation (p 136), a wonderful necessity (p 114), to want it in a gender-equal way (p 96), courage (p 74), a return ticket around the world for endless travelling (p 50) and rock and roll all night and party every day (p 40) (Skugge et al, 1999a).

The individual discourses on feminism are also reflected in the book's layout, which consists of individual contributions with the author's name, year of birth, photo and the above definitions. This differs from the collective orientation of the feminist literature of the 1970s (Dahlerup, 1998). An analysis of young Norwegian women born in the early 1970s reveals that a central value is to be original, to realise oneself as an individual and to focus on aesthetics and art. This can be seen as a way of realising generation-specific individuality (Nielsen, 1999):

Feminism should not be standardising. You don't have to wear specific clothes, have sex in a specific way, vote for a specific party or belong to a specific religion. There is no specific way to behave as a feminist. You do not even need to be a woman. Actually, we call on all men to become feminists. (Goth et al, 2000, p 11)

Another characteristic of the debate is its specific discursive framework. Feminism is considered a discursive practice, a struggle for a language, and associated with a type of discursive power: 'For the past 20 years, all talk of suppression of women has been met with aggressive ridicule and political indifference. We are told that men and women are equal. That is a lie. There is still much to talk about. That is the reason for this book' (Goth et al, 2000, p 8).

A third characteristic is related to the discourses on the relationship between feminism, men and women. Feminism is not articulated as an idea of an antagonistic relationship between women and men, but as a common solution for both women and men. This discourse can be interpreted as an attempt to spread the notion of women's experiences of gender inequality to cover the gendered norms experienced by both sexes and as an attempt to mobilise men to feminism: 'I do not think that feminism always has to deal with the education of the poor fellow next to you. It is rather a question of dealing with the structural aspects that prevent equality and then elaborating what one considers female in all corners of society' (Kraul, 2000, p 194).

The discourses formulate an inclusive idea about feminism as a project for different groups of women and men – no matter how you choose to live, dress or behave. Men, at least younger men, are potential allies and not enemies: 'Feminism is not about opposition between the sexes, but about responding to the unfair reality right in front of our eyes. We wish for a broader understanding of cultural conceptions of gender and sexuality' (Goth et al, 2000, p 11).

I interpret the three elements of the discourse as a type of 'rehabilitation of the F-word'. This has been termed a 'recapturing of feminism' as a concept, an idea and as a strategy by a group of young women (Bråten, 2002, p 45). The category 'feminist' is deconstructed and transformed to new meanings, defining new labels and understandings that are different from the ones employed by the women's movement of the 1970s.

Discourse of public recognition

The discourse of public recognition articulates narratives on sexual harassment and bodily disciplining. I understand public recognition as the movement of taking problem complexes from the private and intimate sphere into the public arena with the intention of gaining recognition. Recognition is not only viewed in terms of identity. It is the status of individual group members as full partners in social interaction that requires recognition, not group-specific identity (Fraser and Honneth, 2003).

The discourses on sexual harassment are associated with the young women's upbringing, and with the school system in particular. On an individual level, the discourses point at men as the source of discrimination: teachers, schoolmates, the chiropractor or family friends. For example, one narrative deals with the male teacher who harassed the girls in a school class (Skugge et al, 1999b, pp 10–19).

On a structural level, the discourses articulate a type of structural harassment by the growing pornification of public space in films, ads, music, discursive practices, media such as TV and radio where pornography is interpreted as a mainstream phenomenon (Bom and Bjerke, 2002, pp 50–65), and by the gendered norms the young women encounter in relation to their growing sexuality in their teenage years:

> The teachers noticed everything, but did not react. In the sixth grade when we were 12 years old, the teacher asked the girls to stay behind in the classroom while the boys went for the break. 'I see that the boys feel you up', she said. 'Make sure that you do not turn into tarts. Personally, I only let my husband touch me.' (Skugge et al, 1999b, p 130)

When it comes to bodily disciplining, the debate articulates narratives about eating disorders and other types of bodily control related to weight, sports and body language (Skugge et al, 1999b, pp 20–7, 156–61; Kraul, 2000, pp 249–59).

The discourses are examples of storytelling that challenges a view of the Scandinavian gender-equal welfare states by expressing the particularity of experiences. It is a kind of storytelling that is not based on rational arguments for equality and equal opportunities, but works via emotion, irony and humour. In taking action and establishing the debate, the actors claim a voice by politicising everyday experiences of gender inequality. Publicity is used to heighten the awareness of gender (in)equality across Scandinavia.

The debate focuses on ways of creating a stronger sense of bodily integrity. The actors insist on a sense of agency and autonomy across the experience presented above:

> We want to give girls a forum where they are not edited and put into place. This is an uncensored free zone, an outlet for aggression. Everybody's opinion is of equal value, and we are proud of the honesty of all the girls (participating) in this book. We hope that girls, by reading this book, perhaps will learn to draw the line earlier, recognize their personal worth and realize that they have power over their own lives. (Skugge et al, 1999b, p 9)

I interpret the discourse of public recognition as parallel to the conclusions drawn by Budgeon: that young women have access to a range of choices and to self-determination in many areas of their lives but also that 'coexisting with these conditions are those which counter women's equality, thereby making resistance an issue of ongoing relevance' (Budgeon, 2001, p 16).

Discourse of consciousness raising

The final analysis covers a discourse of consciousness raising and can be interpreted as an inward-orientated type of discourse as the key actors emphasise their autonomy and agency by pointing at the inward-looking space of the debate. The discourse works around self-reflection, construction of identities and self-determination and creates awareness of the necessity for teenage girls and young women of changing society. It contributes to the development of a conscious sense of agency:

> It was not the least tedious, but very refreshing (and somewhat shocking) to talk realising how each of us individually have hidden away big and small problems of gender equality. It was also a common experience that if it did not work out perfectly at home, it was not necessarily because oneself or the husband was an idiot. It was also because there still is some way to go before we can talk about gender equality in Denmark. (Kraul, 2000, p 11)

The discourse also mirrors the expressions of individuality in the debate – there are very few references to a 'collective we' or to types of collective political action. Participation in the public sphere opens up for the realisation of the articulated problems' collective character. In my interpretation, a type of collectivity is linked to publishing and participating in a public sphere. Individualism privileges the worth of the individual at the expense of the collectivity – it can also be a source of agency at the micro-level of everyday practice (Budgeon, 2001, p 18).

Discussion

Returning to the second question of the chapter – in what ways the new feminist debate challenges the official Scandinavian state discourses on gender equality – an answer can now be given. The three discourses I have analysed illustrate how participants in general publics employ narratives and storytelling to identify with each other, as a means of politicising their situation and as a consciousness-raising process. Communicating helps name a problem that previously had no name (Young, 2000). Hence, the public sphere forms a constructive arena for exchanges of convictions and various facets of 'hermeneutic self-understanding' on the part of the individual and the collective (Gimmler, 2001). It is used as a platform for creating awareness in a broader society of otherwise relatively 'invisible' problems. The new feminist debate can lead to collective recognition of private, individualised experiences especially related to bodily integrity. By airing problems in the public sphere, the individual and private dimension is transformed into a collective and public one. Everyday individual experiences are transformed from the single actors' horizon of experiences. The processes of agency which the public sphere hosts can be interpreted within a framework of discursive power: it contributes to the production of identities and capabilities for action and to politicising the key actors' life situations.

The public sphere becomes an arena for reconceptualisation of the political vocabulary on feminism and gender equality. The arena of the debate de facto contributes to a thematisation of issues and articulation of discourses, which Giddens terms a life-political agenda, an agenda that puts moral and existential questions in the centre of the debate, helping to identify societal problems (Beck et al, 1994). In comparison with the women's movement of the 1970s and its related women's publics, the new feminist debate differs in one main way. Approached as a type of general public, it is not characterised by social movements and a collective perspective but by individual actors and an individual perspective.

Many issues raised in the debate, for instance 'the tyranny of beauty', are framed in a way that is far from a terminology employed in parliamentary politics. By taking a debate on personal issues from the private, intimate sphere into the public, the debate becomes a dialogue on gender equality and feminism.

The discourse of rehabilitation and the new meanings ascribed to 'feminist' and 'feminism' can, in a perspective of post-modernity, be interpreted as a part of a political process where politics is enacted through signs and spectacles (Roseneil, 1999). The discourses on feminism articulated in the debate point towards new ways of approaching and formulating policies related to gender issues. These are based neither on a mobilised women's movement nor on strong pressure on the political system, from below, for initiatives.

The political transformation identified in the debate is not related to party politics. It includes 'the power of participation', that is, people's active engagement in creating and transforming the conditions of their own lives, such as non-institutional forms of political action. The discourses on feminism do not include any of the brands into which feminism is commonly categorised – '"radical, socialist, liberal, lesbian or eco' (Roseneil, 1999, p 167).

It remains an open, empirical question whether the discourses of the debate will turn into issues formulated in terms of party politics and the logic of strong publics. That is, whether a general public will foster debates and further initiatives in a strong, parliamentary public. Eriksen and Fossum (2002) argue for the reverse order: that the strong publics in the EU-system foster general publics. In the case of the new feminist debate, I would put it the other way around.

The debate points towards a vision of everyday life with more gender equality and less discrimination, which does not, however, refer to an explicit political strategy, party politics or political institutions. Neither does it reflect an antagonistic relationship with the state or with the political system. The question is whether narratives, storytelling and testimonies of, for example, sexual harassment and discrimination can make the audience reflect critically and, in combination with conventional politics in formal political institutions, lead to political initiatives as was the case in the UN (Ackerly and Okin, 1999). Some political actions are results of the new feminist debate. The actors gather around web pages, internet-based networks, campaigns and, in the Danish case, as political actors campaigning for a maternity–paternity leave fund, parliamentarian 'coffee clubs' and feminist networks within and across the political parties.

Conclusion

The chapter raises the question of the meaning of a generation and of whether there is a political difference between the new feminist debate and the second-wavers of the women's movement. The analysis illustrates the complex relationship between the two generations of feminists. On the one side, the feminist mum has become a feminist heroine and paved the way for societal changes providing young women with more life choices. On the other side, the feminist daughters reformulate the concepts of feminism, distancing themselves from the feminist ideals and icons of the 1970s and early 1980s. Age is a source of difference (Budgeon, 2001) and so is the relationship between feminism and the media. Feminism is now part of the cultural field and expressed within the media rather than simply being external, independent, critical voices. It might be argued that much of what counts as feminist debate in western countries today takes place in rather than outside the media (Gill, 2006).

The actors in the debate transform private matters into public ones and use the public sphere to improve conditions in the private realm. In relation to the generational question, the public sphere works as a way of gaining access to recognition and representation. This particular way of employing the public–private split in the Scandinavian welfare state is different from the way it is done by the young Danish women analysed by Ann-Dorte Christensen (see Chapter Ten). These women insist on reinstalling the public–private split, so that a clear line is drawn between their public and private lives. The public life – such as their work life – is approached as a barrier to their private, family life.

The study suggests that gender inequality is still a key issue in women's lives in Scandinavia among educated young women and feminists. It remains to be seen whether – quoting the American black public sphere – the new feminist debate's critical memories are 'the faculty of revolution' (Baker, 1995).

Notes
[1] This chapter is based on my PhD thesis, 'A Feminist Public Sphere. An Analysis of the Habermasian Public Sphere in a Danish Gender Political Context' (Fiig, 2003). I would like to thank the editors of this anthology and Fiona Williams, Leeds University, and Richard Herriott for constructive criticism.

[2] For empirical analysis of the public sphere see Eriksen and Weigård (1999), Eriksen and Fossum (2002), Fiig (2003, 2006) and Loftager (2003).

[3] Bergman (2002) has pointed out that women's social and economic rights, bodily and sexual integrity and (political) empowerment are important themes for feminist movements everywhere.

[4] The first book *Fittstim* (*The Cunt Cascade*) was initially published in Sweden in 1999 and translated into Danish. Other publications followed in Danish, Norwegian and Swedish. In 2004 came the book *Femkamp* (2004), which consists of analyses from the five Nordic countries. This book, based on a common Nordic initiative, illustrates the idea of a feminist public sphere existing across the countries. I have chosen to use the term 'Scandinavian' about the public sphere as most of the analytical material is published in the three Scandinavian languages.

[5] Nielsen (2002) interprets the general focus on bodily matters in the debate in a class perspective.

[6] The following quotations are translated from Danish, Norwegian and Swedish by the author.

[7] In this section, I draw on my previous analyses (see Fiig, 2006) and on Nielsen (2002) and Budgeon (2001).

[8] Both Christensen (1994) and Jensen (2001) refer to Mannheim's idea of a link between general societal changes and generations and the common framework in which a generation is brought up (see Mannheim, 1952).

Bibliography

Ackerly, B. and Okin, S.M. (1999) 'Feminist Social Criticism and the International Movement for Women's Rights as Human Rights', in I. Shapiro and C. Hacker-Cordón (eds) *Democracy's Edges*, Cambridge: Cambridge University Press, pp 134–62.

Baker, H., Jr. (1995) 'Critical Memory and the Black Public Sphere', in The Black Public Sphere Collective (eds) *The Black Culture Book*, Chicago and London: The University of Chicago Press, pp 5–38.

BANG, Feministisk Kulturtidsskrift. Various issues.

Beck, U., Giddens, A. and Lash, C. (1994) *Reflexive Modernisation. Politics, tradition and aesthetics in the modern social order*, Cambridge: Polity Press.

Bergman, S. (2002) *The Politics of Feminism. Automomous feminist movements in Finland and West Germany from the 1960s to the 1980s*, Åbo: Akademisk Forlag-Åbo University Press.

Bergqvist, C., Borchorst, A., Christensen, A.-D., Ramstedt-Silén, V., Raaum, N.C. and Styrkárdóttir, A. (eds) (1999) *Equal Democracies? Gender and politics in the Nordic countries*, Oslo: Scandinavian University Press.

Bom, M. and Bjerke, N.K. (2002) *Udslag-hverdagsfeminisme i det 21. århundrede*, Copenhagen: Elkjaeroghansen.

Borchorst, A. (2003) *Køn, magt og beslutninger. Politiske forhandlinger om barselsorlov 1901–2002*, Aarhus: Magtudredningen.

Bråten, B. (2002) "'... Det er kanskje noe i veien med de jævla hyllene da". Unge feminristers valg av arbeidsformer for at få endringer i samfunnet', Master's thesis, Oslo: University of Oslo, Department of Sociology and Social Geography.

Budgeon, S. (2001) 'Emergent Feminist (?) Identities. Young women and the practice of micropolitics', *The European Journal of Women's Studies*, vol 8, pp 7–28.

Christensen, A.-D. (1994) 'Køn, ungdom og værdiopbrud', in J. Andersen and L. Torpe (eds) *Demokrati og politisk kultur*, Herning: Systime, pp 175–210.

Christensen, A.-D. (2003) *Fortællinger om identitet og magt. Unge kvinder i senmoderniteten*, Aarhus: Magtudredningen.

Dahlerup, D. (1998) *Rødstrømperne. Den danske Rødstrømpebevægelses udvikling, nytænkning og gennemslag 1970–1985, Bd. I, II*, Copenhagen: Gyldendal.

Dahlerup, D. (2004) 'Feministisk partipolitik? Om skillnader i dansk och svensk jämstalldhetsdebatt', in C. Florin and C. Bergqvist (eds) *Framtiden i samtiden. Könsrelationer i förändring i Sverige och omvärlden*, Stockholm: Institut for Framtidsstudier, pp 234–63.

Eriksen, E.O. and Fossum, J.E. (2002) 'Democracy through *Strong Publics* in the European Union?', *Journal of Common Market Studies*, vol 40, pp 401–23.

Eriksen, E.O., Fossum, J.E. and Weigård, J. (1999) *Kommunikativ handling og deliberativt demokrati. Jürgen Habermas' teori om politikk og samfunn*, Oslo: Fagbokforlaget.

Femkamp, various editors (2004). *Femkamp-Bang om Nordisk Feminism*, Viborg: Denmark.

Ferguson, K. (1987) 'Male-Ordered Politics: Feminism and political science', in T. Ball (ed) *Idioms of Inquiry: Critique and renewal in political science*, Albany, NY: State University of New York Press, pp 209–29.

Fiig, C. (2003) 'A Feminist Public Sphere. An analysis of the Habermasian public sphere in a Danish gender political context', PhD thesis, Aalborg: Aalborg University.

Fiig, C. (2006) '"Det vigtigste er debatten" – Feministiske stemmer i den danske offentlighed', in A. Borchorst and A.-D. Christensen (eds) *Kønsrefleksioner – om magt og mangfoldighed. Festskrift til Birte Siim*, Aalborg: Aalborg University Press, pp 155–72.

Fiig, C. (2008) 'Women in Danish Politics: Challenges to the notion of gender equality', in J. Gelb and M.L. Palley (eds) *Women and Politics Around the World. A comparative encyclopedia*, Santa Barbara CA: ABC-CLIO (forthcoming).

Fraser, N. (1992) 'Rethinking the Public Sphere: A contribution to the critique of actually existing democracy', in C. Calhuon (ed) *Habermas and the Public Sphere*, Cambridge, MA: MIT Press, pp 109–42.

Fraser, N. and Honneth, A. (2003) *Redistribution or Recognition? A political-philosophical exchange*, London:Verso.

Gill, R. (2006) *Gender and the Media*, Cambridge: Polity Press.

Gimmler,A. (2001).'Deliberative Democracy, the Public Sphere and the Internet', *Philosophy and Social Criticism*, vol 27, 21–39.

Gomard, K. and Krogstad,A. (eds) (2001) *Instead of the Ideal Debate. Doing politics and doing gender in Nordic political campain discourse*,Aarhus: Aarhus University Press.

Goth, A.F., Maclean, H.K., Petersen, L.M. and Schelin, K. (2000) *Nu er det nok. Så er det sagt*, Copenhagen: Rosinante.

Habermas, J. (1989) *The Structural Transformation of the Public Sphere*, Cambridge: MIT Press.

Habermas, J. (1996/orig. 1992) *Between Facts and Norms. Contributions to a discourse theory of law and democracy*, Cambridge, MA: MIT Press.

Hagemann, G. (2004) 'Norsk nyfeminisme – amerikansk import?', *Nytt Norsk Tidsskrift*, vol 3–4, pp 275–87.

Hagemann, G. and Krogstad, A. (eds) (1994) *Høydeskrekk-kvinder og Offentlighed*, Oslo: Ad Notam, Gyldendal.

Jensen, U.H. (2001) *Man skal være sig selv – teoretisk og empirisk belysning af unges politiske univers*, Copenhagen: Department of Political Science, University of Copenhagen.

Karvonen, L. and Selle, P. (eds) (1995) *Closing the Gap. Women in Nordic politics*, Dartmouth: Aldershot.

Kraul, M. (2000) *Fem@il*, Copenhagen: Aschehoug.

Loftager, J. (2003) *Politisk offentlighed og demokrati i Danmark*, Aarhus: Aarhus University Press.

Mannheim, K. (1952) *Essays on the Sociology of Knowledge*, London: Routledge and Kegan Paul.

Marshall, B.L. (1995) 'Communication as Politics. Feminist print media in English Canada', *Women's Studies International Forum*, vol 18, pp 463–74.

Nielsen, A. (1999) 'The Cunt Cascade Takes on Denmark', *Forum*, 6 December at www.kvinfo.dk/forum.

Nielsen, H.B. (1999) 'Utdanning, kjønn og kjærlighed i tre generationer', in G.E. Birkelund,A.K. Broch-Due and A. Nielsen (eds) *Ansvar og Protest, Kjønn, Klasse og utdanning i senmoderniteten, Festskrift til professor Hildur Ve*, Bergen: University of Bergen, pp 309–38.

Nielsen, H.B. (2002) 'Næsvise Piger', in J. Cramer, O.Togeby and P.Widell (eds) *M/K – Mod og Kvindehjerte. Festskrift til Mette Kunøe 5. november 2002*, Aarhus: Modtryk, pp 65–79.

Nielsen, H.B. and Rudberg, M. (2006) *Moderne jenter. Tre generasjoner på vei*, Oslo: Universitetsforlaget.

Øvald, C.B. and Lode, V. (2000) *Feminisjon*, Socialistisk Oplysningsforbund, Norway.

Ravn, A.-B. (1989) 'Mål og midler i den nye gl. og nye kvindebevægelse', *Nyt forum for kvindeforskning*, vol 9, pp 3–20.

Richard, A.B. (1978) *Kvindeoffentlighed 1968–1975. Om kvindelitteratur og kvindebevægelse i Danmark*, Copenhagen: Gyldendal.

Roseneil, S. (1999) 'Postmodern Feminist Politics', *The European Journal of Women's Studies*, vol 6, pp 161–82.

Sandness, C., Nossum, B. and Smith-Erichsen, C. (1999) *Matriark: Nesten sanne historier om å være kvinne*, Oslo: Gyldendal.

Skeggs, B. (1997) *Formation of Class and Gender. Becoming respectable*, London: Sage.

Skov, L.C. (ed) (2002). *De Røde Sko. Feminisme nu.* Copenhagen: Tiderne Skifter.

Skugge, L.N., Olsson, B. and Zilg, B. (1999a) *Fittstim*, Stockholm: Bokförlaget DN.

Skugge, L.N., Olsson, B. and Zilg, B. (1999b) *Fisseflokken*, Copenhagen: Informations Forlag.

Solheim, H.C. and Vaagland, H. (1999) *RÅTEKST*, Oslo: Aschehoug.

Streijffert, H. (1983) *Studier i den svenske kvinnorörelsen*, Monograph nr. 30, Sociologi, Gothenburg: Gothenburg University.

Tong, R. (1998) *Feminist Thought. A more comprehensive introduction*, London: Westview Press.

Young, I.M. (2000) *Inclusion and Democracy*, Oxford: Oxford University Press.

Websites

www.forum.kvinfo.dk

www.kvindeligtselskab.dk

www.feministiskforum.dk

www. bang.a.se

www.fet.no

www.groups.yahoo.com/group/femail-bonding

Gender, citizenship and social justice in the Nordic welfare states: a view from the outside[1]

Ruth Lister

This postscript offers an outsider's assessment of the political ambition represented by the Nordic welfare-state model from a gender perspective. More than any other welfare-state model, the Nordic or social-democratic model is not just a label applied by welfare-regime analysts but is worn with pride by Scandinavian governments and citizens. As this volume demonstrates, gender equality is treated as a hallmark of this model (even if there are differences between the Nordic countries). The original class-based 'passion for equality' was gradually extended explicitly to embrace gender so that, according to Arnlaug Leira, gender equality is now 'integral to Scandinavian citizenship' (Ellingsæter and Leira, 2006, p 7). This shapes the gender culture within which specific policies operate in the Nordic welfare states.

Nevertheless, as this volume again demonstrates, there are considerable differences between the Nordic countries. In particular, while the Nordic welfare states tend broadly to be characterised as among those that have moved furthest towards a dual earner or adult worker model, the policy mechanisms deployed to support those with care responsibilities differ in terms both of the specifics of policy and of the gendered citizenship models underlying them.

Just as there are differences between policies for gendered citizenship between the Nordic countries, so there are differences among feminist scholars in their evaluation of the Nordic model. Such differences can reflect differing normative positions as to whether the goal is an ostensibly gender-neutral or an explicitly gender-differentiated model of citizenship or some combination of the two (Lister, 1997/2003). Nordic policy discourses have generally been gender neutral, with the explicit aim of promoting equality between women and men. However, some policies, even though still couched in gender-neutral language, arguably are more consistent with gender-differentiated models of citizenship, in which women's particular responsibilities and needs are recognised.

Distinctive too, among some Nordic welfare states, has been the attempt, however tentative, to promote a more gender-inclusive model of citizenship in which men as well as women are able to play a part as citizen-earner/carers and carer/earners. This points towards what Nancy Fraser (1997) has termed the universal-caregiver model in which men become more like women, rather than the universal-breadwinner model in which women are expected to become more like men. Nowhere, needless to say, has achieved the universal-caregiver model.

The relative success or not of such policies is important to overall empirically based judgements as to the extent to which the Nordic welfare states have achieved their goal of gender equality and their potential as 'women-friendly' welfare states (Hernes, 1987). Again, the degree of progress is a source of dispute between feminist scholars. Crudely, it is a question of whether the glass is half full or half empty. It is also a question as to 'which women?' In the 20 years since Hernes coined the term 'women-friendly' state, there has been increased recognition of the diversity among women, to the extent that some feminist scholars have now rejected the term as biased in its failure to acknowledge this diversity, particularly racial/ethnic diversity.

The 'half-full' analysis

In terms of women's overall position, as measured by the UN gender-equality indices, the Nordic countries lead the world and they hold the top five places in the World Economic Forum gender-gap index. Women have advanced further as political citizens in the formal public sphere than elsewhere. The extent to which this has been the product of women organising 'from below' in the feminist movement or from 'within' the established political parties has varied between countries, but either way the improvement in women's political representation has transformed the face of Scandinavian politics and social life (Karvonen and Selle, 1995).

It is important not just as a marker of women's political citizenship but also because of its potential implications for policy, particularly the policies that underpin social citizenship. Key here to the half-full analysis is the highly developed social infrastructure of services and leave provisions, which have contributed to women's increased economic independence through paid employment and low levels of poverty. It can be argued that it is the infrastructure of services that is key to understanding the distinctive Nordic welfare model, particularly from a gendered perspective.

Despite the differences highlighted in this volume, there are sufficient similarities among social care services in the Nordic countries (with the exception of Iceland) to allow identification of what Arnlaug Leira terms 'a 'caring' state' (2006, p 30) and Anttonen and Sipilä a Nordic 'social care regime' (1996). This is characterised by extensive provision of public care services for both children and frail older people, in line with the value of universalism, even if the universalist trademark does not always fulfil its promise (Anttonen, 2002). Anttonen argues that 'from the feminist point of view, a radical extension of social citizenship has taken place, and citizens have won the right to certain social care services, for example a comprehensive and universal municipal day-care system' (2002, p 76). Important from the perspective of gendered social citizenship (and also the rights of children) is the characterisation of childcare as a citizenship right, most explicit in Finland but effectively realised in Denmark and Sweden also and aimed for in Norway (Lister et al, 2007).

As well as, for the most part, being in the vanguard of developing childcare provisions to support an emergent dual-earner model, the Nordic welfare states have pioneered new parental leave arrangements to enable parents (not just mothers) to look after very young children at home. Interestingly, the Nordic countries have not all followed the same model of parental leave in terms of the relationship between leave and public childcare provision. Nor is there a single position with regard to encouraging fathers' use of parental leave and involvement in childcare more generally. This last issue is an element of the Nordic welfare model which is particularly important for gendered citizenship: it represents recognition that men's and women's access to citizenship rights and ability to act as citizens in the public sphere is differentially affected by their responsibilities in the private sphere (Lister, 1997/2003).

It is important to acknowledge the significance of what has been attempted, in particular when writing in the British context. As Leira observes, 'the schemes, and especially the father's quota, are remarkable as examples of state intervention not only in the general framework of employment, but also in the internal organisation of the family. Everyday family life has been made into an arena for the promotion of gender equality' (2002, p 85). Particularly striking here is Iceland, which tends to be left out of many accounts of the Nordic welfare state but which has not just a daddy month or two but three months. The father's quota has been most successful in increasing fathers' use of the leave there and in Norway (up to 80% and 90% respectively from tiny proportions); Lammi-Taskula (2006) suggests this may be because it was added on to the existing parental leave period, whereas in other countries it involved some loss of the leave previously available to mothers.

Taking the range of social policies together, cross-national comparisons tend to support the half-full analysis: the Nordic countries generally score well on most indicators of gender equality and gendered social citizenship (Daly and Rake, 2003; Gornick and Meyers, 2003). However, if one takes 'gender equality' as the benchmark rather than comparison with other industrialised societies, as does, for instance, the Swedish Political Platform for a Feminist Initiative (www. transnational.org/SAJT/forum/meet/2005/Schyman_FeministInitiative.html), then the glass starts to look half empty.

The 'half-empty' analysis

Anette Borchorst (2006) observes that, for all the achievements in embedding gender equality in public policies, policy inconsistencies and gaps between objectives and outcomes can be found in all the Nordic countries. This can be seen in the gender division of labour in both public and private spheres, the effects of which interact with each other. As a result, on the one side, gender divisions in the labour market affect decisions about who uses parental leave and homecare allowances and on the other side, policies to help parents reconcile paid work and family responsibilities are seen by some as contributing to inequality in the labour market, because it is still primarily mothers who make use of them. In other words, it is a vicious circle in which policies and practices reinforce each other to undermine the very commitment to gender equality that frames those policies.

Despite women's educational achievements and increased labour market participation, they enter a labour market that remains highly segregated both horizontally and vertically. Women are more likely to work in the public sector (where leave arrangements are more generous) and men in the private (where pay is, on average, higher); they are more likely to work reduced hours when children are young and are less likely to achieve top positions in the private sector. The degree of occupational segregation often comes as a surprise to outside observers. That said, because these are relatively egalitarian societies overall, the gender pay inequalities that result from occupational segregation do not translate into such wide economic inequalities as segregated labour markets do elsewhere.

In the private, domestic sphere, where women still do the bulk of the caring work, two very different policy logics can be observed. On the one hand there is the gender-explicit policy logic of the 'daddy leave' (in Norway, Sweden and Iceland) or extended paternity leave (in Finland, provided the father also takes the two last weeks of parental leave), in which the stated aim is to shift the gendered division of labour by encouraging men's greater participation in the care of young children. On the other hand, there is the supposedly gender-neutral policy logic of childcare allowances (again Finland and Norway), which are highly gendered in their effect. Here is an example of Danish exceptionalism (Borchorst, 2006), as it appears in neither list, having abandoned its short-lived 'daddy leave' policy with the change of government.

Unfortunately, the embedded resistance of the gendered domestic division of labour to significant change means that the gender-neutral policies seem to have more of an impact in inadvertently reinforcing the gendered division of labour than do the gender-explicit policies in shifting it. It is overwhelmingly women who make use of homecare allowances. The significance of this for gender equality and women's citizenship is disputed (Bergman, 2004). Some point to the temporary nature of the break from the labour market and the value to those mothers who would otherwise be unemployed (Salmi, 2006). Others, including the OECD (2005), argue that it harms women's longer-term labour market position and reinforces the gendered division of labour, particularly for less-educated women in lower-skilled jobs (Mahon, 2002; Morgan and Zippel, 2003). Thus, the policies can also exacerbate class stratification.

Highly gendered labour markets, together with workplace cultures that emphasise male indispensability, also blunt the impact of the daddy month policies. Even in Norway and Iceland, where they are most successful, mothers still take more parental leave overall than fathers. Only in Iceland have the number of fathers taking parental leave and the length of leave taken by fathers been growing at the same time (Lammi-Taskula, 2006). Thus, some conclude that the value of the policies lies more in what they symbolise – a belief in the importance of a more equitable division of labour and the role of public policy in achieving that – than in their impact on the actual division of labour.

Interestingly, while the Nordic governments (other than in Denmark) stand out in their willingness to treat the domestic division of labour as 'a structural problem' (Andersson, 2005, p 176), they were generally slow to acknowledge issues of bodily integrity as matters of public citizenship requiring rights of protection – more so than in liberal welfare states like the UK. While this did change, thanks to feminist movements, a recent evaluation of the major reform package adopted by the Swedish government in the late 1990s to counteract male violence against women identifies significant shortcomings in its implementation (Leander, 2006).

However, according to Maria Eriksson, male violence is more readily acknowledged in the immigrant population. In other words, male violence is racialised and, she argues, 'gender equality and child-friendliness become ethnic and racialised markers' of Swedishness (2005, p 28). Similarly in Denmark the political Right have adopted the rhetoric of gender equality as a means of framing, particularly Muslim, minorities as the Other. This raises the wider issue of the challenges to the Nordic model in general and the women-friendly state in particular, created by immigration and multiculturalism.

While the Nordic welfare states are said to belong to the same worlds of welfare and gender, they are, to some extent, responding to these challenges in different ways (Lister et al, 2007). In some accounts, immigration is presented as the answer to the demographic challenges facing the Nordic welfare states; at the same time, in Denmark at least, the immigration regime has become much more restrictive and the principle of universality of social rights has been breached for immigrants and refugees. However, despite the Danish exceptionalism, Birte Siim (2006) notes that 'studies of lived citizenship of ethnic minority women have identified common problems in the relation between the Nordic gender equality norm, women's rights and multiculturalism'.

A number of Nordic feminists have drawn attention to how not all women fare equally in women-friendly states and, in the Danish context, Birte Siim (2000) has pointed to new patterns of class polarisation and the need for new forms of gender solidarity able to embrace women of different ethnic and religious backgrounds. More recently, she and others have argued the need for mechanisms that enable immigrant women to be full, participating citizens so that their voices are heard in their own right rather than lost in translation when mediated by others (Siim, 2006).

More generally, a number of commentators have been warning that diversity stands in tension with the values of solidarity and universalism that are so central to the Nordic model. This is a challenge that faces not just the Nordic welfare states, but it is perhaps here that it stands in particularly sharp relief. Others have argued that empirical analysis does not support the thesis that we have to choose between diversity and solidaristic welfare states (for instance, Taylor-Gooby, 2005). Indeed, in a globalising world it is possible to identify alternative, more inclusive, conceptualisations of solidarity that go beyond the cross-class solidarity identified as underpinning universalist welfare: for instance, a 'cosmopolitan solidarity', which values diversity and 'multiplicity' over 'sameness and unity' (Beck, 2005, pp 140–1), or 'reflective solidarity', appeals to which rest on 'our awareness of and regard for those multiple interconnections in which differences emerge' (Dean, 1996, p 16). Perhaps one of the biggest challenges for the Nordic model, therefore, is to develop new forms of gender-inclusive citizenship rooted in these cosmopolitan or reflective forms of solidarity.

Note
[1] This is a much shortened version of a keynote address to the Nordic Council of Ministers conference in Oslo, May 2006.

Bibliography
Andersson, M. (2005) 'Why Gender Equality?', in A. Giddens and P. Diamond (eds) *The New Egalitarianism*, Cambridge: Polity Press, pp 171–82.

Anttonen, A. (2002) 'Universalism and Social Policy: a Nordic-feminist revaluation', *Nordic Journal of Women's Studies*, vol 10, no 2, pp 71–80.

Anttonen, A. and Sipilä, J. (1996) 'European Social Care Services: Is it possible to identify models?', *Journal of European Social Policy*, vol 6, no 2, pp 87–100.

Beck, U. (2005) 'Inequality and Recognition: Pan-European social conflicts and their political dynamic', in A. Giddens and P. Diamond (eds) *The New Egalitarianism*, Cambridge: Polity Press, pp 120–42

Bergman, S. (2004) 'Collective Organising and Claim Making on Child Care in Norden: Blurring the boundaries between the inside and the outside', *Social Politics*, vol 11, no 2, pp 217–46.

Borchorst, A. (2006) *Daddy Leave and Gender Equality – the Danish case in a Scandinavian perspective*, Tekst no 60, Aalborg: FREIA, Centre for Feminist Research, Aalborg University.

Daly, M. and Rake, K. (2003) *Gender and the Welfare State*, Cambridge: Polity Press.

Dean, J. (1996) *Solidarity of Strangers. Feminism after identity politics*, Berkeley: University of California Press.

Ellingsæter, A.L. and Leira, A. (2006) 'Introduction: Politicising parenthood in Scandinavia', in A.L. Ellingsæter and A. Leira (eds) *Politicising Parenthood in Scandinavia*, Bristol: The Policy Press, pp 1–18.

Eriksson, M. (2005) 'The issue of violent fathers', *Gender Research in Sweden 2005*, p 28.

Fraser, N. (1997) *Justice Interruptus*, New York and London: Routledge.

Gornick, J.C. and Meyers, M.K. (2003) *Families that Work*, New York: Russell Sage Foundation.

Hernes, H. (1987) *Welfare State and Woman Power*, Oslo: Norwegian University Press.

Karvonen, L. and Selle P. (eds) (1995) *Women in Nordic Politics: Closing the gap*, Aldershot: Dartmouth.

Lammi-Taskula, J. (2006) 'Nordic Men on Parental Leave: Can the welfare state change gender relations?', in A.L. Ellingsæter and A. Leira (eds) *Politicising Parenthood in Scandinavia*, Bristol: The Policy Press, pp 79–99.

Leander, K. (2006) 'Reflections on Sweden's Measures against Men's Violence against Women', *Social Policy and Society*, vol 5, no 1, pp 115–25.

Leira, A. (2002) 'Updating the "gender contract"? Childcare reforms in the Nordic countries in the 1990s', *Nordic Journal of Women's Studies*, vol 10, no 2, pp 81–9.

Leira, A. (2006) 'Parenthood Change and Policy Reform in Scandinavia, 1970s–2000s' in A.L. Ellingsæter and A. Leira (eds) *Politicising Parenthood in Scandinavia*, Bristol: The Policy Press, pp 27–51.

Lister, R. (1997/2003) *Citizenship: Feminist Perspectives*, Basingstoke: Palgrave.

Lister, R., Williams, F., Anttonen, A., Bussemaker, J., Gerhard, U., Heinen, J., Johansson, S., Leira, A., Siim, B., Tobío, C., with Gavanas, A. (2007) *Gendering Citizenship in Western Europe: New challenges for citizenship research in a cross-national context*, Bristol: The Policy Press.

Mahon, R. (2002) 'Child Care: Toward what kind of "Social Europe"', *Social Politics*, vol 9, no 3, pp 343–79.

Morgan, K.J. and Zippel, K. (2003) 'Paid to Care: The origins and effects of care leave policies in Western Europe', *Social Politics*, vol 10, no 1, pp 49–85.

OECD (Organization for Economic Co-operation and Development) (2001) *Starting Strong: Early childhood and education and care*, Paris: OECD.

OECD (2005) *Babies and Bosses*, Paris: OECD.

Salmi, M. (2006) 'Parental Choice and the Passion for Equality in Finland', in A.L. Ellingsæter and A. Leira (eds) *Politicising Parenthood in Scandinavia*, Bristol: The Policy Press, pp 145–68.

Siim, B. (2000) *Gender and Citizenship*, Cambridge: Cambridge University Press.

Siim, B. (2006) 'The multicultural challenge to citizenship: the recognition struggles of ethnic minority women in Denmark', paper given at the Gender, Citizenship and Participation conference, London School of Economics, 23–24 March.

Taylor-Gooby, P. (2005) 'Is the Future American? Or, can Left politics preserve European welfare states from erosion through growing "racial" diversity?', *Journal of Social Policy*, vol 34, no 4, pp 661–72.

Future research on gender equality in the Scandinavian countries

Keith Pringle

This postscript does not provide a systematic summary of the book. Nor does it seek to provide a detailed commentary on each of its chapters. Instead, based on the themes which I interpret as emerging from across the various contributions, I attempt to suggest some main directions for future research on gender equality in the Scandinavian countries.

The Scandinavian countries are often seen in the 'outside' world (that is, the world from which I come originally) as the most successful social 'experiment' so far in the creation and implementation of gender-equality policies. The contributions to this volume make a very significant contribution to the development of a more sophisticated and nuanced understanding of this 'experiment' by exploring the complexities of these policies across both time and space. They also provide the so-called 'English-speaking' world with access to some excellent Scandinavian scholarship that might otherwise go relatively unnoticed in that world. What, then, are the themes that I suggest emerge from this range of studies?

Heterogeneity and homogeneity

The first one is the complex interplay of heterogeneity and homogeneity that characterises the Scandinavian countries around issues of gender equality (as well as many other issues). It is brought into striking relief by the comparative perspectives employed by many of the book's contributors in terms of time and space. In future, we need more such explorations and, based on them, development of interpretative frames to help us understand why and how such patterns of hetero/homogeneity exist. For instance, in this volume Borchorst suggests that the timing of specific policies, the role of specific political discourses and economic/political opportunity structures have all been central to differential developments in gender-equality policies across the Scandinavian region. Other commentators, focused on a different level of analysis (Balkmar, Iovanni and Pringle, 2005; Balkmar and Pringle, 2005; Iovanni and Pringle, 2005), attribute such differential developments to largely cultural and historical factors. These two levels of explanation are not, however, mutually exclusive. In future research attention could usefully be devoted to further exploring multilevel analyses of patterns of hetero/homogeneity.

Research and policy: a two-way relationship

Another recurring theme in this volume is the complexity that exists in the relationship between research and policy related to gender equality, a complexity that the book explores very helpfully. On the whole, most analyses in the book emphasise the way research has impacted upon policy. However, some contributions (for instance that by Annfelt) hint at the important impact of policy on research. It is vital to explore further the sensitive question of how, at various times, policy priorities may have influenced research, directly or indirectly: which forms of research are financed; which research discourses are officially supported and which are silenced according to the requirements of policy or ideology? It is especially important that those of us engaged in the research field make clear that the institution of research is shaped by relations of power just as much as any other social institution, rather than making simplistic claims of absolute neutrality about it.

Conceptualising power: intersectionality and processes of mutual constitution

A clearly central focus of the book is on the interplay of different forms of power relationships in terms of social processes that generate gender-equality policies. Many chapters in this volume usefully focus on gender and class together. Some also investigate the dimension of age and others address ethnicity in relation to gender. Future research needs to develop such multidimensional analyses more often and more fully, not forgetting other dimensions of inequality such as disability and sexuality. One vital means of achieving that goal is, as Mulinari admirably demonstrates in this collection, to make use of more sophisticated conceptual frames for understanding how different dimensions of power impact upon one another in complex and contradictory ways: frames such as intersectionality and processes of mutual constitution (West and Fensternmaker, 1995; Brah, 2001; de los Reyes and Mulinari, 2005).

Gender, class, age and ethnicity

Although the issue of intersectionality is relevant to all dimensions of power relations, it seems clear from contributions in this book that there are some interconnections that are especially crucial for the Scandinavian countries in terms of policy and practice. These require much further research attention in the future. I pick out three constellations of power relations here.

The first concerns gender and ethnicity. As is hinted at in a number of chapters, minority-group ethnicity is being socially constructed as an allegedly key 'marker' of oppressive patriarchal relations in many of the Scandinavian countries. Conversely, majority-group ethnicity is also becoming constructed as an alleged 'marker' of 'gender equal' relations. Such a trend has already been heavily critiqued by a number of commentators (Eriksson, 2005a; Pringle, 2006); but this critique urgently needs further development.

A second especially significant constellation of power dimensions concerns gender and age. There is a real need in the Scandinavian countries for more research to focus on the way some men 'do' oppressive gender not only in their relationships with women but also with children (Eriksson, 2003, 2005b). For instance, there remains a relative absence of research exploring the linkages between, on the one hand, fatherhood and, on the other hand, men's violence to their partners and/or to children within partner relationships (Eriksson, 2005a; Pringle, 2005).

The third and final constellation to emphasise here is that involving class and ethnicity, for in many of the Scandinavian countries there is a rapidly developing convergence between social marginalisation and minority-group ethnicity (CASA, 2006) – to an extent that threatens to seriously destabilise those societies (see for example de los Reyes, 2006). Consequently, there is an urgent need to research ways in which such a process of convergence can be reversed by means of policy and practice.

Broadening comparative welfare analysis

In terms of illuminating the dynamics of gender relations, many chapters successfully focus on issues of labour in the home and/or in the market place. A few chapters broaden this analysis by also focusing on, or at least acknowledging, other important aspects of gendered relations (see for example the chapters by Annfelt, Borchorst and Roman). This is especially significant because, as has recently been pointed out (Hearn and Pringle, 2006), patterns of comparative welfare responsiveness look very different when seen through the lens of gendered violence rather than through the lens of gendered labour activities. In particular, the Scandinavian countries look far less successful in terms of welfare on the former measure as compared to the latter. Moreover, it has also been suggested that a similarly negative outcome for the Scandinavian welfare systems occurs if one assesses them in terms of their responsiveness to issues of racism (Pringle, 2006) and (young) ageism (Pringle, 2005). Thus, to obtain a fuller appreciation of how far the Scandinavian countries deserve their positive welfare reputation, it is vital that future research seeks to explore welfare responses to all aspects of well-being beyond the dimensions of class, financial disadvantage and work. Such research must also embrace dimensions like gendered violence, racism, ageism, heterosexism and disablism.

Which form of gender equality are we talking about?

Another key theme in this volume is the helpful exploration it provides of the complex variations around the meanings of 'gender equality' in the Scandinavian countries across time (for example Christensen, Lundqvist, Ravn, Roman, Carlsson Wetterberg and Melby) and space (for example Annfelt, Borchorst, Mulinari). Much remains to be further explored in this area, especially the complex and contradictory interplay between discourses of gender equality emphasising gender sameness and discourses stressing gender difference/complementarity (Eriksson, 2003; 2005b).

Difference as a barrier to the achievement of equality?

Throughout the book an underlying central tension recurs across time and space in Scandinavian gender politics between, on the one hand, pursuing the principle of equality and, on the other hand, recognising and managing difference.

A number of alternative interpretations regarding this phenomenon are suggested, or hinted at, in the book. For example, one interpretation is founded on the judgement that Scandinavian societies have managed rather well to deal with gender difference and equality. The question then posed in such an interpretation is why those societies have found it much harder to deal with ethnic diversity in the same way. A contrasting interpretation is based on the judgement that the Scandinavian countries have only dealt with gender difference and equality to a very limited extent: it is therefore suggested that there may be some connection between problems in managing gender difference and ethnic diversity. Further research is required to explore both possibilities – and others. My own view is that the facts support the latter interpretation more than the former. For the 'success' of the Scandinavian societies in achieving gender equality seems quite partial if one takes in the following considerations, which apply to most of the Scandinavian countries: a highly gender-segregated labour market, horizontally and vertically; the concentration of wealth and industrial power largely remaining in the hands of men; the large proportion of childcare still carried out by women in terms of the parental leave available to both parents; the high levels of gendered violence to women that we know prevail in Finland (Heiskanen and Piispa, 1998) and Sweden (Lundgren et al, 2001).

Of course, we should not assume the dynamics of racism are the same as those associated with sexism: quite the contrary, in fact. So, other factors are clearly relevant to processes of ethnic oppression which may not be relevant, or so relevant, to gendered oppression, and vice versa. Nevertheless, it may well be that at least some of the dynamics associated with institutional and societal racism in the Scandinavian countries are also operative in relation to gender oppression there. We need to explore all these possibilities much more carefully in future research.

Difference as a barrier, or as a pathway, to equality?

However defined, this recurring tension between difference and equality does not appear to represent such a massive challenge in some other European countries. In fact, struggles for equality have sometimes actually been premised upon recognition of difference in certain cultural locations such as the United Kingdom (Pringle, 1998; Pringle et al, 2006). The question to be answered then becomes this: why is it that British society seems to have embraced – sometimes even cherished – diversity as a potential path to equality in a context of great economic inequality and welfare inadequacy? Even more relevant to this book is the parallel question: why is it that the Scandinavian societies often seem to find it so hard to cherish diversity and largely perceive it as a societal problem, despite their relative material equality and relative welfare richness? Based on two recent European-wide studies, a group of researchers (including myself) have suggested that part of the answer lies in the fact that dominant discourses of individualism and collectivism have been shaped differently over time in specific cultural locations. It is suggested that in the Scandinavian countries this has produced – albeit in contrasting ways and to various extents – a marked rigidity and inflexibility towards issues of diversity in relation to equality (including gender equality), compared with the United Kingdom (Balkmar, Iovanni and Pringle, 2005). Moreover, we further suggest that such an analytical frame, centred on dominant discourses around individualism and collectivism, can also illuminate why problems of rigidity seem considerably more intense in Denmark than in Sweden (Dahlerup, 2002; Siim, 2004). Much more analysis along these lines is required to confirm – or dismiss – such suggestions.

An uncertain future

We live (as ever) in a dynamic situation, with the social kaleidoscope turning particularly fast in relation to issues of difference and equality across the western world. For instance, as I write this in November 2007, it seems that the United Kingdom is hurtling towards a breakdown in its previous, relatively stable, management of ethnic diversity; thereby rapidly losing any advantage it had over its Scandinavian neighbours in this respect. Over recent years Sweden has travelled in the opposite direction, towards more sensitivity in matters of ethnicity – and of gendered violence. At the same time, Denmark has increasingly differentiated itself from Sweden by actually managing to further increase its already high levels of unresponsiveness towards issues of diversity and difference: most clearly in relation to ethnicity; but a significant gap has also opened up between the two countries in terms of responses to gendered violence to women and children. Of course, all this could easily change yet again and no doubt is changing. In this unstable context there is at least one thing about which we can be certain: the study of gender equality in the Scandinavian countries and beyond will definitely continue to require clever, sensitive and skilful feminist scholarship such as is exemplified by the present volume.

Bibliography

Balkmar, D. and Pringle, K. (2005) *A Review of Academic Studies Relating to Men's Practices in Sweden*, Critical Research on Men in Europe, www.cromenet.org.

Balkmar, D., Iovanni, L. and Pringle, K. (2005) 'Mäns Våld i Danmark och Sverige', *NIKK Magasin*, vol 2, pp 18–20.

Brah, A. (2001) 'Re-framing Europe: Gendered racisms, ethnicities and nationalisms in contemporary Western Europe', in J. Fink, G. Lewis and J. Clarke (eds) *Rethinking European Welfare: Transformations of Europe and social policy*, London: Sage, pp 207–30.

CASA (Center for Alternative Samfundsanalyse) (2006) *Social Årsrapport 2005*, Copenhagen: Socialpolitisk Forlag.

Dahlerup, D. (2002) 'Er ligestillingen opnået? Ligestillingsdebattens forskellighed i Danmark og Sverige', in A. Borchorst (ed) *Kønsmagt under forandring*, Copenhagen: Hans Reitzel Publishers, pp 226–46.

de los Reyes, P. (ed) (2006) *Om Välfärdens Gränser och det Villkorade Medborgarskapet*, rapport av Utredningen om makt, integration och strukturell diskriminering, Stockholm: SOU:37.

de los Reyes, P. and Mulinari, D. (2005) *Intersektionalitet*, Malmö: Liber.

Eriksson, M. (2003) *I skuggan av Pappa. Familjerätten och hanteringen av fäders våld*, Stehag: Gondolin.

Eriksson, M. (2005a) 'Den onda och den normala fadersmakten? Fäders våld i svensk offentlig politik', *Tidsskrift for Kjønnsforskning*, Journal of Women's Studies, Norway, vol 2, pp 56–72.

Eriksson, M. (2005b) 'A Visible or Invisible Child? Professionals' approaches to children whose father is violent to the mother', in M. Eriksson, M. Hester, S. Keskinen and K. Pringle (eds) *Tackling Men's Violence in Families: Nordic issues and dilemmas*, Bristol: The Policy Press, pp 119–35.

Hearn, J. and Pringle, K. (2006) *European Perspectives on Men and Masculinities*, London: Palgrave.

Heiskanen, M. and Piispa, M. (1998) *Faith, Hope, Battering. a survey of men's violence against women in Finland*, Helsinki: Statistics Finland/Council for Equality between Women and Men.

Iovanni, L. and Pringle, K. (2005) *A Review of Academic Studies Relating to Men's Practices in Denmark*, Critical Research on Men in Europe, www.cromenet.org.

Lundgren, E., Heimer, G., Westerstrand, J. and Kalliokoski, A.-M. (2001) *Captured Queen: Men's Violence against Women in 'Equal' Sweden – A Prevalence Study*, Stockholm: Fritzes Offentliga Publikationer.

Pringle, K. (1998) *Children and Social Welfare in Europe*, Buckingham: Open University Press.

Pringle, K. (2005) 'Neglected Issues in Swedish Child Protection Policy and Practice: Age, ethnicity and gender', in M. Eriksson, M. Hester, S. Keskinen and K. Pringle (eds) *Tackling Men's Violence in Families – Nordic issues and dilemmas*, Bristol: The Policy Press, pp 155–70.

Pringle, K. (2006) 'Svenska välfärdssvar på etnicitet. Intersektionella perspektiv på barn och barnfamiljer', in P. de los Reyes (ed) *Om Välfärdens Gränser och det Villkorade Medborgarskapet*, rapport av Utredningen om makt, integration och strukturell diskriminering, Stockholm: SOU:37, pp 217–48.

Pringle, K., Hearn, J. et al (2006) *Men and Masculinities in Europe*, London: Whiting and Birch.

Siim, B. (2004) 'Globalisation, democracy and the politics of every day life', in J. Andersen and B. Siim (eds) *The Politics of Inclusion and Empowerment: Gender, class and citizenship*, London: Palgrave Macmillan, pp 64–83.

West, C. and Fenstermaker, S. (1995) 'Doing Difference', *Gender and Society*, vol 9, no 1, pp 8–37.

Appendix

Table 1: Milestones in the history of Scandinavian women

	Denmark	Norway	Sweden
General			
Equal inheritance rights for women and men	1857	1854	1845
Unmarried women attain majority status	1857	1863	1863
Married women attain majority status	1899	1888	1921
Marriage and family			
Formal economic equality within marriage	1925	1927	1920
Acceptance of no-fault divorce	1922	1909	1915
Equality within marriage in regard to:			
– custody of children	1922	1859	1920
– guardianship of children	1957	1958	1950
Individual taxation of spouses	1967	1959	1970
Parental leave*	1984	1978	1974
Politics			
Women are granted the right to vote and become eligible for office:			
– in elections to local authorities	1908	1910	1918
– in general elections	1915	1913	1919
First woman elected to parliament	1918	1922	1922
First woman minister	1924	1945	1947
First woman prime minister	–	1981	–
Education and work life			
Women are allowed to enrol for university studies	1875	1884	1873
Women achieve equal rights in appointments to public offices	1921	1938	1925
Women can be ordained as priests	1947	1952	1958
Equal pay for the same work in the public sector	1919	1959	1947
Equal pay for the same work in the private sector	1973	1961	1960

* Fathers get rights to statutory leave.

Sources: Bergqvist et al (1999, p 296). Additional information on marriage and family: Melby et al (2006a; 2006b); Chapters One, Two, Three and Seven in this volume.

Table 2: Early marriage reforms in Scandinavia

Country	Laws on the formation and dissolution of marriage	Laws on the legal effects of marriage
Denmark	1922	1925
Norway*	1918	1927
Sweden	1915 (1920)	1920

* Norway had already adopted a liberal law on divorce in 1909.
Sources: Melby et al (2006a; 2006b, pp 651–61).

Table 3: Women's labour force participation in Scandinavia, 1900–1970 (%)

	1900	1910	1920	1930	1940	1950	1960	1970
Including agriculture								
Denmark	36	35	34	36	46	41	35	43
Norway	36	35	32	30	27	26	24	27
Sweden	29	30	36	38	31	30	33	37
Excluding agriculture								
Denmark	23	23	24	27	32	31	32	-
Norway	23	23	23	23	22	23	23	-
Sweden	11	15	21	25	26	27	31	-

Source: Åmark (2006, pp 327-8, Tables F and G).

Table 4: Women's labour force participation (15–64 years) in Scandinavia and OECD–Europe, 1960-2000, per cent of female population and of total labour force

	1960	1968	1974	1985	1990	1995	2000
Per cent of female population							
Denmark	43.5	56.4	63.2	74.5	78.5	73.6	75.9
Norway	36.3	37.7	50.0	68.0	71.2	72.4	76.3
Sweden	50.1	56.6	64.9	78.1	80.1	74.5	75.0
OECD-Europe	44.2	43.5	46.3	49.1	53.2	54.0	58.0
Per cent of total labour force							
Denmark	30.9	37.7	40.9	45.6	46.1	45.7	46.8
Norway	28.2	29.4	36.1	43.2	44.9	45.5	46.5
Sweden	33.6	38.1	41.8	47.1	47.9	47.9	47.7
OECD-Europe	32.7	32.8	34.7	37.5	39.4	40.4	42.4

Source: Åmark (2006), pp 330-1, Tables M and N) (Table M corrected by K. Åmark in e-mail to the editors, August 2007).

Table 5: Persons with foreign citizenship in Scandinavia and the UK

Country	1991 1,000 persons	1991 Per cent	1995 1,000 persons	1995 Per cent	2000 1,000 persons	2000 Per cent
Denmark	170	3.3	223	4.2	259	4.8
Norway	148	3.5	161	3.7	184	4.1
Sweden	494	5.7	532	5.2	477	5.4
UK	1,750	3.1	1,948	3.4	2,342	4.0

Source: The Danish National Centre for Social Research (2004), Tables 1A and 1B.

Table 6: Population in Scandinavia and the UK by native country and labour-market status (15–64 years), 2002 (%)

Country	Classification*	Employed	Unemployed	Outside labour force	Total	1,000 persons
Denmark	Non-Western	53.7	6.1	40.2	100.0	128.2
	Western	74.1	5.6	20.4	100.0	103.2
	National	77.5	3.3	19.2	100.0	3,289.4
	Unknown	49.9	10.9	39.3	100.0	11.2
	Total	76.4	3.5	20.1	100.0	3,532.0
Norway	Non-Western	60.3	9.0	30.7	100.0	119.9
	Western	81.5	2.6	15.9	100.0	83.3
	National	78.0	3.1	19.0	100.0	2,716.2
	Unknown	100.0	0.0	0.0	100.0	0.2
	Total	77.3	3.3	19.4	100.0	2,919.6
Sweden	Non-Western	55.0	9.0	36.0	100.0	467.9
	Western	70.3	4.5	25.3	100.0	254.9
	National	76.0	3.4	20.6	100.0	49,62.9
	Unknown	76.4	4.1	19.5	100.0	84.1
	Total	74.0	3.9	22.0	100.0	5,769.8
UK	Non-Western	58.9	6.0	35.1	100.0	2,558.0
	Western	72.7	3.4	23.9	100.0	1249.3
	National	72.4	3.7	23.9	100.0	35,145.8
	Unknown	56.1	0.0	43.9	100.0	4.6
	Total	71.5	3.8	24.7	100.0	38,957.7

* 'Western' countries include EU (2003), Iceland, Lichtenstein, Norway, Switzerland, Canada, USA, Japan, Israel, Australia and New Zealand. 'Non-Western' is defined as the rest of Europe, Asia and North America as well as Africa, Central America, the Caribbean, South America and Oceania.
Source: The Danish National Centre for Social Research (2004), Table 7A.

Table 7: Employment rates in Scandinavia and the UK by native country and gender (15–64 years), 2002 (%)

Country	Classification*	Women	Men
Denmark	Non-Western	44.0	65.5
	Western	71.4	76.7
	National	73.9	81.0
	Unknown	52.2	48.3
	Total	72.6	80.2
Norway	Non-Western	56.8	64.0
	Western	75.1	88.3
	National	75.0	80.8
	Unknown	100.0	0.0
	Total	74.2	80.3
Sweden	Non-Western	50.1	60.1
	Western	70.0	70.6
	National	74.8	77.1
	Unknown	76.7	75.9
	Total	72.5	75.5
UK	Non-Western	49.2	68.6
	Western	65.4	80.6
	National	66.4	78.2
	Unknown	37.1	75.1
	Total	65.3	77.7

* See Table 6.

Source: The Danish National Centre for Social Research (2004), Table 8A.

Table 8: Families in Scandinavia by family type, 2004

	Denmark*	Norway	Sweden**
Number of families with children aged 0–17 years (1,000)	670	581	1,093
Percentage of whom are:			
– married couples	62.4	60.1	77.1
– cohabiting couples	17.4	20.2	
– single parents	20.2	19.7	22.9
Total	100.0	100.0	100.00
Number of childless families (1,000)	2.219	1.444	4.053
Percentage of whom are:			
– married couples	27.3	33.6	29.9
– cohabiting couples	7.9	6.0	
– single persons	64.8	60.4	70.1
Total	100.0	100.0	100.0
Single parents (per cent)			
– men	13.9	14.1	19.4
– women	86.1	85.9	80.6
Single childless persons (per cent)			
– men	50.3	46.6	50.3
– women	49.7	53.4	49.7
Average number of persons per family	1.9	2.2	1.8

*A further 16,513 families consist of children under 18 not living at home.

** Cohabiting couples included as married couples.

Source: Social Protection in the Nordic Countries 2004: Scope, Expenditure, and Financing (2006), p 281, Table 4.2.a.

Table 9: Total fertility rate in Scandinavia and selected EU countries, 2004

Denmark	Norway	Sweden	France	Germany	Ireland	Italy	Netherlands	Spain	UK
1.78	1.83	1.72	1.90*	1.37**	1.99**	1.33	1.73*	1.32**	1.74**

* Preliminary data.

** Estimate.

Source: Social Protection in the Nordic Countries 2004: Scope, Expenditure, and Financing (2006), p 31, Table 3.1.

Table 10: Children enrolled in day-care institutions and municipal family day care in Scandinavia, by age as percentage of the respective age groups, 1995–2004

	Denmark	Norway*	Sweden**
1995			
0–2 years	48	22	37
3–6 years	83	61	74
0–6 years, total	68	44	59
7–10 years	53	–	45
2000			
< 1 year	15	2	–
1–2 years	77	37	60
3–5 years	92	78	86
0–5 years, total	75	52	66
6 years	90	–	77
0–6 years, total	77	–	68
7–10 years	63	–	51
2004			
< 1 year	12	2	0
1–2 years	83	48	66
3–5 years	95	87	95
0–5 years, total	77	61	71
6 years	87	–	83
0–6 years, total	79	–	72
7–10 years	63	–	59

* As from 2000, only children between 0 and 5.

** As from 1998, a special pre-school class was introduced for the 6-year-olds. These children are not included, unless they also attend a day-care institution.

Source: Social Protection in the Nordic Countries 2004: Scope, Expenditure, and Financing (2006), p 283, Table 4.11.b.

Bibliography

Åmark, K. (2006) 'Women's Labour Force Participation in the Nordic Countries during the Twentieth Century', in N.F. Christiansen, K. Petersen, N. Edling and P. Haave (eds) *The Nordic Model of Welfare. A Historical Reappraisal*, Copenhagen: Museum Tusculanum Press, pp 299–333.

Bergqvist, C., Borchorst, A., Christensen, A-D., Ramstedt-Silén, V., Raaum, N. C. and Styrkársdóttir, A. (eds) (1999) *Equal Democracies? Gender and Politics in the Nordic Countries*, Oslo: Scandinavian University Press.

Melby, K., Pylkkänen, A., Rosenbeck, B. and Carlsson Wetterberg, C. (2006a) *Inte ett ord om kärlek. Äktenskap och politik i Norden ca. 1850–1930*, Stockholm: Makadam Förlag.

Melby, K., Pylkkänen, A., Rosenbeck, B. and Carlsson Wetterberg, C. (2006b) 'The Nordic Model of Marriage', *Women's History Review*, vol 15, no 4.

Social Protection in the Nordic Countries 2004: Scope, Expenditure, and Financing (2006), Copenhagen: Nordic Social-Statistical Committee (NOSOSCO)(www. mom-nos/nososco.htm).

The Danish National Centre for Social Research (1.12.03) 'Notat til Integrationsministeriets tænketank', in *Udlændinge- og integrationspolitikken i Danmark og udvalgte lande – Baggrundsrapport* (2004), Copenhagen: Ministry of Refugee, Immigrant and Integration Affairs.

Index

Page references for notes are followed by n